Secrets of the Lord's Prayer and Our World Today

Jennifer Safoah Awuah, PhD

Secrets of *the Lord's Prayer* and Our World Today

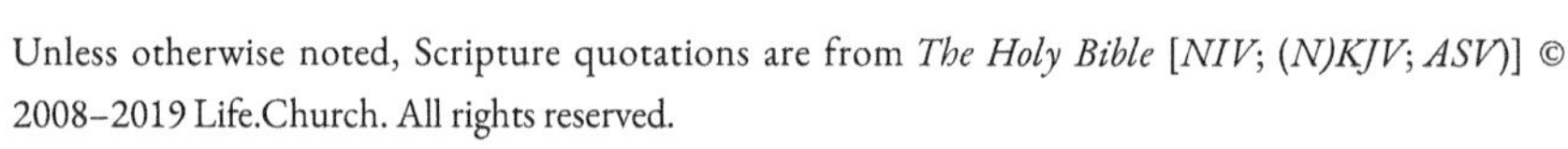

Details in some anecdotes and stories have been changed to protect the identities of the persons involved.

Trade Paperback ISBN 979-8-9896737-1-1

God bless you.

Printed in the United States of America.

2024

1 2 3 4

Contents

Contents

Acknowledgements

All praise and glory, honor, and thanksgiving be to our God the Father, the Son, and the Holy Spirit. Amen!

Many thanks go to my son, Joseph, for his assistance designing the cover, and to my son, Ebenezer, for his hard work editing, typesetting, and putting all the finishing touches on this book. I am grateful to Nicole (daughter-in-law), Matthew Yabe (nephew), Mr. Doug Halvorsen, and Mrs. Delores Flannigan, and Lizelle Torres for proofreading this manuscript. May God bless you all!

I am also indebted to the publisher, as well as Ms. Diane Flores, Ms. Carolyn Chung, Rev. Awuah, Rev. Dr. Danny Diaz, Apostle Ameyaw, Rev. Elaine, and Rev. and Mrs. Stretch, and all my prayer leaders at One&All who helped me with their prayer supports, feedback, and encouragement to bring this book completion.

All of you are so much appreciated. May God bless you all! Amen!

Foreword

I have known the author, Dr. Jennifer Safoah Awuah, who likes to be called "Ama" or "Princess." I prefer to call her "Mama" because she is my dear mother. Unbeknownst to me, the Holy Spirit had been imparting to her the knowledge and wisdom for this book for several years after she encountered the Lord, who taught her the truth about His prayer called *the Lord's Prayer*. After I completed my doctorate degrees and entered the field of scientific/medical editing, she informed me of her book, and I had the privilege to review the first draft.

She was born in Ghana, West Africa, and has lived in the United States for many years. After completing school, my mother was deterred from her educational goals because her parents believed it was not necessary for a girl have higher educational ambitions. But she never gave up on her dreams. After she got married, she and my dad worked in the ministry for over 10 years before travelling as missionaries to the US, where she had the opportunity to further her education. Although she struggled for her statistics requirement for university, she never gave up. She strove hard and consequently qualified for a transfer to San Diego State University where she studied to be a gerontologist. Through her hard work, she received her AA in 4 years and her BA in 2 years. However, her ambitions helped her to further her education in a field that relates to her calling to help her prepare people's souls for the afterlife: Christian counseling.

Therefore, years later, after asking the Lord about the reason she had studied gerontology, He connected the dots for her and revealed that it was truly His purpose (read her book *He Turned My Nothing Into Something*

Beautiful) for the full story. After having a clear revelation from God to further her education, she did not waste any time. She obtained her MA and PhD in Christian Counseling in less than 5 years, marking the culmination of the numerous years that she had been blessed as a beneficiary of the gift of faith; what an amazing journey with an amazing God!!! In total, she has now been working in ministry for over 40 years.

Since her early years, the most recognizable part of my mom's entire being has been her spiritual life. That's not to say that the importance of the physical, psychological, and emotional aspects of her being has not been emphasized, but her faith has always been her driving force. Her faith leads her to love people. She loves to connect with all people, regardless of their race/ethnicity, age, gender, socioeconomic background, or political or religious beliefs. She has lived by her calling to share her faith with everyone God has allowed her to cross paths with. For me, hearing about her encounter with God regarding *the Lord's Prayer* and the underlying explanation has been remarkable but not shocking at all!

While I helped Mama edit certain parts of this book, we explored how best to use her voice to channel the messages she received from God. What I gained spiritually, even while editing her book, cannot be overstated. Sometimes, the things that have the greatest impact on our Christian lives are the foundational truths that we previously assumed we already understood. I am grateful to be part of this wonderful prayer book.

By Ebenezer M. Awuah-Yeboah, MD.

Overview

Matthew 6:5–15 & Luke 11:1–13:

In teaching His disciples how to pray, our Lord Jesus said, "When you pray, say 'Our Father in Heaven'..." (**Matthew 6:9–13**). What if I had told you that, prayer would get you to the throne of God in less than 1 minute? And what if this 1-minute prayer will get you through Heaven's gates, take a tour through Heaven, and access all that is in Heaven each day within 1 hour? It would be so-so delightful than visiting the king of England.

What you are about to read is *the Lord's Prayer* and my encounter with the Lord regarding its importance. You will get to see the mysteries of His Prayer which I called the 'hidden secrets', and how it was revealed to me. It has everything that each of us ought to know to pray according to the Will of the Father. As you read through the pages, you will see all the three parts of His Prayer and what they entail. You will also find that prayer is not just a set of words but a mighty weapon in the supernatural realm.

The first part of His prayer is thanksgiving, which involves giving thanks to God. We give thanks for everything in life. **Ephesians 1:7** says, "In Him we have redemption through His blood, the forgiveness of our sins, according to the riches of His grace." We give thanks for God's great work of salvation done on our behalf. In this, we receive forgiveness through the inexpressible love of God in Christ Jesus. **John 3:16** declares, "For God so loved the world, that He gave His only Begotten Son – [Jesus]..." This is the greatest act of God's unspeakable love for humanity. So, saying "Our Father who art in Heaven" gives us a sense of belonging to God's family. Once we understand what God has done through salvation, and all His goodness to us, we and give thanks to Him as our *Awesome Heavenly Father*.

The second part of His Prayer is supplication or making our requests known to the Father through Christ, our Savior. This is the part where we ask God for all our needs. **James 1:17** says, "Every good gift comes from above." This means all our needs come from God. **Philippians 4:19** – "God shall supply all your need..." **Psalm 23** – the Lord is my shepherd; I shall not want. Jesus made it clear that God is the only provider – the One capable of fully supplying our every need if we ask according to *His Will*. **In Matthew 7:7, He says,** ask, seek, and knock.

The third part of His prayer is adoration, which is basically about the supremacy or the reign of God – His superiority, His power, control, authority, glory, and honor. He said to Moses, "I AM that I AM," (**Exodus 3:14**). In all the heavens and on the earth, God the Father cannot be compared with anyone or anything. No one has ever been and will ever be equal to Him. He is who He is and is above all. He is the Alpha and Omega, the Beginning, and the End, the First and the Last. Having existed since the "Ancient of Days", He is the great and mighty God, the great deliverer, the rock of ages, the everlasting God, the giver of life. He deserves all glory, honor, and praise because they belong to Him. This is the reason why we worship and adore God. So, when we say, "For thine is the kingdom, the power...**Matthew 6:13**, we are saying that God is worthy of praise.

What does *the Lord's Prayer* contain?

I have given you a general insight into the prayer, but don't be surprised that this simple prayer from the Lord contains everything we need to know to live our lives and serve the Lord faithfully. The Lord separates and divides His prayer into distinct parts for easy access and comprehension. He opens His prayer with admiration for the Father by saying, (a) "Our Heavenly Father." Then, He adds (b) His Holy name, (c) His kingdom, (d) *His Will*, (e) Forgiveness and the gift of salvation, (f) His protection, and (g) His reign. All these elements make *the Lord's Prayer* perfect throughout life. With His Prayer, the

Holy Spirit is your intercessor. Whatever questions you have, He will answer it all! His Prayer makes it possible for us to know how to enter the *THRONE ROOM* of God which is the most secret place of the Most-High.

This book covers everything in His prayer to make it a very effective daily prayer book. The goal is for you to appreciate the gift of prayer. I will explain each of these areas in a simple yet effective manner to make it easy to understand.

The Lord's Prayer is about:

1. God the Father. 2. His power. 3. Our salvation journey on earth. 4. Establishing and maintaining a personal relationship with God and others. 5. Knowing how to develop a consistent prayer life. 6. Where we came from, why we are here, and where we go from here. Know all these basics prayer concept, and it will help you pray for God's Kingdom to come fast. His Prayer is a mystery. May God grant us the desire for prayer because surviving what is ahead of humanity will depend on how we keep our focus on the Lord in prayer. Our effective prayer will keep us close to the Lord. Nothing can help humans survive more than *God's Word* and Prayer through faith. Amen!

Our Father, Who Art in Heaven

Do you know what it means to say, *our Father?* This part helps us with the understanding of God the Father through Jesus Christ the Savior – salvation. You become part of God's family right after salvation, and it helps you to have a personal relationship with Him. For instance, if I say, 'Father in Heaven', it means I know who He is and where He is. Apart from Him being in Heaven, I also know He lives inside my heart and reigns in me. What about you? Do you know what it signifies to say, *Our Father, who art in Heaven?* If you do, then it means you are part of God's Family. Some of us do, but unfortunately, not everyone. So, let me ask you, and be honest with yourself. Do you know who you are? Do you know you are a child of the Most-High God – the Father in Heaven? The King of all kings? If you do, then it means you are a prince or a princess. Our Father is loving, kind, caring, and gentle. He is full of compassion and has eternal life! **Read 1 John 3.**

Hallowed Be Thy Name

This is about the Holiness of God. It means God has a Name, and His Name is Holy. **Hebrews 12:14** tells us that it is impossible to see God without holiness. Do I know His Name? What is His Name? Do I keep His Name Holy? In what way? **1 Peter 1:15** says "Be holy, because I am Holy." Why do we need God's Name and make His Name Holy in our lives? **Proverbs 18:10** says, "The name of the Lord is a strong tower: the righteous run to it and are safe." God's Name is our place of safety. So, we need His Name, but without holiness, it will be impossible!

When we think of what happened during *World Wars 1 and 2, the Great Depression, the 9/11 Terrorist Attack,* all the lives that AIDS, Polio, Cholera, Ebola, and COVID-19 viruses, etc. have caused, we can say it is very troubling; but it is not over yet. Read **Matthew 24.** The worse is yet to come. What would you have said if someone had told you in 2017 or 2018 that there would be a pandemic a year or two later that would affect the whole world and require people to wear masks, be unable to 'interact with others, shake hands, hug, travel, and despite all human efforts, still destroy many lives? Right now, the virus has come to stay. We still see and hear about many troubles in our world. Some come from the media, governments, communities, businesses, schools, street corners, homes, individual lives, and almost every part of life. We have seen it all, but the question is, is it over? Well, the troubles of this life are not yet over. Probably future disasters would be even worse! Have you thought of it? Is there any hope at all for humanity?

Yes, there is! There is a song that says, "We have an anchor that keeps the souls..." Jehovah is our anchor! He has sent His Son, Jesus, to bring us hope. So yes, we have a solution to every problem, and that solution is Jesus! In His Name, we can make it to the end successfully. He is the only One that can help us survive whatever is ahead of time. In the Name of Jesus, we have hope. Therefore, it is vital to know the only Name that can save you in times of trouble and keep you holy in all you do. **Psalm 9:10** states, "Those who know Your Name will trust in You, for You, Lord, have never forsaken those who seek

You." In **Romans 10:13**, we are told, "Whoever calls on the name of the Lord shall be saved." This means we must know, keep, and use His Holy Name!

We are living in a tumultuous world today. Most people know that something is not right in this world, and yet, they cannot put their finger on it. They come up with many explanations, but still, they do not know for sure what the problem is. People are getting worried, anxious, and depressed. Each day, there are troubles everywhere. We know that something is ahead of humanity, but other than death, which is our final destination, we do not know exactly what is ahead of us in order to fix it. This is because no one knows what tomorrow holds. Even if we know what is ahead of us, we cannot fix it because we have limited abilities. But there is One God who knows it all. This has nothing to do with being rich or poor; young or old; vibrant or feeble; smart or simple; or knowledgeable or ignorant. We are all going to face what is ahead. And depending on whom you have put your hope, you will perish or survive. If you know there is going to be a flood, fire, hurricane, tornado, earthquake, or other natural disaster, you will be prepared. It is written in **Luke 12:39–40**, "*If* the *owner* of the *house* had known at what time of night the thief was coming, *he would* have kept watch and *would* have done whatever he could to prevent the thief from breaking into the house." The truth is, we don't know what is ahead, but thankfully, God is All-Knowing. He knows everything ahead of time and prepares us. At this point in time, He is preparing His people who know His Name and wait upon Him in prayer.

I was editing this section of the book when the news came out that our dear Dr. Charles Stanley had passed. Then, a friend who had no idea what was on my mind sent me the last message of our dear Dr. Stanley before his passing. He said, "The question I want to ask is, what is God's message to us is in these troublesome and trying times we are facing?" He explained that we have responsibilities to everyone, including our government and Almighty God. With this, he read **Psalm 130:19** for direction and assurance. The reading says, "The LORD has established His throne in Heaven, and His Kingdom rules overall?" Yes, the Lord has established His Kingdom in His people and has chosen us to send the message of salvation to the end of the world, but that can only be done through the Word and prayer in His Holy Name. **Some are sent with warning messages and teachings, some carry empowerment and encouragement messages, some carry messages of salvation, and there are those with healing messages.** But we are all in for the same goal; we must do it out of love and compassion; there is no need for criticism because what is ahead of humanity requires unity and *God's Name* as our strong tower.

Regardless of who you are and what you do, know that the Lord has established His Kingdom on earth. You and I are not the ones ruling; He is. If His Kingdom is established in your heart and my heart, we will be safe, because as the verse above states: "God Almighty is in control." That is the reality. Whatever happens, God knows because nothing is hidden from Him. He knows everything; He knows why everything happens and how long it will take. And He alone has power in His Name to solve all our problems in this world; but we must depend on Him and ask for His help through prayer and thanksgiving. So, what is our response to holiness? I will say, for the sake of holiness, 'this is not a time to hate, but a time to love.' 'It is not a time for war, but a time for peace.' 'It is not a time for fear, but a time for courage.'

My question to you is what will be your response to whatever happens? Are you prepared? How prepared are you? According to Dr. Stanley, he was only 9 years old when WWII broke out. He described how fear gripped everyone for some time, but after a while, they learned to keep their faith in God. With this, they began to pray for God's intervention. With boldness and assurance, they won the battle. The same Name they relied for victory in the past, is the same Name we have been given. But before we can have victory in our time, we must play our part, and that is to keep His Name Holy. This is our requirement before trouble hits; because the Name of the Lord is the only 'Strong Tower' which we can run to.

It was very shocking when I received Dr. Stanley's message from my friend who had no idea what I was writing about at that moment. Was it a coincidence? No, I believe it was part of God's divine plan to confirm what

I was writing. In the same way, God is using each of us to touch the lives of others through the Word and prayer. Everything I was writing at that moment was confirmed. That means God has everything under His control. If this little prayer book I am writing is under God's control, then nothing can be hidden from Him. Everything is in His divine plan; this means it is important to live for God and do *His Will*. He is the One who can order our footsteps – **Psalm 37:24–25**. God knows all our needs and can supply them in due time, but we must honor His Name first through our services to Him. We must give to Him our lives and praise Him because it is our responsibility. We also must live wisely because we owe our lives to Him. So, each day that we live to say, *"Hallowed Be Thy Name,"* we are living in the awareness of God's salvation through forgiveness, and we are also relying on His mercy to help us choose the right path.

If there has ever been a time when humans needed God and His supernatural intervention, it is today. With all the troubles in this life, we can trust God and the power in His Holy Name for our survival. In **2 Chronicles 7:14**, God has promised to listen if we call on His Name. So, let's turn to God, fill our hearts and minds with peace, our lives with holiness, and call upon His Name each day for all our needs. In Him, we can always find refuge – **Psalm 91 & 118**.

The Lord knew what would come into this world before giving us His prayer. In His Prayer, His Holy Spirit will help us to pray to cover every area of life and conquer fear. So, this is not the time for worries but a time for prayer. **We must pray, depend on God, trust Him more, and seek Him like never before, and all through *His Name*.** The time is now! We must encourage ourselves, go on our knees, and pray to the One who is our Rock and our Refuge! We must build our faith in Him, stand strong, join people who are called to pray, encourage one another, pray, and to bring about a change. We are not to send hateful messages, but to proclaim the good news to the lost, and pray for those who destroy God's work without realizing.

We are thankful that prayer has been made available to us freely; so, let's be alert, encouraged, and pray. Fear is deadly, but faith and prayer conquer. Faith can help us defeat fear. We must do as we are told to do. Prayer is our mighty weapon to counter and frustrate the plans of the enemy. Prayer can do many great things. Through prayer, He can thwart every plan of the devil that causes commotions, whether it is through wars, diseases, natural disaster, division, or any evil. Unless it is part of God's plans, no plans of the evil one shall succeed if we pray according to the *Will of our Heavenly Father*. If we pray in His Name, God can bring salvation by causing people to renounce their evil ways and turn to Him. Everything is possible through His Name. The powerful Name of Jesus Christ can accomplish many amazing things; it undeniably does. In His Name, we are equipped and empowered. So, it is time, let's go on our knees and pray.

The most important thing is that we build our relationship with God through prayer and His Word, that is why we are commanded to pray. So, we must pray because our victory is established and assured through the relationship we have with the Father through the Word and Prayer. With these, God makes the impossible, possible. **Ephesians 6:10–12 tells us t**o "put on the full armor of God" and pray. **James 5:16** says, "The prayer of the righteous avails much." In that case, let's pray without ceasing as it is written in **1 Thessalonians 5:17**. The devil may try to stop us, but with prayer, he will have no power over us. God Almighty has instructed us; so, let's prepare ourselves as good soldiers. He is in control; therefore, we are not to be afraid. The Bible says that no weapon formed against us shall prosper, but the Word and prayer must come first.

We have a Good Father who hears us when we call out to Him. So, instead of wasting time talking about our problems and worrying about them, we can spend the same amount of time calling upon His Holy Name in prayer about the problems we have, because any problem can be solved in God's Mighty Name. *Christ is the answer for the world today.* Therefore, instead of wasting time engaging in worldly pleasures and the worries of this life, we can channel that energy into prayer, and leave the rest to God. He always has an answer. The solution to every situation is found in Him. As it is written in **Matthew 24:35,** "Heaven and earth shall pass away, but the Word shall never pass away." This means our troubles and pains shall also pass away; but, for that to happen, we must pray.

One morning, during COVID-19, I was praying for the world, when **Matthew 24:35** came to me. The Lord gave me this verse and said, "Just as WW1, WW2, the Great Depression, AIDS, cholera, etc., became history, so shall this pandemic pass and become history." The message came at a time when COVID-19 was at its peak and fear had gripped humanity. I immediately texted some friends to encourage them. Truly, the Lord saw us through. Today, we see that the impact of COVID-19 is not the same even though it has come to stay. It was all because we called upon His Holy Name.

The same prayer that helped the disciples is also available for us to use. Throughout the time of the plague, my continuous prayer was through the *Lord's Prayer*: for the Lord to deliver me, my family, and the world from evil, and I'm sure many people prayed the same. When we pray according to *the Lord's Prayer*, the Lord does mighty things in our midst through the Holy Spirit. He delivers, rescues, protects, and builds His Kingdom among us for *His Will to be done*. As it is written in **Revelation 3:20,** He says, "Behold, I stand at the door and knock...." This means that Jesus wants to build His Kingdom of righteousness in us, individually, for us to live according to His Kingdom's Rules. That is what His Holy Name does. God's Kingdom on earth will make everything perfect. Every good thing comes from above," and so is God's gift of salvation through Jesus Holy Name.

The concept of prayer. This requires salvation, a relationship with God, faith, holiness, and the power of the Holy Spirit through His *Holy Name*. God has provided His guidelines. They are the solutions to our problems on earth, and we must do our best to follow because without that, we cannot receive answers to our prayers. Therefore, let's live our lives in a way that brings glory to God's Name, and He will take care of the rest. With God's prayer requirement, our prayers will be answered, and His blessings will follow. Just think of it from this perspective: In your everyday life, you cannot just go to the bank to withdraw money unless you have savings. It is the same with prayer. For your prayer to be answered, you must first be saved and then you must follow the prayer concept. Today, I encourage you that whoever you are, wherever you are, and whatever you do, you must turn to God, *know His Name, depend on His Name,* and *pray in His Name*; if you do, it shall be well with you and your family.

God is not respecter of persons. The world and everything in it will soon pass away. But whoever you are—whether a president, governor, mayor, assemblyman, military man or woman, police officer, schoolteacher, doctor, nurse, scientist, businessperson, farmer, churchgoer, church leader, a priest, a minister, an atheist, rich, poor, et al.—you must truly know God and *His Name*; accept His Plan for humanity through salvation; learn how to communicate with Him through prayer; and build your relationship with Him. This is because very soon, life is going to become more difficult. However, if you know God, then He will lead and guide you in every step of the way because you believe in Him. If you don't know God, you will get to know Him if you confess your sins and turn from your evil ways. He will not reject you if you turn to Him. If you are living in faith, you have His word, so, there is nothing to be afraid or worried about.

Some people say life is going to be easy because of technology, but unfortunately, that is not the case. If whatever we come up is out of *God's Will*, it will definitely cause a chaos in the future. It seems as if we are building the tower of babel in our time, but no plans of humans last forever. Read **Matthew 24:35.** All we need is to walk in His path of righteousness, obey God, and learn to spend time with Him in prayer and in His Word. If you do this, *the peace of God that surpasses all understanding* will be yours and you will not be afraid of whatever obstacle you face or anything that is ahead of humanity. So, abide with Him, keep His promises, and His light will always guide you. With that, His Name will become your strong tower.

Thy Kingdom Come and Thy Will Be Done on Earth as It Is...

God's Kingdom is the only government that can repair this broken world. **Daniel 2** states that, "The God of heaven will set up a kingdom that will never be destroyed. The earth is overwhelmed with all kinds of calamities, but God's Kingdom brings peace, even in the midst of the storm. During His earthly ministry, Jesus dealt with many issues, and among all that He did, the subject of the Kingdom of God was His main goal. Today, the end of the message is that God's Kingdom is the only solution to all our problems. Everything we see in this life is troubling, but God's Word assures us not to be troubled because we can be confident that His Kingdom will soon bring an end to all such problems. This is what Jesus means when He says to pray and say, *Thy Kingdom Come.* The Lord knew that the awful things happening on the earth are not what God wants and that His Kingdom is the only government that can bring the solution. So, He came to establish that; it is done already through salvation. In **Revelation 12**, the Bible says that Jesus overcame Satan and his demons. Right now, we have the responsibility to improve our lives, enjoy everything God has given to us, and not allow anything to enslave us.

Today, while some of us have rested our hope on God and in His Kingdom, some are relying on their money, wealth, power, and knowledge. But as **Revelation 20 says**, the Lord will eliminate Satan's rulings; All his agents, his wicked followers, false religions, false teachers, lovers of money, and deceivers will be no more. Soon, the earth will be destroyed. God will bring relief to all who have obeyed Him. His government will rule over us, but those who oppose Him will find no rest for their souls. So, be thankful if you are blessed with riches, but don't depend on your wealth; instead, rely on God and His plans for your life.

On earth, the Kingdom is through salvation. When God's Kingdom of salvation comes, (this means when we accept Christ), *His Will* shall be done, and this must be our primary goal. According to **Matthew 6:10 and 24,** when we accept Jesus as our Savior, the Kingdom of God will come into our lives to help us do what is right and acceptable unto God. It will help keep us alert and prepare ourselves for the end times. Because troubles are part of life, they will surely come, but we shall not be afraid.

Today, I challenge you to think about how you view the world and how eagerly you want God's Kingdom and *His Will to come and take over*. From the beginning of time, humanity has faced several challenges. This is because evil rules on earth. This is the reason why Jesus came. But since not everyone is saved, the enemy still possesses the world and control people and their doings. The devil schemes in the darkest places before enacting his plan. In every way, he replaces the truth with lies, light with darkness, love with hatred, unity with divisions, and soundness with confusion. So, you see, *God's Will* is not being done on earth as it is done in Heaven. But you can trust that life under the rule of God's government will accomplish one thing – peace on earth.

In summary, God's Kingdom is how He rules, and *His Will* refersto-Hissovereign plan and His decree. God's Kingdom and *His Will* work together and can never be altered. And it is important to know this because it shows us what is good and what is requires of us. To humans, it is His salvation to us. Thus, we get to live in the Will of God when we become saved. It is what pleases Him – **Romans 12.** It tells us to not be conformed to the habits of this world. It also transforms us to the likeness of God. In *His Will*, our minds are renewed; and it also helps us to stay humble–**Micah 6:8.** In *His Will*, we are able to walk with joy and with a thankful Heart – **1 Thess. 5:16-18. Not only that, but** it helps us to study and keep the commandments of the Lord – **Psalm 119** & **John 14:15.**

Give Us This Day Our Daily Bread

Who can meet your needs? Human needs that are out of *God's Will* have taken them far away from God's grace. **James 4:2** says, "You desire but do not have, so you kill. You covet but you can't get what you want, so you quarrel and fight. You do not have because you do not ask God." Today, many people have gone to the extreme all in the name of power and riches. We must therefore seek all our physical, emotional, and spiritual needs directly from God because He is our Great Provider.

Forgive Us Our Sins As We Also Forgive Those...Sin Against Us

Unforgiveness has brought about so much evil. We see bitterness, hatred, riots, street gangs, killings, shootings, divorce, and all kinds of evil due to unforgiveness. They are all generated from not being able to forgive one another. From homes and neighborhoods to communities to cities, and worldwide, unforgiveness is ruling. How can we learn to forgive genuinely? Jesus said, "For if you forgive others, your Heavenly Father will also forgive you," **(Matthew 6:14).** Forgiveness is a powerful medicine to your soul. What it does is it brings changes into you. Forgiveness is as a scar. Just like we cannot overlook a scar, so it is with forgiveness. Though, you can never forget about what someone did to you because it became a scar. What you should never do is keep remembering what was done to you in a painful way; it will be like taking a knife and cutting your scar open. This is important because forgiveness is a daily medicine. Thus, the scar will help you to have the chance to forgive every time you remember what was done to you, but not to remember the pain. You must forgive in order to receive what God has for you. So, put forgiveness into practice daily. If you fail to do that, you will hold yourself hostage, and block your own blessings.

If you forget everything about forgiveness, then keep in mind that if you take forgiveness as a daily sacrifice, it will help you enter God's gate with thanksgiving to praise and worship Him in the majesty of His Holiness.

Lead Us Not Into Temptation But Deliver Us From Evil

There are temptations all around us. They can be found in many things in life and can cause us to sin if we are not watchful. For example, integrating and assimilating are causing us to become conformed to the things of the world. For this reason, we can be tempted by people we encounter or interact with on social media. We can be tempted by what we see on television or listen to on the radio. We can also be tempted by our style of clothes, the lifestyle we want to copy, and so on. This is because the world we live in is filled with all kinds of things that are easily attracted. The question is can we ever stop temptation and evil from coming? The answer is no. Jesus was tempted and we will be tempted as well. But God is faithful; He will not let us be tempted beyond what we can bear. As **1 Corinthians 10:13** declares, God will provide a way out so that we can overcome, but we must model Jesus and His victory over temptation. What did He do? Jesus overcame Satan with nothing but the *Word* by saying, "It is written" three times (**Matthew 4:4).** With the Word and prayer, we too shall overcome temptation. And if we fall into temptation, then we can pray and say, '*Deliver us....*' Thus, we must pray each day and say, '*Lead us not into temptation;* and say, *'but deliver us from evil.*' God is merciful.

NB: Never enjoy living in sin. If you find yourself trapped, cry out to God to deliver you ASAP. Don't delay, because sin is deadly. *The wage of sin is death* – **Romans 6:23.**

For Thine is the Kingdom, the Power, and the Glory, Forever...

Do you know what belongs to God, and do you give to Him what He deserves? The question is, what do you do as you live your life on earth? Be it at home, outside, or in the church, what do you do? Is your lifestyle a reflection of God's Kingdom and its Glory? How do you live your life. Does is reflect God's praises? Do you get up each day thinking of what must be given to God from your heart? Read **Psalm 100**.

Conclusion – *The Lord's Prayer* is simple, but the secret behind the prayer makes it powerful. It impacts lives in every way. Knowing this secret will have a profound impact on your life. This book has all the info you need to understand *the Lord's Prayer*, to pray with the prayer, and to help bring changes into your life and the world. If you desire to be a prayerful man or woman, then follow *the Lord's Prayer* guidelines.

The Lord knows all about prayer, and He tells it all!

Chapter 1 – What Is the Lord's Prayer About?

Matthew 6:5-15 & Luke 11:1-13

The Lord's Prayer was Jesus' answer to His disciples when they asked Him to teach them how to pray. In response, He said, "When you pray, say 'Our Father'..." (Matthew 6:9–13; Luke 11:1–4). It is a prayer guideline and a real foundational for prayer. With this, they were able to know everything they were to pray for and about. Praying as they were taught, they received answer to their prayers; they were guided, strengthened, and empowered daily. Thus, the Lord's prayer is not just any prayer but a powerful prayer for every believer who understands the power of prayer. The starting of the prayer speaks a volume. He started out by saying, *Our Father in Heaven.* This means when I am praying, I am not just throwing words into the air. Rather, I'm communicating with a Supreme Being - my Father in Heaven, as a true child. Knowing this, is the key. With this, I am already anticipating in faith toward what I am petitioning or decreeing because I know that the Father is a Good Father. He is great and Awesome!

His Prayer contains everything we must know to pray effectively. In **Matthew 7:11**, Jesus said, "If you then, being humans, know how to give good gifts to your children, how much more will your Father who is in Heaven give what is good to those who ask Him!" There is a sense of hope when we pray to our Heavenly Father because **James 1:17 says**, every good gift comes from Him. With this, I already know that my Father in Heaven will supply my needs of healing, good health, peace of mind, prosperity, joy, wisdom, and so on, even before I start to pray. And it won't matter my needs once I ask according to *His Will*. Today, we call it the Lord's Prayer because it was directly taught by the Lord Jesus Christ, who knew everything about Heaven, the concept of prayer, and how prayer works. In His prayer, Jesus taught His disciples the personality of the Father and everything they needed to know about Him. Since He knew the importance of communicating with the Father through prayer, He willingly taught His disciples to pray according to the Will of the Father so that their prayers will not be hindered.

The Lord's Prayer is simple yet profound and powerful, with divine insights. It is known as the favorite prayer among many Christians who recite it daily. But *th*is Prayer is not just a recitation. It covers all areas of life and teaches us how we should live our lives. It contains the glue that holds our Christian life together and connects us to our Heavenly Father. This makes the Prayer of the Lord a way of life. The impact of His prayer is properly felt when it is said phrase by phrase, with a deliberate attempt to understand the words. To grasp the truth behind the prayer, you must understand the meaning of each phrase in a much deeper way beyond a mere recitation.

The Lord's Prayer is a mystery that needs to be unraveled, and I am humbled to be part of those chosen to unveil the hidden truth which has never been revealed clearly for a better understanding. I have heard complaints about how people spend too much or too little time in prayer, but there is no right or wrong duration of prayer when the Spirit Himself is in control (**Romans 8:26**). With the understanding of His Prayer through the Holy Spirit, no prayer is useless. Every prayer is powerful when it is led by the Holy Spirit. When the Holy Spirit is in the lead, we pray according to the Father's Will, and that is the key. Once you get to know the true depths of the Lord's Prayer and the power of the Holy Spirit concerning prayer, you will see why the *Lord Prayer* is powerful. And spending time in prayer will not be a minute or 3 hours, but until the Spirit is done with His work. This is what I have been instructed to write, and I am determined to explain it in the same way it was revealed to me for everyone to see that His Prayer is simple, yet powerful!

What is our earthly purpose? This book will further enhance your understanding of God and draw you closer to Him because that is its purpose. Part of our calling is do the Kingdom's Work here on earth; but that can't be done effectively without effective prayer. That is why the Lord Jesus taught us to pray as such. This is not to say that one does not know how to pray. It is just that sometimes, we miss important things that must be prayed about. But this simple but powerful prayer of the Lord teaches us everything we need to know, so we can do the Kingdom's Work here on earth for *God's Will to be done as it is done in Heaven*. With His Prayer, we get to know about the Father; His Holiness; His Kingdom; His Love, *His Will*, His provision, and His forgiveness. Not only that, but His Prayer can also help deepen our love for Him, for ourselves, and for others. We can also learn how to surrender to Him our freewill; live according to *His Will*; get a better understanding of God's Power, His Goodness, His Protection, His Reign, and everything that involves Him and His Kingdom's Work here on earth. It is how we live according to the Father's Will. So, this simple Prayer of the Lord involves everything we need to live our Christian journey here on earth. It is how it becomes our way of life.

What makes the Lord's Prayer remarkable is that it helps us understand that our lives here on earth do not revolve around us and what we can do for ourselves only. Life on earth is more about what we are here for, which includes serving God until the end. And how do we serve Him? In **Galatians 2:20,** Paul says, "I have been crucified with Christ and I no longer live, but Christ lives in me..." Understanding the Lord's Prayer helps us to know our purpose in this life. Jesus was sent from Heaven to give His life, to reveal to us our purpose in life, and show us the way to God to fulfill that purpose. That is His purpose. Similarly, each of us should be able to identify our purpose and work towards fulfilling that purpose. The understanding of the Lord's Prayer led me to write this book; it is part of my purpose on earth, and I take great delight in fulfilling that purpose. I am glad to have found my purpose and so can you. I want to live a life worthy of my calling, to imitate Christ, and abide by His commands. I pray for everyone to be able to tap into their earthly purpose.

When we receive salvation, we are cleansed of sin and enabled to know the Father personally and share in His goodness. However, this cannot happen without taking the time to read, pray, and meditate on God's Word. Although each one of us has a different assignment and purpose, we have the same goal, which is, the Kingdom's Work, where prayer, God's Word and salvation are intertwined. In His own words, Jesus gives us guidelines for praying because He knows that the most intimate way to know the Father, His Kingdom, and our purpose is through prayer. Jesus knew that prayer is the work of the Holy Spirit. Therefore, He promised us a helper, the Holy Spirit, who intercedes on our behalf and strengthens our foundations in Christ (**John 16:7**).

The Lord's Prayer is the *Word of God* which applies to us as well. It takes someone who understands everything about Heaven and what prayer does to reveal these simple words of mystery for us to follow. Christ revealed the Father and connected us to Him. This means that *the Lord's Prayer* is not only for the disciples. **2 Timothy 3:16** says, "All Scripture is given by the inspiration of God, and is useful for teaching, rebuking, correcting, and training in righteousness." For example, when He says in **Matthew 28:20,** "Go therefore and make disciples of all nations...," it applies to us all.

The Lord's Prayer helps us know that we are children of God. In His Prayer, Jesus says, "Our Father." **John 3:16** makes it clear that salvation is offered to the whole world so that we can all call God "our Father." This gives us the assurance that we are God's children through salvation, which grants us equal access to say His prayer and communicate with Him through that in Jesus' Name! This is because the contents of the prayer reveal the kind of Father we have and the relationship He desires to have with us. It requires constant effort to establish a bond with Him and get to know Him better. Once we set our path to the road of salvation, build our relationship with God, and communicate with Him through Christ, our relationship starts to grow. Therefore, our salvation's foundation depends on constant prayer in His Word. I am fascinated by the idea of communicating with God, with the help of the Holy Spirit because it is *God's Will.*

The Lord's Prayer helps us to know that prayer is an important aspect of the Christian life, and so we ought to pray ceaselessly because we cannot survive without prayer. In Gethsemane, Jesus noticed that His disciples were weak in prayer. On His return to them and seeing that they were sleeping, He asked them, "Could you not pray with me for one hour?" (Matthew 26:40–45). In 1 Thessalonians 5:17, we are encouraged to pray without ceasing. When people say it is not necessary to pray for long, I always say, 'let the Holy Spirit have His way. If you do not understand the purpose of the Lord's Prayer, you will think praying for 1–2 minutes is okay. Yes, it can be okay, but not always. We can pray for a short time whilst in public, but not in our closet. In our world today, there are too many things to pray for, and we cannot do so in 2 minutes. I am certain a Holy Spirit led prayer for intercession will be more than just a minute or two.

People who do not seek God through His Word, seek answers elsewhere. Some seek answers from family, friends, or academics. Others go to the extreme of becoming polytheistic, because they think many gods can produce practical results for them – both good and bad. Others involve themselves in witchcraft and divination, hoping that their hunger for answers will be gratified. As for us Christians, we have no doubt that Jesus Christ is the only answer. He has given us the answer we need in His Word. This is because each phrase of His Prayer helps us find supporting Scriptures for more insight into what we are searching for or troubled about. The phrases in the Prayer of the Lord help us to pray and cover a wide range of things, and referring to Scripture for added clarity helps us to pray and meditate affectively. As we search through the Bible, we obtain the answers we need for our questions, without the need for sorcerers, enchanters, or anyone/thing else, because the word of God has it all! He says, "...ask, knock, and seek...and you shall find" (**Luke 11:10**). This gives us the confidence that we are praying in *God's Will*, and that our question will be answered in due time when we pray diligently.

The Lord's Prayer makes it more practical because it acts as our guide to effective prayer. It is easy to access. Its effectiveness comes from the fact that it covers every area of life. You can use it to pray for yourself, your family, and the world, to counteract the works of the evil doings that affect lives.

The Parts of *the Lord's Prayer*:

The first part, thanksgiving/exaltation deals with God's Fatherly nature, power, and glory. This is to know the Father who resides in Heaven: who He is, what His Name is, His Holiness, His Kingdom, *His Will*, our salvation, and our appreciation of Him.

The second part is a request. This is about the Goodness of the Father; It is because of His Goodness that we ask and give thanks for the things which He does in our lives.

The third part is praise/worship. This section tells of God's eternal Kingdom and His reign, which is the reason behind our praise and worship of Him.

The Holy Spirit is the power behind **prayer**. He helps us to pray in *God's Will*. Knowing these simple steps will help you build your prayer life. In His prayer, Jesus speaks about the Will of the Father. With this, we understand that *His Will* is perfect and that anything we do must be directed toward fulfilling *it*. The Bible tells us that "Whatever we bind on earth shall be bound in Heaven, and what is bind in Heaven is bound on earth" as a confirmation of the *Will of God* (**Matthew 18:18**). In any relationship, whether with our family or friends, communication is essential. It is the same with our Heavenly Father. He wants to hear from us daily. When we pray, He listens. When He speaks through His Word, we also must listen. It is how we get our answers to what we requested in our prayer. He is a Great Father who knows all our struggles. Sometimes even if we cannot speak out laud, He still can hear us. So, our prayers in the form of thoughts, feelings, reading of scripture, and through actions, are all known to Him. Thus, praying in the Lord's Prayer helps us prioritize our prayer life, develop a relationship with God, so that our prayers can be answered.

Living in the *Will of God* is a concept that every true believer finds as essential to our spiritual lives. It brings profound meaning and satisfaction. 1 **Thessalonians 5:16-18** teaches us the three dimensions of the *Will of God*: rejoicing, giving thanks, and praying without ceasing. These bring us the sense of purpose to have priorities, make good plans, and stand strong. The pursuit of the *Will* of *God* also helps us with a deeper relationship with the Father and get a better understanding of our purpose in life so we can live a life that reflects our values and beliefs. It's about aligning our actions, decisions, and life direction with God's desires. In *His Will*, we can lead a life that is not only pleasing to God but also fulfilling. Living in the will of God involves seeking guidance through prayer, scripture, and the counsel of the Holy Spirit. It is a believe that that helps us to discern the plans God has for each of us. For example, **Ephesians 5** tells us to understand what *God's Will* is so we can live wisely.

Praying in *God's Will* helps us unlock Heaven's gates for anointing to do God's work zealously. In *His Will*, we can break loose from the shackles of the evil one, release Heavenly blessings of salvation, healing, and wisdom. Most importantly, praying according to the Father's Will helps us to enjoy praying, because in *His Will*, we see God's best. But none of these will happen without the word of God because *God's Will* works through His Word to perfect everything. We shall get to that later.

I know these few secrets in the Lord's Prayer that have been disclosed are preparing your heart. After the whole secret is unfolded, your understanding of His Prayer will be broadened. The Lord wants us to be involved in His Kingdom's Work, which is nothing like earthly business. Thus, knowing the details of His Prayer and expanding it in prayer is how it works, because His Prayer is about everyone and everything, including the unsaved, and the challenges in our lives and in the whole world, which is why Christ came.

This reminds me of a lady who believed that she did not need to pray for anyone or about anything because she had her own problems to worry about. She also believed that we could pray for just 1 or 2 minutes because God knows everything already anyway. So why waste time in prayer? Sadly, she was misled about the Lord's Prayer until she was hit by a severe life storm. From that time, her prayer life changed completely. If the Lord urges us to pray without ceasing, it means to pray, pray, and pray, 1) always, 2) for all people, and 3) for everything. Yes, I am aware that prayer can never be too short or too long once the Holy Spirit is leading.

Communicating with the Lord makes His Kingdom Work easy, fun, and effective no matter the challenges. However, there is no short cut. It must be led by the Holy Spirit because that is the Will of God. He gives us the power to do the work through prayer. That is why Jesus models prayer. It was the Word and prayer that aided Him to conquer Satan. In **Matthew 21:13**, He says, "My house shall be called a house of prayer." **Isaiah 56:7** also says, "I will bring them to my holy mountain of Jerusalem and will fill them with joy...prayer. I will accept their burnt offerings and sacrifices because my temple will be called a house of prayer for all nations." Therefore, we should not take the notion that says we must pray for just a minute.

We must follow the rule of prayer. In **Luke 5:35**, Jesus said, "But the time will come when the bridegroom will be taken from them; in those days, they will fast." So, as you can see, this is not the time to pray between 1–2 minutes and think that it is okay. It is okay only *if* the Holy Spirit is done praying through you.

***The Lord's Prayer* is for effective prayer.** Before God can do greater things including those that seem impossible on our behalf, we must pray like that of Moses, Daniel, Esther, Elijah, Mary, Peter, Paul, etc. But that is impossible without a fervent prayer. A fervent prayer is a key to unlocking the unknown. Once you have the right key, unlocking the door would be so easy. I remember one time I misplaced my key. I tried them all, but none worked. It was very frustrating, but the door easily unlocked when I got the right key. I was stuck behind the door for several minutes, trying to open it with the wrong key. The same can be said about prayer. Yes, it is true, it is not about how long we pray, the sweet words we use, and how perfect our words may sound. Rather, they must be aligned or supported by God's Word with the help of the Holy Spirit. He oversees prayer.

That means prayer in general is not just about being eloquent. **We cannot use persuasiveness or expressiveness to convince and influence God in anything. It is also not about having the ability to say the right words to sound logical. Instead, it is about opening ourselves and allowing the Holy Spirit to help us pray.** With His help, our prayers will be as that of Abel's offering and not as Cain's. God answers us when we pray according to *His Will*. It is written in **1 John 5:14,** "This is the confidence we have in approaching God: that if we ask anything according to *His will*, He hears us." When we pray according to the Father's Will, we are joined by a multitude of angels to give thanks, sing praises, worship the Father, and petition Him.

Effective prayer is also like solving a jigsaw puzzle. Prayer is a way of communicating directly with God, so, knowing how to pray according to *God's Will* is important. When the Holy Spirit is leading you in prayer, He helps you solve the prayer puzzle easily. With His help, the hidden puzzle pieces of the Lord's Prayer will fit together perfectly! He helps us connect all the pieces together as we pray, and according to the Will of God so we can yield the most results. We cannot just say whatever we want in prayer, because the Lord does not teach us to pray anyhow. In the Lord's Prayer, our prayers are effective. Read **James 5:16.** You can be a righteous person, but if your prayers are contrary to *God's Will*, it will not be effective. As **Jeremiah 33:3** states, if we call to Him, He will answer and show us many great things. This is what the Lord's Prayer is about. So, it is not just about praying. It is about praying to get the work done as the Master requires. We may face serious adversities, but prayer with fasting will empower us.

In essence, the purpose of the Lord's Prayer is to remind us that we have an awesome Father. It is to help us communicate and bond with Him, bond with one another, and do the Kingdom's Work together. Many things are going on in today's world, and if we are not bound to Jesus Christ and the power of His Word and Prayer, we will drift away. But knowing God intimately, will prevent us from being deceived.

Chapter 2 – What Brought About the Lord's Prayer?

Do you have any questions you wish you could ask our Father in Heaven? Well, you are not alone, so did the disciples.

When Jesus was on the earth, He had 12 disciples who accompanied Him wherever He went. Because the disciples were with Jesus most of the time, they observed that prayer was an integral part of His life. They witnessed how He communicated daily with His Father through prayer. Jesus never did anything without asking His Father first. He prayed when laying hands on the sick, casting out demons, and resurrecting the dead. The miracles He did clearly showed that His prayers never went unanswered. His disciples saw that Jesus performed all those miracles through prayer. However, I am sure what drove the disciples to ask Jesus to teach them to pray was a divine plan. I have put together some possible reasons. You may also have different reasons and that is okay.

> Could it be that they wanted their faith to be increased? Jesus said all His simple prayers with faith. **Hebrews 11:6** says, "It is impossible to please God without faith." Therefore, could it be that the disciples were motivated by His faith-filled prayers? Our reading of Scripture makes it clear that sometimes no lengthy prayers were said before healing the sick, casting out demons, resurrecting the dead, or performing countless other miracles. Sometimes He didn't have to say much, yet miracles happened. For instance, in **John 11**, Jesus prayed a short prayer and still Lazarus came back to life. On the other hand, He also prayed for 40 days. In **John 17**, He prayed for us all. He also prayed long in

the garden of Gethsemane. This means that prayer has no time or length limits. So, I am sure, Jesus wanted to build their faith and their prayer endurance by giving them a prayer guidance.

> Sometimes prayer, fasting, and faith are all required. In **Matthew 17:16–21**, (KJV) a man brought his son to the disciples to be prayed for, but they could not help the boy. Jesus questioned them of their faith when they failed to heal the boy. He also told them this kind of healing can come forth by nothing except prayer and fasting. I chose KJV because some of the Bible verses do not acknowledge fasting. But according to Jesus, there are times when we must fast and pray if we want good results. We cannot ignore that fact! In **Matthew 4:1–11,** we read of Jesus and His 40 days fasting. So, it was prayer, the Word, fasting, and faith. Jesus did all four. Were they inspired by that?

> What about sin? As humans, we are usually entangled by sin and that makes it impossible for our prayers to easily reach the throne of grace. But the disciples never saw Jesus commit any sin. **1 John 3:21** says, "if our hearts do not condemn us, we have confidence before God and receive from Him..." Were they inspired by His Holiness? That is why Jesus taught us to reconcile with those who have wronged us before making an offering. In **Matthew 5:24**, Jesus said, "Leave your gift there in front of the altar. First go and be reconciled to them; then come and offer your gift." What do you think? I think by the time we leave our offering at the altar and run to find the person with whom we must reconcile, we would have already run out of time (I don't think this is funny). Were they inspired by the fact that Jesus always forgave people right away, even those that had done Him wrong? Though it may seem improbable, we can heal the sick and cast out demons by the authority given to us if we immediately forgive. So, I am sure true forgiveness could be one reason why the disciples wanted to know the concept of prayer. If they failed to heal the boy, imagine what would have happened in the absence of Jesus. He knew the challenges ahead of them after His departure, and, as a result, He prompted them to ask to be taught how to pray.

> Did the disciples want to distinguish themselves from the Pharisees? Could it also be that the disciples did not want to be perceived as the self-righteous Pharisees who were praying to impress or show off? The Pharisees portrayed themselves as the purest and most righteous people. They prayed in public places, prayed for everyone to see, and they also condemned others. Was that right? **Luke 18:9–14** tells us of the parable about two men, a Pharisee and a tax collector who went into the temple to pray. The Pharisee compared his prayer to the tax collector's prayer and thought he was more righteous. In **Matthew 6:5,** Jesus said, "When you pray, you shall not be like the hypocrites." First, they were to go before God in prayer in humility and with a heart desiring forgiveness. Second, they were not to judge others, so that they won't be judged. Clearly, by comparing the prayers of the Pharisees and hypocrites to that of Jesus', the disciples saw a difference and immediately knew which one they wanted to learn.

> Did the disciples want a personal relationship with God through prayer? Did they want their prayers to please God? Could it be that they observed that Jesus gave more thanks as it is written in **1Thessalonians 5:17**? Yes, all these can be true. Can you think of other reasons of why they wanted to be taught to pray?

> Let's conclude that the *Lord's Prayer* was a divine plan.

Prayer is a way to communicate with GOD the Father, our creator. It is a way of building a personal relationship with Him. I have listened to some people and their argument on prayer. Someone said, GOD don't need my prayer if He already knows what we need. Another said, isn't it absurd to pray? Another, if GOD knows my problems already, then why do I need to pray? I see no reason to pray; another also said, GOD will do whatever pleases Him, anyway. And on and on, it goes! No not at all, because prayer is the way that you have to get to know God on a personal level. Prayer helps you to build your personal relationship with GOD Almighty, your creator, which is what, God, wants us to pray.

Chapter 3 – The Purpose of the Lord's Prayer

Why the Lord's Prayer is so important?

Why *the Lord's Prayer* is so important? *The Lord's Prayer* was a prayer given to the disciples as their guide. But it is also for us. The reason why it is so important is that it is to build a relationship with God the Father through Jesus Christ the Son, with the help of the Holy Spirit. The Prayer of the Lord sets up a system where we can communicate, meditate, and focus on the Father, to help us enrich our relationship with Him and with one another. With this, we can accept *His Will*, get rid of worldly things, build a strong Christian foundation though love, obedience, and faith to help us maintain our focus on the things of Heaven so we can grow. As **Psalm 16:11** states, "In His presence, there is fullness of joy." As we know, people without relationships are lonely; sometimes, that can cause them to be disheartened. But *the Lord's Prayer* helps us to build a good relationship with Him and assure us that we are never alone. Our intimacy with the Father in Heaven through Christ, with the help of the Holy Spirit, bond us to the Heavenly family. Jesus says we are not orphans –**John 14:18**.

***The Lord's Prayer* is our inheritance.** His Prayer has it all! It is just like any good *will* that a person leaves behind for his family. The contents of the *Lord's Prayer* encourage us to pray in very productive ways. It aids us in building our relationship with God the Father, helps us with problem-solving skills, and gives us a passionate spirit for fervent prayer. If you know the importance of a '*good living will*,' then you will know what I'm talking about. The

Prayer of Jesus is as a living will. It has everything we need to pray and build our relationship with God. It is not just for recitation, but to help us pray, and keeps us focused on the Kingdom's Work. Through it, we are encouraged to pray for everything and everyone, every day, anytime, and anywhere. If we use each line as a major topic, then the subtopics will unfold as we start to pray for what we ought to pray for. With the *Lord's Prayer,* you can fulfill your purpose of attaining the Kingdom's Mindset. For example, even if you had no idea how to pray or what to pray for, you can give thanks, ask, and practice holiness, ask for your needs, pray for salvation for all, ask for forgiveness, learn to forgive, ask for protection, and know how to praise and worship God. All these must be a daily request. Each phrase helps us to pray constantly and tackle a major issue in life.

***The Lord's Prayer* reveals the mysteries of Heaven and what prayer does for us.** Under the shadow of the Almighty God, there are secrets, and we get to know some of these secrets as we pray and seek His face. In **Jeremiah 33:3** we are told that secrets would be revealed if we call unto Him in prayer. **Psalm 91:1** says, "He who dwells in the secret place of the Most-High will abide under the shadow of the Almighty." Many hidden secrets are revealed to those that dwell in the secret place of the Most-High God. When we dwell in His most secret place, the Almighty God shields us under His shadow. Just as human relationships depend upon communication, the more we communicate with people, the more we become familiar with them and their secrets. A close relationship with the Lord helps us get to know Him in a personal way and learn some secrets about Him. If we become familiar with His ways, He will not hide things from us. Thus, a relationship with God through prayer is vital.

***The Lord's Prayer* also helps us understand the concept of prayer.** There are many ways to do things. Some are good and others are bad. Some yield good results whereas others produce bad results. The same can be said about prayer. *The Lord's Prayer* points us specifically to the things of which we must become aware. For example, you do not need to be told how to worship God if you properly understand it, because *the Lord's Prayer* is self-explanatory.

Also, if you know how to give thanks, praise the Lord, and forgive, you will do so easily. What I like about *the Lord's Prayer* is that no one can ever teach us how to pray better than the Lord Himself. This makes His prayer divine, and that is what I find inspiring.

***The Lord's Prayer* helps us to intercede.** Esther's story teaches us the importance of intercession. In times of trouble, Esther put her life in danger and said, "If I perish, I perish" **(Esther 4:16).** Her story shows that prayer is not just for us, but also, for everyone in our circle and around the world. In **John 17:15**, Jesus prayed a prayer of protection for us. Just like Abraham, Moses, Joshua, Elijah, Daniel, Esther, etc., our prayers can make a big difference. So, we too must pray. In times of trouble, they interceded. We have been called just like them. We are God's faithful servants just like them. When we pray and intercede, we align ourselves with *God's Will*, and our prayers are not wasted.

We can be assigned to pray for different things in many ways. Can you count the number of times the Holy Spirit woke you up in the middle of the night to pray or intercede for someone? Yes, it happens. It can be for anyone, for anything, or something that has nothing to do with any concerns you may have. Sometimes, you may be assigned to intercede on behalf of someone who is tempted, undergoing a surgical procedure, getting married, having a baby, looking for a job, needing salvation, or being attacked by the deeds of the devil. Because of this unique prayer guideline from the Lord, you can pray specifically.

Just keep in mind that every fervent prayer requires determination. We can become distracted, discouraged, or feel tired when we want to pray because the enemy always works against our efforts; but again, the steps in *the Lord's Prayer* can keep us focus. His prayer provides a significant guideline for easy, enjoyable, and effective prayer. A closer look at *the Lord's Prayer* says it all. *You will notice that it is a collection of phrases and statements that have been put together to form a whole and meaningful set of prayer guidelines.* Each phrase explains the purpose of the prayer and the need to pray. With understanding, you will have the confidence to pray anytime and anywhere.

The Lord's Prayer help us to communicate better with God through prayer. It is to help us get a better insight of God and His plans for the world; but without understanding its implications, we will never be able to apply it correctly.

As communication is essential in any relationship, so it is with our Heavenly Father. He wants to hear from us daily, and we also want to hear from Him. This is how we get our answers. He is a Great Father who knows all our struggles. Our prayers in the forms of thoughts, feelings, reading of scripture, and through actions, are all known to Him. Sometimes even if we cannot speak out loud, He still hears us. Thus, it is good to know that communication is a two-way street. Any communication that gives only one person the opportunity to talk is not a communication. It's like calling a friend on the phone and hanging up after you are done talking. If you fail to grant the person on the other end a chance to speak, that is not a proper way to communicate. It is the same with prayer. It is wrong to just talk to God and walk away when we are done talking without giving Him any chance to speak. We pray, read the Word, meditate, give thanks, praise, worship, and listen to God in prayer. These are rules of prayer.

Chapter 4 – My Encounter: Why I Chose to Write About the Lord's Prayer

Joel 2:1-32

"You are the God who performs miracles; you display your power among the peoples" (**Psalm 77:14**). Sometimes, as humans, we tend to think that God is far from our reach. But He is closer than we could ever imagine. So, let what you are about to read resonate in your mind and stay in your heart for the rest of your life to help you know that "GOD is Omnipresent. He is the God that is everywhere.

It's been a while now since I encountered the Lord concerning His prayer, and I must say that I am humbled to share its details with you. The Lord explained that many believers barely believe in Him and His love as a true Father. Many doubt His capability to provide for their needs; therefore, they look for other ways and means to meet their own needs. As the Lord spoke, I realized that most of the things He said were true about my own life as well. I thought I knew all about God as my true Heavenly Father, but I was wrong. I thought I knew how to ask for all my needs including wisdom, protection, forgiveness, but I was wrong. I thought I knew about temptations, how to give thanks, praise, and worship the Father, but I was wrong. So, when I asked for my needs, praised God, or forgave others, I did so based on how it suited me, even though I have always been a strong believer in God.

When the Lord told me to write about this encounter, I thought of it as a joke. So, for some time, I tried to hide it as if nothing had transpired between me and the Lord even though the Holy Spirit kept reminding me. This went on for some time until I prayed for His Will to be done. After that, I became delighted. Until now, He has made my desire to write clear, which directed me to write this book to disclose what was revealed to me about His prayer after telling me that it wasn't meant just for me. The opportunity to write about the Lord's Prayer has been such a blessing. It was a surprise to me because this encounter with the Lord was something I never thought could evolve into a writing assignment. If I had my way, I would have chosen to write about something else. Besides, I don't enjoy writing. Nevertheless, I thank God for giving me the strength and motivation to make this book possible. I am thankful that the Lord chose His Prayer as my first book assignment and motivated me through the contents of His Prayer. I have come to know how to give thanks, praise, and worship God sincerely.

Through the Prayer of the Lord, I have now come to appreciate that my past, present, and future sins have all been taken care of, and I can also let go and forgive myself and others. I know how to ask for my needs. I know without a shadow of doubt that I am a child of the Father. I am protected against evil because God has promised to supply all my needs, which include His protection. I also know that I have peace that surpasses all understanding, that joy, love, kindness, compassion, blessings, etc., are all part of His provisions for me. Because of His faithfulness, I can always trust Him. I am delighted to pray, and I know God hears me when I pray. After the encounter with the Lord, my realization of prayer and God's Will has broadened. I have learned a lot about His Prayer, its purpose, and its ability to change circumstances. Moreover, this encounter has improved my prayer life significantly. It has broadened my understanding to better appreciate the things of God from a spiritual perspective. It has also given me more insight into God the Father, His kingdom, and His plans and purposes for our lives. Today, I am thankful for this encounter and the way it has increased my faith and dependence on Him. I am confident that this amazing encounter that has transformed my life will also have a positive impact on your life even before you finish reading this divine prayer book.

My encounter with the Lord regarding His prayer began with two visions during my visit to Ghana in the latter part of 2013. From that time, the Lord revealed many things to me and used me in many ways to pray for people even without their knowledge. I had always prayed for people, but after the secret of His Prayer was revealed, the Lord intensified this need and gave me a clear insight into why intercessory prayer is so important. When the Lord told me to write this book, I thought all Christians knew about the Lord's Prayer and how to pray based on it, but after receiving the deepest revelation that prayer is not just mere words, I attained the understanding that though we all pray, we end up missing several important pieces. There are concepts in prayer; these include caring about worldwide issues apart from my own. It is about sin, forgiveness, praise, thanksgiving, worship, faith, trust, fear, doubts, prayer, the world, individuals, and so on. And they all must be in God's Will, but the Lord explained to me that not everyone fully understands this. Sometimes we mostly pray for our own needs above those of others, or pray for others, and forget ourselves, and that can be wrong.

The Lord explained that it is time for His people to fully understand the purpose behind His Prayer, because we will need it in the times ahead. Because of lack of proper understanding, the things that need to be tackled for the world, are sometimes missing in our prayers. Our prayers cannot only be centered on our needs. I am so thrilled to know that the Lord's Prayer, with the help of the Holy Spirit, can help bring our concerns before the Lord in daily prayer for everyone and for everything. I am delighted to have become more passionate and compassionate. The concerns I have for my own needs, as well as those of others, have helped me to know how to intercede. Finally, I have gotten a better understanding that truly, in His presence there is fullness of joy!" I am thankful for the gift of prayer, and better than before. I delight to be in His presence, but more so for the profound insight He has given me through His Prayer.

The Lord Jesus wants us to become familiar with His Prayer so it can educate us on the concept of praying to have a deeper appreciation of the Father, the Son, and the Holy Spirit. He wants us to understand His Kingdom and its rules. I know that this book will guide you to know the truth and the power behind prayer by the time you are done reading. The Holy Spirit is the only one who can help you understand this piece of writing and help you pray according to the Will of God. So, as you flip through the pages of this book, I pray that the Holy Spirit will help you gain a deeper understanding.

Childhood Memories About the Lord's Prayer: Now, let's go deeper to know how the Lord's Prayer became part of my story. During my childhood, I attended Christian schools. Our education was a system that combined traditional and Christian teachings, without any proper explanation to what Christianity was truly about. It was at the age of five when I attended kindergarten. Because it was mandatory to recite the Lord's Prayer even at that early age, I did my best, but with no understanding. If it was explained, then I never got the idea of who Jesus Christ was or about what the church was. The Lord's Prayer was a daily routine at assemblies where my country's flag was displayed, and a ceremony of morning prayers was said at the start of every school day. This forced every child in the school to learn and recite the Lord's Prayer as part of the school's routine. This continued into my teenage years. Although I prayed, I was clueless about what prayer truly represented. I had no relationship with God, neither did I know about His salvation. I celebrated Christmas, Easter, and a host of other Christian holidays, yet I couldn't appreciate God and His Kingdom, and who God the Father, the Son, and the Holy Spirit were. I guess that throughout my journey toward knowing God, He knew me and my struggles because that is what His word says in **Psalm 139:3.** In my case, Christian education at an early age had no significant impact on my life until the age of 21, when I accepted the Lord as my Savior. This means, back in my early school years, His Prayer was just a recitation and nothing more.

I have had many encounters with the Lord after salvation, but His Prayer is the most profound one. By the age of 21, after coming to know the Lord, I prayed, and my understanding of God began to grow. I got to know who God is because I was determined to learn more about Him. I developed love, faith, and trust in Him. I had a strong bond and a solid foundation in Him, yet I never even paid much attention to the Lord's Prayer. Though I understood the Father and His holiness, power, grace, mercy, forgiveness, and above all, His love for me, but it was not in the same way as I came to after the encounter. With the help of the Holy Spirit, I made significant progress in my walk with God after I accepted Jesus as my Lord and Savior and was able to pray fervently. Still, one major thing was missing: the hidden truth of the Lord's Prayer.

In the church, not much emphasis was placed on the Lord's Prayer, and I'm sure it was one reason why many of us struggled to forgive one another, praise God, or give thanks sincerely. This was because the insight of His Prayer was missing. Most of us grumbled instead of giving thanks, grew bitter instead of forgiving, or took our own ways in choosing life partners instead of God's ways. Thus, we failed to live our lives and pray according to how the Lord intended for us to live our lives. We thought of it as a prayer for the disciples, certain groups of people, or churches, but that is wrong because His prayer is for us all. It is for teaching us how to pray, how to know and serve God, and how to serve one another. It is how we incorporate the Kingdom of God into our earthly lives for His Will to be done through us as it is done in Heaven. Do not get me wrong; Almost all of us were very devoted, and yet the church was filled with many things that hindered prayer.

It was amazing to see how the Lord clarified His Prayer and allowed me to see it in detailed. God is our Lord and Savior and the words that proceed out of His mouth are more powerful than anything. That is why it takes most of us so long to know what the concepts of loving one another, forgiving one another, and living according to God's Will are. I once met a lady, who despite being a church leader, told me she would never forgive a friend. There was another church leader who kept record of all the wrongs done to her for years. This is just to name a couple. Were they counting each other's sins or forgiving only 77 times? Forgiveness must come from the heart; though it is not to say go and party with them, but you must forgive wholeheartedly and let go. I did not keep records on paper, but for many years my forgiveness was not from my heart.

What about choosing life partner, a career, or making a move? Some of us did these on our own without involving God, (out of God's Will). Some have no idea what it means to give thanks, praise, worship, meditate, and wait upon the Lord in prayer, and have Him speak. So, most of us stumbled and fell into temptations. This helps to clarify the point that many important subjects in the Lord's Prayer are not carefully addressed, and no emphasis is put on what it truly represents. So, even when we are not on good terms with someone, we act as if nothing is wrong; and we take actions even if God has not spoken yet.

The encounter was amazing because the understanding of prayer became so clear. The transformation that it brought into my life completely revitalized my walk with the Lord. It was as if a veil had been lifted from my eyes. I say this because I have experienced a great change after the encounter, and I can only be thankful to God for that. There are many things that I have learned. Here are few that were emphasized:

How do I honor God's Name? How do I seek Him? How do I live according to His Will? How do I ask for my needs? Do I honestly seek forgiveness and give the same to others? Do I genuinely repent? Do I have victory over temptation and evil? Do I give thanks, praise, and worship God daily, meditate on His Word, wait upon Him until He speaks?

My prayer is that this book will make a difference in your prayer life.

The Divine Encounter continues: The day after my encounter with the Lord, I started praying daily based upon His prayer. But every time I did, the Holy Spirit directed me to pray for my sins, for the world, and the dark days ahead. One morning while in prayer, I heard the Lord saying, "I am a True Father, and My children must know how to call on me in the days of trouble, and I will hear their cries for mercy and deliver them from evil and all troubles that are ahead." Every time the Lord spoke to me, I began writing His words, which gave me a clear picture of what He wanted me to write. From that time,

I knew something was about to happen, but I had no idea what it was, at least not until COVID-19 came as a first warning, but it is not over yet.

God explained that He had given each of us specific assignments that we must accomplish, and each of us must do our part for the sake of the Gospel and the Kingdom, and prayer must be the driving force behind whatever we do because it is prayer that will make all things possible. This is because prayer is part of His Word and the Kingdom's Work. It has been years now since my encounter, yet every detail is so real. I can only compare this with the Ethiopian eunuch who was reading the book of Isaiah without comprehension, as it is written in **Acts 8:26–39**. It was exactly how I felt; I didn't know what was happening. Although the Lord did not appear to me physically, I knew from what transpired that it was the LORD.

Your calling: Please pay attention to the little things that the Lord is trying to show or tell you. It could lead you to your calling.

My Testimony: It all began few years ago when I traveled to Africa to visit my sick mother. The distance from the airport to her city was about 100 miles. From the airport, I drove straight to her home. My mom felt better within a few weeks after being with her; therefore, I decided to travel back to the capital. My relatives agreed to send a house helper to aid me, so I would not be alone. Living in the house alone was not comfortable for personal reasons, and locking and unlocking the gate was only one of the issues. The gate bell had been broken; therefore, it was hard to hear when a visitor was knocking. One morning, I was expecting a handyman. So, I got up early, still in my nightgown, to unlock the gate. Stepping out in my nightgown was not a problem because I was alone, and the gate was just a few yards out. But on that morning, I slammed the door only to realize that I didn't have my keys with me. I had practically locked myself out of my house wearing only a nightgown! I felt distressed. Being outside without proper clothes and knowing a stranger was on the way to the house to fix something was very disturbing. I didn't know what to do. While I was worrying miserably, the Lord caused four things to happen, which I viewed as miracles. This is how it all happened:

(1) The first miracle was realizing I had my phone in my hand. Since arriving in my home city from my mom's town, I had never taken my phone with me when unlocking or locking the gate, so I wondered how my phone was in my hand that morning. I would soon understand that it was all part of God's plan.

(2) The second miracle occurred when the Lord confirmed His power as a true provider. In **Genesis 22:14,** God instructed Abraham to sacrifice his son, Isaac. When Isaac asked his father about the lamb for the sacrifice, Abraham replied that the Lord would provide it. As God is omniscient, He knows everything ahead of time and works behind the scenes so that what does not make sense will come to light in good time. As I paced around the compound troubled, I felt the urge to go behind the house. To my surprise, I saw a large beach towel hanging on the clothesline. That was strange because I hadn't fully unpacked my suitcases since I arrived, so how the towel turned up on the clothesline was a miracle! To this day, I wonder how that happened. I grabbed the towel and wrapped it around myself perfectly. God surely provided for me that morning like He did for Abraham. Although my situation was not a big deal like Abraham's, I believe that in every situation God provides through His power for His glory. God is our Great Provider. He is truly great and awesome, and nothing is impossible for Him.

(3) I needed someone whom I could trust to unlock the door. Many thoughts kept flashing through my mind, but I did not pray. This was strange because in situations like these, I would usually find myself praying and asking God for help. But I guess my desperation got the better of me or maybe it was God's own doing for me not to pray at that moment. This didn't stop God from what He was ready to do on that day. I turned on my phone hoping to call someone for help with the situation, but I realized that I hadn't saved any phone numbers. My desperation then became even worse. I needed the right number. But I had made several phone calls since my arrival, so even if I wanted to call each of those numbers to ensure that I had the right person, it would take some time. I couldn't call any of my relatives because they lived in deferent cities, and

it would take hours for them to arrive due to traffic. As I scrolled through the unsaved numbers, I heard a voice telling me to call a particular number, so I did. Surprisingly, it was the right person who could get me a trustworthy locksmith. That was unbelievable!

He told me he would arrive in the next 3 minutes. A few minutes later, I began thinking about the phone in my hand, the beach towel behind the house, and the specific number that the Holy Spirit directed me to call. I felt relieved, knowing that God was controlling the situation. My heart was filled with so much joy. However, after half an hour had passed without the locksmith's arrival and I couldn't reach him on his cell phone, my anxiety level increased. But the amazing thing that happened was that instead of focusing on the problem, suddenly, I began singing and immediately felt the touch of the Holy Spirit. It was as if an angelic choir was singing with me. I completely forgot about the locked door and the carpenter. Then, the Holy Spirit changed the song and brought my attention to The Lord's Prayer. I started reciting it over and over without paying much attention to what I was saying. As I kept reciting it, I heard a voice asking, "Do you understand it? Do you understand what you are saying?" I answered "Yes" and kept reciting it. The voice continued to ask the same question repeatedly. Thinking the voice was my own thoughts, my childhood memories of the Lord's Prayer started playing in my mind. Then I started thinking about when I use to recited the Lord's Prayer in school at the age of five. I said, "Oh yeah, I remember when I was a little girl reciting it, blah, blah, blah..." Then the voice came back again, and again, but this time even louder. Without realizing where the voice was coming from, I wondered, "Why this question?" At that point, the Holy Spirit drew my attention to what was going on. I kept quiet for a minute and began deeply analyzing the words in the Lord's Prayer. From that moment, I was drawn away in the spirit, and I completely lost my sense of awareness. I didn't remember where I was, what had happened, what I was doing, or what was going on.

I felt as though I was being controlled. I was neither sleeping nor sitting, and I was not aware of myself anymore. The Lord kept me in the same spot in the compound, without moving. It was as if I was watching a movie about the truth of the Lord's Prayer phrase by phrase. I recall it being a beautiful moment. The words were pouring into my heart like a fountain. I pray that this will excite you as it had been for me! So let me make it simple by saying that we truly serve a Mighty God whose name is Yahweh. He is Omnipotent (all powerful and has power over everything), Omnipresent (always present and there is no place we can be without Him being there), and Omniscient (He has all knowledge and is all-knowing).

On that day, the Spirit of God revealed to me the mystery behind the Lord's Prayer and taught me all I needed to know about it. Today, anytime I say the words "Our Father who art in Heaven," or "My Father who art in Heaven" (if I want to make it personal); Hallowed be Thy name," it makes more sense to me now than it did before. The Lord knew that it was time for me to stop simply reciting His prayer and put it into practice. Later, the Lord said to me, "Write about what I have revealed to you because there would be challenges ahead, and when it happens, I want My people to know that I am a true Father to whom they can turn." A year after the encounter, I returned to America and have never stopped working on this assignment. I have never liked writing and so I initially hesitated, but after starting to write this story, the Lord has never stopped revealing the hidden truths of His prayer to me. Now, I have come to realize that indeed He is the All-Knowing God. Even when I encountered difficulties, such as my hard drive breaking down, and I had to start everything afresh, still I never got discouraged. One time, I wanted to give up writing, but the Lord revealed two past visions to me, which made me realize that indeed God had a purpose. Since that time, writing has been a delightful assignment. So, believe it when I say, the more I tried to quit, the more I became delighted to write. Today, I am still writing because I know He has a purpose.

There has always been a father-daughter bond with the Lord from the time of my salvation. God cares for me; He protects and guides me through all things. What I know not, He explains. He clears my doubt from all confusion. He encourages and comforts whenever I need them. Even when I think that I do not deserve His goodness, He never leaves me to my fate, He always makes sure it is right with my soul. Sometime ago, I faced many challenges enough to make me feel as if God had forsaken me. But throughout my difficulties, God proved Himself as the faithful God and Father, whom He has always been. He has always kept me by His side. He helps me when I need help and rebukes me when I need to be admonished. Whenever I need answers and solutions to my problems, His presence is always there. But regarding this encounter, I never expected it to be as huge a writing assignment as it has become today. This has been a life-changing event that I will cherish forever. Thank You Lord!

God indeed has a plan. In His plan, everything happens for a reason. **Romans 8:28** states, "For those who love the Lord, all things work together for good." This means that in every circumstance, no matter how critical, God already has a plan that will surely work for our good if we love Him, because our love shows how much we trust in Him. Even if our challenges are caused by the devil, God is not surprised. He will always work things together for our good. Therefore, it won't matter how hard the devil tries, God will cause faith in place of doubt, love in place of fear, and certainty in place of anxiety. God will use any disadvantage for our advantage because everything is for His purpose. That is why Jesus taught us to pray according to the 'Will' of the Father; because if we do, we shall combat the works of the evil one on earth.

During the whole encounter, I was unaware of my surroundings. My thoughts shifted from all my worries about the locked door to a place of tranquility. It was only when the Lord finished communicating with me that I realized what had transpired. God knows all about us and our needs. Be it physical, emotional, or spiritual, He knows them all. The Bible says in **Psalm 14:1** that "Only a fool says in his heart that there is no God." Anyone who says there is no God is pitiful because God is within and around us.

(4) Final miracle: This takes us to the fourth and the final miracle. This occurred less than 30 seconds after I came out of the trance. My rescuer had arrived with a locksmith. I immediately checked the time on my phone and surprisingly, what was supposed to take 30 minutes had lasted almost 3 hours.

"Three hours!" I exclaimed! The Lord had been working on me for almost 3 hours without my realization. That was how I knew it was the Lord's doing. I was stunned! So, put simply, I would say, 1) the Holy Spirit put me in a trance, 2) worked in me, and right after He finished, 3) He sent those two men to my aid. Thus, the Lord stopped the handyman from coming and brought the rescuers instead. He also made my wasted time a meaningful one. The following day, the handyman came over to apologize for not showing up. But knowing it was all God's plan, I took no offense because I was certain that the Lord stopped him from coming for a reason. In fact, I was in awe of everything. It made me know how closer God is to us than we could ever imagine!

Looking back at all that occurred that day, I can say that God knows how, and when to supply our needs, but we must rely on Him. Going to bed that night, I couldn't help but think about the encounter. As I lay down, I began pondering of the goodness of God. I thought of how He establishes His Kingdom in us through salvation; how He helps us to live according to His Will and moves us to work toward expanding His Kingdom. All these are part of God's wonders through grace. I also thought about His delivering power. The Lord's Prayer sounded and felt completely different after that encounter. I could only be grateful. My encounter with the Lord transformed my life. Some time ago, I had a conversation with someone about prayer. According to this person, there is no need to pray too long and for anyone but herself. When I asked why, she responded, "Because the Lord's Prayer is short." I smiled, knowing that this was exactly what I am assigned to write. This was a few years before the 'COVID-19 pandemic struck. After the encounter, I always knew that something terrible was about to happen, and that the LORD was preparing me. Although I had no idea what was ahead, I trusted God in His capacity to do what no one can and prayed. As a compassionate Father, He protects and rescues us from all forms of calamity no matter the affliction, if we pray.

After the encounter, I kept praying that people will come to the saving grace of Our Father and that whatever was yet to befall us would not occur.

Even if it must come, I pray that the Lord would see us through. With this feeling, my prayer topics are: Lord, 1) let Your Name be known to all, 2) let Your Kingdom of righteousness come and rule in our midst, 3) let Your Will be done on earth as it is done in Heaven, 4) help us to depend on You for all our needs, 5) forgive us of all our sins, and help us to forgive one another, 6) lead us not into temptation but deliver us from evil, and 7) teach us to know You more, love You dearly, and worship You daily. I have expanded and extended my prayer to all people! My prayer is shifted from 'me' to more of 'us.'

I can confidently say that the Lord's Prayer has increased my faith and dependence on God because surely, during the COVID-19 outbreak, my prayer each day in my closet was for the Lord's Will to be done, and I prayed for protection for the whole world. My acknowledgment of God and His Kingdom has eradicated my sense of self-dependence and self-righteousness, turning it into complete reliance on God. I have come to understand His Fatherly love as it is written in **1 John 4:19**. Now more than ever, I am determined to experience His glory and submit myself completely to His Will. I am not worried about what tomorrow holds because I know that with God, I can face whatever obstacles life will bring. This is because my understanding of the Lord's Prayer has brought me peace of mind.

The Lord saw my shortcomings and filled in whatever was lacking, and now, my life is filled with songs of thanksgiving, praise, and worship. I am encouraged to work toward my salvation and to spread the gospel of Jesus Christ. I know that the Lord will continue to use this book as His tool to spread the good news for all to know that we truly have a Father in Heaven who cares so much. His Holy Name must be known to entire world. I am thankful that the Holy Spirit explained everything that I needed to know about the Lord's Prayer, phrase by phrase. Lately, if something doesn't work out the way I want, I give thanks instead of murmuring, because I trust in His ways. I can also forgive quickly. Though I am not perfect, I am no longer confused, frustrated, impatient, or filled with doubt. I ask for forgiveness if I become frustrated or upset about something. I know how to ask for all my needs, not just some, but all my needs including patience, wisdom, and protection. I know I am under the Lord's protection. I call it 'divine insurance coverage.' It is paid in full, and I have nothing to worry about. Because **Psalm 91:1** says, "He who dwells in the secret place of the Most-High, shall abide under the shadow of the Almighty."

For decades, my thoughts were repleted with so much negativity that they caused me to run away from God instead of running to Him when trouble arose. I was angry with myself and others and there were times when I even directed my confusion toward God, although I knew He was my Heavenly Father. The difference today is that I do not doubt His Fatherhood. Years ago, when trouble arose, I thought He could not be reached. Today, I know He is closer than I could ever imagine. Years ago, I became confused and frustrated. Although I knew God was good and merciful, I allowed doubt and fear to push me away from God by blaming Him as if He was not a good Father. Today, there is no doubt in my mind that He is indeed my reliable, dependable, and unfailing Father. I have no worries because my deep love for Him has conquered every fear. The negative mindset that allowed the devil to manipulate my situation and caused confusion is no more. I now know how to oppose and resist the devil all because I have come to know that I am 100% under the canopy of God. Amen! All the negativities that previously allowed the devil to manipulate my situations are no more. Now, I have moved past running from God to running to Him. I don't run from His presence because according to **Psalm 139:7**, there is nowhere to turn to where He won't be present. When we are confronted with an obstacle, the solution is not to question, doubt, or be angry with God out of frustration. This insight into the Lord's Prayer helps me to realize that praying, thy will be done, humbles my heart and give me a desire to submit to God, rely, and depend on Him. In **Psalm 34:18,** we read, "The Lord is near to the brokenhearted and saves the crushed in spirit." We cannot come before the Lord with angry hearts to demand anything from Him. This was exactly what I did because back then, I didn't understand what it meant to say with all sincerity, Thy Will be done in me, as it is in heaven. Although I thought I knew.

Today, by His grace, the moment I say, "Lord, let Your Will be done in this situation as it is in Heaven," I can see the difference. I can see God's mighty hands releasing solution into the situation. This helps me not to be afraid, worried, or anxious. Even if it is not the way I anticipate it to be, I am still thankful that He hears me. In every prayer, I plead for the Father's Will to be done instead of mine. This positive attitude has brought me peace of mind. When I pray, "Lord, let Your Will be done in my children, as it is done in Heaven," I can see positive outcomes. It is so peaceful when God's Will is indeed at work in each of our lives. In the same way, praying for God's Will be done on earth is important. Though troubles still exist and will never be gone until Christ comes, I am certain God will forever be in control when I keep praying, 'Thy Will be done.' It helps us to surrender to God completely. With this, we can bring change into our lives and in our world.

The circumstances surrounding this book make me believe that God has anointed this book for a greater work. Our God is a rescuer who knows when and how to rescue His children. When I needed a locksmith to unlock the door, He came to my aid. He broke through the door of my heart and rescued me from my unholiness. God knew that I needed to be spiritually rescued before anything else. So, He did just that. Today, this encounter with the Lord has brought me to higher levels in my Christian journey. Right when the door locked, I didn't know why, but God knew. I didn't know what to do, but God knew. I didn't know how to solve the problem, but God knew. I didn't have any plans, but God had plans. He always has a plan.

God knew exactly what would happen and what He would do as soon as I walked outside. He caused the door to be locked so He and I could have a Father–daughter moment. The Lord wanted to teach me something. Many years before the encounter, the Lord gave me a vivid vision of something He wanted me to do. In this vision, I was sent to do something, but I was delaying. On my way, I got distracted by some friends and found myself busy doing something unrelated to what I was sent to do. This means I didn't pay much attention to the vision as I should until I was alerted by a second vision. This is true because for years, I occupied myself with other things that had nothing to do with my purpose until the encounter came as reminder.

Today, using the Lord's Prayer as a prayer guideline has deepened and broadened my understanding of how powerful communication with God can be. Using His Prayer as my guide has helped me to focus. I have come to realize that there is a lot of work to be done, and they can be done right if I seriously pray. I have come to realize that there are many things to pray for and about: Not only my problems but everyone else's. There is also no such thing as too short or too long of a prayer. For me, it has been nothing but peace within my soul after I started using the Lord's Prayer as my guide because the Holy Spirit is always in control. Today, I can assure you that a good understanding of the Lord's Prayer will cause you to delight yourself in the Lord and in prayer. It will help you give thanks in every situation, rely on God more, and cause you to never lose hope. Even if your faith is tested, your attention will never be shifted away from Christ, the Solid Rock on which we stand.

Let me tell you a little about myself and why I faced many problems having all my needs. Previously, I never asked for anything from the Lord other than healing when I was sick. Today, I appreciate what it means to say, "Give us this day our daily bread" (**Matthew 6:11**). Here was the problem; All my life, I never knew what poverty was because of the home in which I grew up. We had a place to called home, plenty to eat, and clothes to wear. Though we were not millionaires, we were not poor either, and so I never learned to ask God for anything other than physical healing and spiritual blessings. I thought that was all I needed to ask for. So, I never asked God for food, money, or shelter. I did not think of those as part of His provisions, because I could provide those. Once I had money to buy what I needed and to pay my bills; I was okay. This was my life in Africa until I traveled to America. Because my husband was a missionary, we were okay until our mission work ended. That was the time we faced real-life challenges. Even with that, I still did not know how to ask God for the things I needed. So, I struggled for a while. I have a Father who has promised to supply all my needs. Yet, I did not ask for material things. Why? Are those not part of His provisions? I asked not; therefore, I received not. That is what **James 4:2** says. This was simply because I did not know how to ask. But after my encounter with God, He taught me the importance of asking accordingly. Today, knowing how to ask for my needs has helped me to focus on my calling.

I also lived in fear because I misinterpreted the whole concept of what it meant to be under God's protection. I was in Christ, but I still worried about who or what was coming after me, mostly spiritual attacks. The Lord taught me that under His coverage, I am fully protected. After fully understanding His divine protection, I have become rest assured because in Christ, I have nothing to worry about. I know my family and I are protected. The only thing we must do is to trust and obey because 'no weapon formed against us shall prosper' under God's Protection.

Jealousy was another thing the Lord revealed to me. After my encounter, the LORD explained to me how many people are plagued with jealousy and envy, which causes a lot of hatred and division. The way to remove these from the church is by establishing confidence in one another and praying for others and our weaknesses. Many years ago, it was people's jealousy and envy that destroyed my family and I while doing the Lord's work on the mission field. Instead of praying for them, we allowed their insults to build frustration in us and overrule us. If the Lord is our supplier, then there is no need to envy others and what they have or where the Lord places them. We must trust Him for His blessings instead of being jealous. Rather, we can rejoice with them. Also, there is no need to be sad if you are being treated bad. I was offended because I was insulted for something I knew nothing about. But it was wrong to think that way, because in **Matthew 5,** the Lord said, "Blessed are you when people insult you and falsely say all kinds of evil against you because of Me."

Another issue is judging and condemning – **Romans 8:34**. The Lord says we must uphold people in prayer rather than condemn them.

Concerning worship, the Lord said we must know how to give thanks, praise, worship, and wait upon Him in prayer. One day, I heard a pastor preach about how he had observed people coming to church and leaving empty. He explained that those were the ones who did not understand what it meant to worship God in the beauty of His holiness. They come to church as spectators. Through observation, I also came to find this to be true. Others check their phones during worship or watch other people worshipping. But everyone must know what to do during praise and worship time. If people are still lacking in this, then the church must teach the members how to give thanks and participate in praise and worship. We must also be taught of the importance of reading the Bible, and making our request known to God. Beside these, we must also know how to meditate upon the Word, be silent before the Lord, and learn to listen. Every believer's responsibility is getting to know the Father and building a good relationship with Him. However, good teachings will help everyone to establish a better understanding. If we practice these things, our personal relationship with God will grow stronger.

As you read this book, pay special attention to each phrase, and examine yourself using all the phrases in the Lord's Prayer. As you do so, you must consistently pray against the things that cause you to fall short in any way. Apply God's Word. The Lord will not forsake you if you seek Him. **1 John 5:14–15** confirms that our prayers are not a waste; It says, "...and this is the confidence that we have toward Him, that if we ask anything according to His Will, He hears us. And if we know that He hears us in whatever we ask, then we know that we have the requests that we have asked of Him."

Something happens when we pray, because prayer is not just words, it is a powerful tool in Heaven. You can see this when you read from **Revelation 8 and 9.** It is a confirmation of the power of prayer. Our prayers do mighty things. Again, keep in mind that when you pray, everyone needs prayer. As **1 Timothy 2:1–3** declares, "Supplications, prayers, and intercessions must be made for all people..." In **Matthew 5:43–45**, the Lord explains that we must love even our enemies and pray for those who persecute us. This is why understanding the phrase, "Thy Kingdom come" is very important. The Kingdom's Rules grant us compassion and love to pray for everyone, including the unsaved and even our enemies. This is God's Will for our lives.

By praying with the Lord's Prayer, we become wiser and more alert. It prevents the devil from causing us to blame, criticize, condemn, and push people away. When we see people's weaknesses and judge them without saying a prayer on their behalf, we sin against God. However, we do this because we lack knowledge of what His Prayer says. But thankfully, the insight of His Prayer teaches us to not condemn. Rather, we learn to love one another, pray, forgive, and be good to all. We find a way to help them by showing love, compassion, and concern. For the sake of their salvation, we must find a way to bring about a change in them.

Sometimes, it is sad to see how believers gather and speak ill of others, without realizing that, just like any other sin, gossip is also against God. But the understanding of the Lord's Prayer helps us to love and care for one another. When we pray using the Lord's Prayer, the Holy Spirit will teach us how to love and care for one another as true family. We can learn how deadly sin is, how it intends to come into our midst and our lives, how it entangles us, and how we can avoid being trapped in any kind of sin that pollutes the righteousness of Christ in us. If murder, abortion, idol worship, sexual immorality, hatred, envy, jealousy, and rage, among others, are sins against God, then so is condemning others. Instead of condemning, we can use the same amount of time to pray on their behalf, because if God's Kingdom through salvation come into them, they will do what is right and acceptable unto God. Thus, intercessory prayer is vital, and there must be no room for condemnation.

In **Matthew 13:30**, the Lord Jesus told the disciple, "Let both grow together until the harvest, and at harvest time I will tell the reapers, "Gather the weeds first and bind them in bundles to be burned but gather the wheat into my barn." In our world today, are we doing it right, or we are doing it the opposite way? Some people have taken the law into their own hands and are pulling the weeds. But what they do not realize is that they are pulling the harvest and the weeds together. Only God knows the difference between the real wheat and the weeds. Those who speak harshly think they know everything or are better than everyone; so, they judge and condemn. But my dear ones, no one on earth is good. The Master's own words in **Luke 18:19** says, (when He was on earth) "Why do you call me good?" This is not to say Jesus is not good.

Today, we are all trying with the help of the Holy Spirit. We cannot replace the Master; we can only imitate His examples of love and compassion. This is not to say we must condone evil. What we are told to do is to be wise, use discernment in every situation, and act out of love by praying for sinners and helping them find the way to the truth because people a lost without knowing the Truth – Jesus. This means we cannot just make videos, go online, or stand on our platforms, and insult others. Instead, we should do it the Lord's way. And what is His way of handling people? To understand this better, read Luke 6:37 and Matthew 7 to see why we must be careful before we judge others. Jesus tells us what we must know before we judge anyone. To do this, we must remove the plank from our own eyes so we can better see and help others. Also, in **Matthew 18:15–20**, He tells us what we must do, "...sins against you, or if you don't understand something, go to the person, and show him his fault, just between the two of you. If he listens to you, you have won your brother over. But if he refuses, take one or two others along, so that every matter may be established by the testimony of two or three witnesses." If these fail, you still have another step to take, and that is taking your brother or sister to the whole church. So, there are 3 steps. However, do we take this approach? Read the whole chapter (18). Here is another Scripture for those that are trying to stop people from doing God's work. In **Mark 9:38–40**, what we read is that John said to Jesus, "Teacher, we saw a man casting out demons in your name, and we forbade him, because he was not following us." But Jesus said, "Do not forbid him; for no one who does a mighty work in My Name will be able soon after to speak evil of me. For he that is not against us is for us." This is the same as condemning others, today in our time. Please let's not insult others in uncertainty. Yes, there are many deceivers or false preachers. For instance, in many parts of the world, including my country, Africa, there are churches that profess Christ but are in reality are Satan worshippers. They are wolves in sheep's clothing, as it is written in **Matthew 7:15**. Yes, those must be exposed.

Still, we must take the right approach in dealing with others because we are not dealing with flesh and blood. Whatever we say must be according to the Word of God.

Sometimes, insults can be a hinderance to an unbeliever or a new member. For this reason, let's do everything according as we are commanded. If we use the right approach, knowing that we are not dealing with flesh and blood but powers of the dark world, we will pray for all people, including those who we think are misleading, and God will convict them and help them to know the truth. In doing so, God will continue using us for the Kingdom Work, which is done through love and compassion. So, if you think someone has wronged you or is doing anything contrary to the truth, you must find the Christ-driven way to approach that person. We must always bear in mind that it is the Lord's Work. He died for us all, but Satan is only a user. Each one of us matters to Christ. Even on the cross, He prayed for those who persecuted Him, because to Him, each person's salvation matters. Yes, it may not matter to someone, but it matters to Christ. **John 3:16** says, "For God so loved the world..."

Today, many people have stopped attending church because of these kinds of things. They think when it comes to unity, Christians lack what it takes to be united, that we are too divisive. As someone preached: "We are too critical, too boastful, and toxic." I am the kind of a person who loves to talk speak with strangers about salvation, and I can honestly say that about 75% of the people are confused... This is very sad. We shouldn't be viewed as such. Please, let's do what we are commanded to do out of love and compassion to help build the Kingdom of God for others to join. Our ways of dealing with things are causing confusion. While we are fighting, the devil is working by pushing people away from wanting to serve God in the church. This is pushing some people to join other religions or stay home.

Social media: Right now, social media is what people are relying on. The question is, are we using the technology given to us to truly build the kingdom of God on earth, or are we looking for attention, followers, and fam or riches? Whatever we are doing, we will have to answer for it. To prevent confusion and division, we must be careful before we say anything or judge incorrectly. Yes, you must do what we are called to do, but we must do all things in love (**1 Corinthians 16:14**). The current times are very challenging. If we pray for Satan's kingdom of evil to be destroyed, many that are put in chains will be set free. So, let's pray for all people, including minister of the gospel to speak the truth and not insults or lies. Speaking the truth in love will break the shackles from people and set them free (**Ephesians 4:15**).

The truth is, if someone is not for Christ, they will not want to speak about Him. If someone uses the Name of Jesus for his or her own personal interest, the Holy Spirit will convict that person through our prayers. Condemning others without praying for them is wrong. People are leaving the church and are turning away from Christianity due to how we deal with people whom we think are not up to our standards. We can't be toxic to win souls. Do you really want to know the truth about a person, spend time in prayer an ask the Lord for His Revelation. And please, be sure that what you saw was truly from the Lord. If you are still confused about the meaning of a vision or something, please continue to pray until everything is clear. "God is not mocked..." (**Galatians 6:7**) Jesus said, "If you love one another, everyone will know that you are my disciples" (**John 13:35**).

Whatever we are called for, please let's speak nothing but the truth because we can't deceive ourselves. If we are working with the God of love and peace, then we must learn from Him. If after reaching out to someone whom we think is doing something wrong, and the person refuses to listen, then we must take the second and third approach. If they refuse, then the Lord says we must regard them as pagans. This is where we need discernment. How do you know you are doing the right thing? Well, be careful because we are all going to be judged one day.

The circumstances leading to my encounter with God, and my experience that followed, have taught me many lessons. It proves that no one can fully understand how God operates, and no one can completely understand the reasons behind the events He causes to happen in our lives. He is our

All-knowing and Great Father, whose ways are perfect. He works in mysterious ways to put things in order, but we can always trust Him because He is a God who always knows what He is doing. Therefore, let's follow Christ's example, and be careful in the way we judge for even those weeds among the wheat can have their lives turned around by God if He so wills.

The work of the Kingdom of Heaven can be done with the mouth, but it must start with prayer, the Word of God, patience, love, and compassion. Scripture tells us in **Psalm12:2–6** that everyone lies to their neighbor; they flatter with their lips but harbor deception in their hearts. If we lie to one another, then who can we believe? May the Lord silence all 'flattering lips.'

Now let's check into some important subjects to get even better insights. The Lord's Prayer has taught me many important things on prayer and dealing with others. It has helped me to know that: 1) I have a Heavenly Father. Though, my earthly father was a good father, I can never compare him to God the Father; 2) The Prayer of the Lord has helped me to know how to share the good news about the Great and Awesome Father we have; 3) Believers are family in Christ; 4) It has taught me to know that I am never alone; 5) It has helped me come to understand my right as a child of God; 6) It has helped me to know where I came from, my purpose in life, where I go after this life, and through what?; 7) I know my sins are forgiven. I can ask for forgiveness each day and forgive people who have hurt me; 8) I know all my needs are met; 9) I know living a holy life is important; 10) I am protected against temptation and evil, and no weapon formed against me shall prosper; 11) I know how to give thanks in all circumstances, praise, worship the Father; meditate upon His Word, and wait for Him in prayer; 12) I know that praying and interceding for the world is important; 13) I have seen that God is closer than I can ever imagine; 14) The Kingdom of God, its righteousness and salvation have become my priority because I want the evil kingdom of the devil to be destroyed completely, in Jesus Mighty Name. Amen!

My dear ones in the Lord, let me remind you of these, Christianity is a journey with a Supreme Being. "It is a relationship with God Almighty, and with one another," so, let's be quick to listen but slow to speak. Today, there are all levels of deception, and we need a discerning spirit. Thus, we need to renew our minds, but how can we do this? We must study God's Word because the Word is living and active. It is alive, and it will speak to our situations, and transform us. Everything you hear, you must take the time to analyze thoroughly. Always ask the Holy Spirit to help you, and don't stop praying until He clears all doubts and confusions. Things are going to get worse, so put on your belt of truth, ask for discernment and wisdom to have the ability to evaluate situations. You can read more of my encounters from my book titled, 1) Is the God of Yesterday, the Same Today? 2) He Turned My Nothing into Something Beautiful (coming soon). 3) The Power of Intercessory – Election 2020.

Chapter 5 – Our Father

Matthew 6:9

We have a Father in Heaven, but who is He? Do you know Him? Have you ever wondered why despite all his efforts your biological father was never perfect?

Let's start with the first phrase of the Lord's Prayer which says, Our Father. The Lord Jesus references God as "Our Father in Heaven"– **Matthew 6:9. Romans 8:16** says, "The Spirit Himself testifies with our spirit that we are children of God. **John 1:12–13** says, "But to all who did receive Him, who believed in His name, He gave the right to become children of God." Listen to this: The verses continue by saying, "who were born, not of blood nor of the will of the flesh, nor of the will of man, but of God." How do you become a child of God? It is not what you or your parents have done, paid, or can do. It is by His grace. The power of salvation has done it all perfectly. It has made us become children of the Great Jehovah, and we also can call Him, our Father *or Abba Father.*

We see that Jesus started teaching the disciples how to address God. Saying Our Father is a salutation. It is a sign of respect. We show God respect by calling Him or addressing Him as "Father." Saying Our Father means that God is not an illusion but a true Father of love. He is a Father with whom we can build a bond and connect with through prayer. So, as Christians, we know there is One True God and Father, but simply knowing God as our Father is not good enough. There is a kind of a personal relationship that we ought to have with Him, which Jesus highlights in His Prayer.

To know this kind of Father, we must keep in mind that God is good and just. He is a Father who shows no favoritism. He does not discriminate between those whom He calls His children and those who are yet to come to Him. As the Lord Jesus says in **Matthew 5:45**, "He allows His rain to fall on the good and the bad." He welcomes everyone with love and compassion and establishes a father-child relationship with all who come to Him. **John 3:16** says, "For God so loved the world that He sent His only Begotten Son, that whosoever believes in Him will...have everlasting life." Jesus came not to condemn, but to show us the way to the Father.

Let's explain what a true Father is. This expresses affection, confidence, and trust. However, when we say, 'Abba Father,' we go deeper. It signifies an intimate relationship with the God of Heaven. It describes a relationship of a father and a child. It shows the trust a child has for his/her father. Abba is like saying 'daddy.' In **Mark 14:36,** we see Jesus in His moment of anguish praying and calling God "Abba Father." He wanted the trouble to pass from Him because of the pain He was enduring. Yet He wanted the Father's Will to be done. We can also call out to God in times of trouble in the same way.

I recently came across a video that talks about Muhammed Ali's daughter, Layla Ali, who followed her dad's footsteps to become a boxer. She had a record of not losing a fight. In one of her fights, she was rematched with somebody who seemed stronger than Layla. In the fight, she had a cut over her eye and bloody nose. It looked like halfway through the fight; Layla was going to lose. But she came back and knocked the girl out stronger than ever and won the fight. When the fight was over, Layla was interviewed. The interviewers said, "Layla, you looked like you were about to lose that fight. How were you able to come back?" She said, I watched my dad fight. I watched him beat Joe Frazier, George Foreman, and Sonny Liston. I watched him look like he was going to lose, but then I saw him come back stronger." Then, she said, "When I think of my daddy (Muhammed Ali), it encourages me to push harder, knowing I will not lose." So, please allow me to ask you, who is your dad? Do you know who your Heavenly Father is? Do you know what He has done in the past? Do you know what He can do now? Do you believe in Him to help you through your difficulties?

The Heavenly Father can help you overcome any challenge that generates fear in you. Although fear will come, it will not have power over you. Any circumstances that arise, He will be the one who can carry you through. So, in pursuing your goals in life, continue to think of Him. Think of some of the things that you know of Him. Think of some of the things He has done for you. Don't focus on the challenges, and don't let it knock you down. Focus on your Heavenly Father and His capabilities. He is the One who can boost your well-being and increase your happiness and efforts in life. He alone can make all things possible. He can renew your strength like the eagle's. He can equip, empower, and strengthen you to do mighty things. Your goals, well–being, relationships, and joy can all come true by His power. He is the Father who can shower you with blessings. He can send rain on your land and bless the work of your hands. I am thankful for this Father above. I am thankful for His amazing love. His love for me is everlasting. It never changes or fails. Even if I think I don't deserve His best, He still loves me unconditionally.

Can we compare our relationship with God to that of our biological or earthly fathers? No! This Father God in Heaven is like no other. He is full of compassion. He is merciful and gracious. He has redeemed us from under the law. He has sent His Holy Spirit into our hearts, and through the Spirit, we call out, Abba, Father. It is the Spirit that joins us to God and bears witness that we are His children. He helps us call out to Him anytime in every situation, and He can hear us.

Who is God to you? Do you accept Him as your Father? What kind of a relationship do you have with Him? Do you call out to Him in your time of need? Do you always depend on Him? If we believe what is written in **John 3:1–8**, then we know that we are the redeemed of the Lord. We are born again, redeemed from the curse of sin, and adopted into the family of God. We are heirs of the Father, appointed to receive a Heavenly inheritance. We have everything good from the Father (**Mark 12:7**). We are children and not strangers. **Roman 17:8** tells us that we are God's children and His glory, and since we are children of God, we have eternal life. We are heirs and co-heirs with Christ because we have been given the same privilege in sharing with Christ His Heavenly inheritance. We are children that can come boldly before the throne trusting that He will hear us as we call out to Him. So, whenever you are you are troubled, you can cry out to God if you take Him as your true Father. **Galatians 4:6** tells us that because we are His children, God has sent His Spirit into our hearts to help us call Him Abba Father.

There are distinctions between God the Father and our earthy fathers. Even if you have a wonderful biological father, he cannot be compared to God the Father. Through faith in Christ, we believe that He exists and that we can trust in Him. God the Father is a self-sufficient God. He lacks nothing. He controls every situation. So, you can never compare Him to any earthly father. If you were raised in an abusive family, you will never understand true fatherhood. Maybe you were abused by your biological father. In that case, it will be difficult to understand what fatherly love is. Maybe you were an unwanted child who grew up feeling rejected and abandoned. No one wanted you, and that rejection has left a scar in your heart. For this reason, you may think all fathers are the same including God the Father. We have received God's Spirit that makes us His children, removing all doubt, but if you perceive God through the experiences of your earthly father, you will be disappointed because God the Father has no equal. So do not compare Him to anyone else. His love, compassion, care, understanding, and everything else about Him is completely different. So, let the depth of God's love reach to the deepest part of your hearts to renew your mind, take away any negativity, and bring wholeness to enjoy His true love. Accept Him and know that He is the only Father who can heal you of any pain. No matter how severely you are wounded, He can heal you.

One of the most common ways fathers express their love is through acts of service. God will work on your behalf to make sure all is well with you. We have His Word and He takes care of us in His love. Therefore, we can trust that we have a great and awesome Father. He is a God of peace and love, full of life and light. In Him is no darkness. **Psalm 84:11** describes our Father as "...a sun and shield who bestows favor and honor..." But you must build your personal relationship with Him *first.* You will get to know His personality and character as a great Father if you do. You will also experience His power and why He does the things He does. For example, knowing that God is omnipresent is important because when you call out to Him, you know that He is a God who is not far from reach or for whom you must wait to come to your rescue. No, because He is right where you are.

Calling God Father means that we have accepted His gift of love (Jesus Christ), which makes us part of His family. He calls us His children, and we call Him our Father. We are told that we were once sinners, but we have been forgiven. **Ephesians 2:13** says, "We have been united with Christ Jesus. Once we were far away from God, but now we have been brought near to Him through the blood of Christ." We were once lost, but now we are found, once outcasts, but now He has brought us home and made us His own. This is love in its complete and purest form. It is called unconditional and everlasting love.

God's love for humanity made Him send His only Son to die for our sins. Christ's death paved the way for us to receive such special and unconditional love from God. We do not deserve this kind of love because we are tainted by sin, yet God made a way through Christ. **1 John 3:1** declares, "Behold what manner of love the Father has bestowed upon us, that we should be called children of God." **Romans 5:8** states, "God demonstrates His love for us that while we were still sinners, Christ died for us." The Spirit you received does not make you slaves to live in fear again. Rather, the Spirit you received brought about your adoption to sonship and by Him, we cry, "Abba, Father" (**Romans 8:15**). Jesus paid a heavy price for us. He purified, sanctified, and washed us with His precious blood. Through the blood of Jesus, our sinful nature has been transformed. He has also reconciled us to the Father, so, it does not matter what our origin, nationality, language, or skin color may be; In Christ, we are simply children of God. This makes salvation through Christ unbelievable and yet believable! As confirmed in **Revelation 5:9,** "With the blood of Jesus, we have been purchased by God—persons from every tribe and language and people and nation."

Through Jesus, we have our freedom, for the chains that held us captive have been broken, and we have been set free (**Galatians 3:13**). God is not ashamed to call us His children, and Christ is not ashamed to call us His own. We are sons and daughters of God through Christ, children of His Kingdom who belong to God's family. It is written in **Romans 8:17**, "We are heirs of the Father and co-heirs with Christ." As children of God, we must be willing to be there for one another because we share a common goal. God has promised to never forsake us; He is with us always and will be with us till the end of time (**Matthew 28:20**). He lives in, among, and around us. He is loving, caring, gentle, merciful, forgiving, gracious, kind, and compassionate. Now, can we compare our relationship with God with that of our earthly father? No!

Although the disciples knew who Jesus was, they didn't know that they had a Heavenly Father who could be closer to them than they ever imagined. **John 1:12** states, "To all who received Jesus and believed in His name, He gave them the right to be called His children." Believing in the name Jesus carries with it the reward of being able to call ourselves children of God. In His Prayer, Christ reveals God as His Father and as our Father by saying "Our Father...." Being children of God means having access to Him and being able to communicate with Him.

This is true because after my experience, whenever I say, "My Father in Heaven," I feel a sense of belonging. I know that God is real, and I can confidently call Him my Heavenly Father. I'm never alone because anytime, anywhere, and in any situation, I can call and communicate with Him through prayer, knowing well that He hears me. In times of trouble, if my faith is tested beyond what I can endure, I can cry out to Him for help. I am not afraid. I know Him as a Father who exercises all power and authority and can turn my difficulties into triumphs. He does not hide from me. In **Jeremiah 29:13**, He says, "You will seek me and find me when you do so with all your heart." This explains why we must build our confidence in Him. He is the Father who has

Good Plans for us. So, by having a relationship with Him, we are set on the path of righteousness because His righteousness covers His children like a garment. We are given opportunity to become His children which enables us to spend eternity with Him in His Kingdom.

When we become Christians, God accepts us just the way we are and He also, wants us to accept Him and accept others. Anyone who thinks less of another cannot be considered part of the Father's peaceful, loving, and righteous family. You can belong to the Father's family by believing 1) you and everyone else were created by God, 2) Jesus Christ is the Savior, 3) Jesus died on the cross and was resurrected for us, 4) we have the Holy Spirit as our counselor, 5) we are one in Christ. 6) we are not of this world; we are here on purpose; 7) one day, when we are out of this world, we shall spend eternity with the Father. If you have never thought of these things, then pray for the Father to show you more of Him and ask His Holy Spirit to be your counselor. If you are not a believer, then accept Jesus Christ as your Lord and savior, become part of His family, bond with Him through prayer and the Word, and get to know His plans for you.

Let's consider something to see the differences. Imagine having a biological father whom you do not pay attention to. You do not know his name, where he lives, what he does, his likes and/or dislikes. You do not care who he is and even refuse to talk to him. When he calls, you do not answer. When he sends you on an errand, you refuse. You behave as if he doesn't exist. Simply put, you do not care about this father. Why? Because you have no relationship with him. This example demonstrates the fact that our relationships with our earthly fathers can turn sour at any moment. Many people have not spoken with their fathers in decades. Relationships are broken sometimes because when apologies are offered and forgiveness is asked for, they are ignored. When apologies are not accepted and forgiveness is not given, then a relationship can never be restored. Our relationship with God will never be this way. The Lord tells us that anytime we offend Him and seek forgiveness, He will forgive us as we forgive others.

I believe that generally parents want their children to succeed and are willing to do anything to make that happen, but sometimes that is not the case. As hard as we may try, we cannot guarantee our children's success in the way that God can. The love of God is indescribable. Sometimes parents discriminate and have conditional love. God does not discriminate, and His unfailing love is unconditional. Our earthly parents can choose to forsake us, but God will never forsake us as Jesus said in **John 14:1.** The greatest gift He offers us is eternal life, which no one else can offer or provide. With this, everything is included: His goodness, mercy, and grace last throughout our lives. Thus, we can say that God the Father is like no other because He is incomparable. We did not choose Him, He chose us. We are undeserving of His love, yet He loves us just the way we are. We do not deserve to be close to Him, yet He chooses to have a relationship with us. Regardless of the gravity of our sins, He still loves us. **Psalm 27:10** states, "Although my father and mother may forsake me, the Lord will take me in."

Our earthly parents cannot provide perfect security. They may try to be protective, yet sometimes they fail. Their inadequate capabilities do not allow them to protect us against all forms of danger. For instance, parents cannot observe all that is going on with their children while they are in school or even at home, but God can because He sees everywhere, knows everything, and has power over everything. He can do everything and can protect His children from danger. This is where our earthly parents fall short. **Matthew 7:11** states, "If we, being human, know how to give good gifts to our children, how much more shall our Father who is in Heaven give good things to those that ask Him?" Our Father is willing and able to provide for us exceedingly, abundantly, and far beyond the capabilities of our earthly parents.

Let us look at some of the personality and attributes of our Heavenly Father. We know God by His attributes. God's attributes tell us how wonderful He is. For instance, He is an eternal God because "His reign has no beginning and no end." **Genesis 1:1** narrates, "In the beginning, God created the heavens and the earth." This proves that God existed even before He created the world.

Our Father is called the Creator because He made all things, and all creation depends on Him for their existence. Our Father is Omniscient; He knows what is, what was, and what is to come. He is an infinite God because His power knows no boundaries. Other attributes of God include the following:

Holiness: God is pure and righteous.

Omnipotence: God is all-powerful.

Omnipresence: God is present everywhere.

Faithfulness: God is sincere and genuine. He is loyal and devoted.

Sovereignty: God is independent and has supreme power and authority over all.

All these unique characteristics make the Father excellent and incomparable. In **Psalm 18:1–2,** David says, "I love you, Lord, my strength. The Lord is my rock...." With these, we perceive that He is who He says He is to us. He is our protector and the Great Provider.

What are some of God's attributes in His own words? Our Father in Heaven is a good listener. In **1 John 5:14**, it is written, "The confidence we have in approaching God is that He hears when we ask according to *His Will.*"

Our Father in Heaven is a Good Teacher. In **Psalm 32:8,** David asked God to teach him the path he should take and guide him on His right path. In **Psalm 25:4–5**, David asks God to "show him His way, teach him His paths, and direct him to the truth."

Our Father in Heaven is a Good Helper. **Psalm 121** also says our help comes from Him.

Our Father in Heaven is a genuine Lover. God's love is genuine, and nothing can separate us from His love. **Romans 8:38–39** says, nothing can separate us from the love of God that is in Christ Jesus?"

Our Father in Heaven is a Protector. **Psalm 121:7** says the Lord will protect us from all evil, keep our souls, and preserve our lives.

Our Father in Heaven is a Healer. He is our great physician. **1 Peter 2:24**—He bore our sins. Similarly, in **Psalm 103:3**, David says, the Lord "forgives us of all our sins and heals us..."

Our Father in Heaven is compassionate. "...our Father shows compassion towards those who fear Him" (**Psalm 103:13**). **Lamentations 3:22–23** says, "...His compassion never fails. They are new every morning. Great is His faithfulness."

Our Father in Heaven is patient. "Return to the Lord our God, for He is gracious, slow to anger, abounding in love." (**Joel 2:13**)

Our Father in Heaven is everlasting. "The Lord is the everlasting God, the Creator..." (**Isaiah 40:28**). God abides forever (**Psalm 102:12**). He existed before the earth was made (**Psalm 90:2**). God is the Alpha and the Omega, the First and the Last; the beginning and the End (**Rev. 22:13**).

These show the great Father we have. We show appreciation to our Father who possesses all these attributes by adoring, elevating, and giving thanks to His name. He is the greatest, and because we know His name, He will satisfy us and show us His salvation. Because we trust in Him, He will teach us His ways and direct our path. He will instruct us, watch over us, and bless us. His Kingdom shall be our portion. If we do not sit on the seat of the wicked, but do *God's Will*, walk in His ways, take delight in Him and in His law, read and meditate on His Word, and apply His Word, we will be like a tree planted by streams of water; our leaves shall not wither, we will bear fruit in season, and prosper in whatever we do–**Psalm 1:1–3**.

Today, if you forget about everything in this chapter, remember this, our God the Father has no equal. He can never be compared to anyone. He is an Awesome Loving Father to all who believe in Him. If you have just heard about the God of Moses because you have watched the Ten Commandment but have no relationship with Him; then know that God loves everyone as recorded in **John 3:16**. Today, He is calling you to come and have relationship with Him because He is your Creator, but more importantly, He is your Father in Heaven.

Now with all that has been said, do you acknowledge God as a Father? Do you feel His presence? Have you surrendered to His Majesty? Can you trust Him enough to call Him your Father? If yes, then, Halleluiah! If not, then ask Him to come into your heart to build a good relationship with Him. He will be your Father and lead you beside still waters. He will comfort and restore your soul. He will never forsake you. He will be your 'Living Bread'; the 'Living Water;' your 'Way'; your Truth, your 'Life' and your 'Light;' your 'Thirst Quencher'; your healer, and comforter. He will supply all your needs. So, open your heart to Him and experience His peace and love.

Chapter 6 – Who Art in Heaven

Matthew 6:9

We have a Father who is in Heaven. On their request that they be taught how to pray, Jesus said to His disciples to pray like this: "Our Father who art in Heaven..." Jesus was referring to the Father's dwelling in the Heaven of heavens when He said, "Who Art in Heaven." With this statement, Jesus was telling His disciples about the existence of God, who is a Father to all humans, and despite being omnipresent (everywhere), He also has a dwelling place in Heaven. Therefore, God is real, and Heaven is not a myth. God and Heaven and all His angels are just as real as the earth and its inhabitants are real.

Heaven is beautiful beyond description. It is where God and His angels reside. It's real, not fake. Jesus confirmed the existence of Heaven as the actual home of God when He said, "Our Father in Heaven." Genesis 1:1 state, "In the beginning, God created the heavens and the earth." Heaven is for Him, and He placed humans on earth. John 3:16 tells us of God's love and what it means. It means God's love for humans and all that He has created is real. The world and its materials exist for temporary enjoyment, but human beings are God's priority. God does not need anything in this world. He is more concerned about our well-being and our time with Him. Revelation 4 tells us that the throne of God is a real throne of love and peace and beauty. God is love, and His city is a city of love. It is love that brightens and shines in that city of God. Love can never be defeated, and that love is God's Glory. What John saw in his vision about Heaven was real, and he tells us that the beauty of Heaven is like a bride. Without God, there is no love. Without love, there is no Heaven.

Without Heaven, there is no God. Also, without Satan, there is no hate nor hell.

Some people continue to ignore God and hate Him and His creation. Though they use God's creations, they tend to abuse and destroy them by killing the innocent out of hatred. They pollute the beauty of human love with evil intentions and replace truth with lies. This makes hatred on earth the beginning of hell, just as love on earth is the beginning of Heaven. In his preaching about The Beauty of Heaven based on Revelation 21:9–21, Pastor Glenn Allen retells the story of Earl Panzram, who murdered 23 people and was executed in 1930. In the sermon, he quoted the Journal of Murder – The ugliness of hate is what will determine the environment of hell. Earl Panzram's last words were, "I wish the whole human race had one neck and I had my hands around it." Can a person be this ugly? Yes, this is how a human can behave when he is under the influence of the devil. Thankfully, the new Heaven and the new earth will have no such people and such things. The world and all its imperfections will be removed and only the beauty of God's creation will remain. Evil will be completely eradicated. Love will take over, peace will reign, and the result will be joyous. Evil will not have any part to play. That is how we can recognize the connection between the God the Father, love, and Heaven.

People believe that the moon and other planets besides ours exist because these are scientifically proven and there is actual evidence that we can go to some of these places. In contrast, Heaven is a place that we cannot see with our mortal eyes. If our God has given humans a place called earth, filled with all kinds of magnificent things, then certainly, He is not a homeless God walking on the street trying to find a place to sleep. He has a place for Himself. Although we cannot see it, we believe in its existence because it is written in His Word. This is a true revelation of the One True God, who tells us that Heaven is real. In Revelation 21:1–5, the Lord shows John a vision of Heaven, the Holy City of Jerusalem coming down from God and His glory illuminating the entire city. John describes the city as dazzling and crystal clear, like precious jasper. He says the foundations of the city's walls are adorned with every kind of jewel: the first is jasper; the second, sapphire; the third, agate; and the fourth is emerald. The city does not need the sun or the moon to shine on it, for the glory of God gives it light, and the Lamb is its lamp. The nations will walk by its light and the kings of the earth will bring their splendor into it. No one impure will ever enter it but only those whose names are written in the Lamb's Book of Life.

Heaven is not a place of chaos. Genesis 1:31 says, "God saw everything He had made, and it was good." Heaven is a place of holiness where God dwells majestically in His glory. I am an eyewitness. 40 years ago, when I became a believer, the Lord showed me a glimpse of Heaven: Thus, I cannot deny the existence of Heaven because I know Heaven is real. With confidence, I can say my Father is in Heaven, though He lives in my heart. If Heaven isn't real, then my visions about Heaven were not real. If Heaven is not real, then God cannot be real. If God is not real, then Jesus' ministry was a lie and in vain. This cannot be the case because God is not a man who lies. I know what I saw was not from anyone but the Lord. In John 14:2, Jesus says, "In my Father's house, there are many mansions... I go to prepare a place for you." When Jesus rose from the dead, He ascended into Heaven right in front of His disciples (Acts 1:9–11). A cloud took Him from their sight as they looked intently at His departure into the sky. Then, two men in white garments appeared and said, "This Jesus taken from you into Heaven will come again, in the same way you have seen Him go into Heaven." In 2 Kings 2:11, Elijah was also taken up into Heaven. All these confirm the existence of Heaven; so, don't be confused or deceived.

After John had baptized Jesus, the Heavens were opened and a Spirit like a dove descended upon Jesus. The Spirit of God came from Heaven in the form of a dove, yet it appeared to John from the sky (Mark 1:10). The apostle Paul said in his writing that he knew a man in Christ who was caught up to the third heaven (2 Corinthians 12:2). Psalm 115:16 declares, "Even the heavens are the Lord's, but the earth He has given to humans." "For this reason, rejoice, O Heavens and you who dwell in them. Woe to the earth and the sea because the devil has come down to you, having great wrath..." (Revelation 12:12). "The Heavens declare the glory of God, and the sky shows His creation" (Psalm

19:1). "In the Heavens, He has pitched a tent for the sun. It rises from one end of the Heavens, and circuits its way to the other end" (Psalm 19:4–5). These confirm what is written in Genesis 1:1, "In the beginning, God created the heavens and the earth." Note the reference to the earth as singular and to the heavens as plural.

Heaven is our eternal home as children of God. When His Kingdom comes, or whatever the New Jerusalem may be, we will be there to spend eternity with Him. The important thing to know is that it is a city of light without darkness. It is a city of joy without sorrow, and a city of comfort without pain. In describing the city of God, John wrote that what he saw was beautiful! There is no celebration on earth that can be compare the all the celebrations that go to Heaven. So, if you really want to enjoy the beauty of this magnificent, glorious, and wonderful place, then I encourage you to never give up! I can imagine the angels singing, "Holy! Holy! Holy is the Lord God Almighty" (Revelation 4:8).

If we serve God till the end, we shall enjoy with Jesus Christ in eternity. Heaven (or the New Jerusalem) will be more beautiful, more enjoyable, and more fun than any place on earth, and there is no place like it. According to some people, there is no Heaven, but doubting of the existence of Heaven is of great concern. If there is no Heaven, it means there is no God. Christ came to save us. He gave us a promise about Heaven; if we believe in Him, then we must also believe in the New Jerusalem as our dwelling place. No human being is of this world. We are all pilgrims. We are just passing through! The enemy is deceiving and confusing humans and making them think they belong in this world, and that they have the right to do whatever seems best to them without thinking of the consequences of what they do. We are not of this world. If you do not agree to this, then think of where we came from and where some have already returned on the day they passed from this life.

Although this book may appear to have been written for believers only, it is also my mission to reach out to unbelievers as well. Unbelievers do not know God; It is not surprising for them to not believe in the existence of Heaven. If you are one of those who has some doubt, I want you to know that there is a God who created everything, including you, and He has a place called Heaven.

In the same way that there is a God of love who cares for people, there is also an evil one who despises everyone, and everything associated with people, including you. Because of this, he would do whatever he can to deceive you. But understand that even if you are serving Satan, you are not his friend because no human being can be friends with the devil. Oh, yes, the devil will pretend to be your friend, but only because he wants to use you. So be aware and let this resonant in your mind that the devil wants nothing than to steal, kill, and destroy. What he does is to pretend to be a friend, takes your mind off the importance of heaven if you let him, and make you behave as if this earth and everything you see are yours forever. However, after he is done using you, he will kick you, push you to the side, throw you away, punish you, and select another, and watch you die in your sin with no hope. This is because 'Satan is only a user'. So, believe in God and believe that the God of Heaven is real. Heaven is not fictional. Heaven is just as real as the earth in which you live!

If you believe in Satan and do not believe in God, you are deceived and allowing yourself to be fooled. Likewise, if you believe in God and do not believe in Heaven too, you are being deceived. God, Heaven and earth, eternal life, and eternal condemnation are all real. So, know that God and Heaven are real, and Satan and hell are also real. The difference is that:

While God is Love, Satan is hateful.

While God is life, Satan is death.

While God is for peace, Satan is for war.

While God is for us, Satan is against us.

Today, I encourage you to ask God to show you a glimpse of Heaven, if it is *His Will*, so you can better understand it. This will help you understand our eternal destination and the requirements.

Chapter 7 – Hallowed Be Thy Name

Matthew 6:9

God's Holiness is His absolute moral purity. You shall not take the name of the LORD your God in vain – **Exodus 20:7.** *God* is Holy; so is His Name, and His Holiness is what distinguishes Him as God. **Isaiah 6:3** – And they were calling to one another: "Holy, Holy, Holy is the Lord God Almighty; the whole earth is full of his glory." **Isaiah 57:15** explains it. His Holiness is exceptional. In Greek, the word hagiazo means to confirm, make, declare, or render sacred or holy, and that is what describes the word "Hallowed." In His Prayer, Jesus said, "Hallowed be Thy name." Jesus first introduces the Father with reverence by saying, Our Father in Heaven; then goes on to say, Holy is His Name. This means that He is set apart as Pure and Holy. Jesus specifically says the prayer in this order because He does not want us to appear before God and begin stating our demands. He wants us to acknowledge the supremacy of the Father before anything else. In this chapter, we shall see the Holiness of God, and the different ways we can achieve our holiness because without it, we cannot see Him.

Hallowed means holy or sacred. Therefore, when we say hallowed be thy name, we imply that God is Holy. It means that He is sacred, that He is pure, and that He is without blemish. **1 John 1:5** tells us that God's qualities contribute to His Holiness. He is light, and in Him, there is no darkness. He is righteous and pure. He is awesome and glorious. His character is flawless. He is full of truth; No lie can be found in Him. He is highly exalted. He relishes holiness and purity. **Revelation 4:8** tells us that the four living creatures never stop saying, "Holy, Holy, Holy, is the Lord God almighty," day and night. In fact, God's Holiness is everything about Him. It is His Power and Glory! It is His Holiness that makes Him substantially unique. Therefore, separating God from His Holiness is impossible! His wisdom, goodness, and glory come from His Holiness. It is His nature, and He cannot be separated from it because it forms part of His very existence.

What is significant about God's Holiness? A) God's Holiness is important because it is His supremacy. It is why He is highly esteemed. There is no one holier than God. He is above and beyond all, and His power is over all His creation. He rules over everything, including His creations in the Heavens, those on earth, and those beneath the earth. **Exodus 15:11** tells us that there is no one among the gods who is like the Lord. He is majestic in Holiness and Awesome in Glory. His character is perfect, and His moral excellence is the absolute standard of integrity and ethical purity that sets Him apart from all creation. In other words, God can't be compared in terms of sovereignty and power because of His Holiness.

B) Keeping God's name Holy means honoring and glorifying Him for His majesty and awesomeness. God's Holiness represents His worship. He is known for who He is; therefore, He must be adored for the sake of His Holy Name. As written in **Joshua 24:19**, God is pure and Holy, and His Holiness demands exclusive worship. His Holiness requires devoting our hearts and time to Him and remaining pure, holy, and faithful. His Holiness is what drives us to worship Him (**John 4:24**). Therefore, we can conclude that God's Holiness is what makes Him deserve our worship.

C) God's Holiness as opposed to human nature. Throughout the Old Testament, we see the gravity of God and His Holiness. Therefore, holiness is not an option for Christians but a requirement. **Hebrew 12:14** says it is impossible to see God without holiness. But can holiness be attained? The difference between God and us is that in His nature, God is Holy. But for us, holiness can only be attained when we begin our journey with the Holy God by having a relationship with Him through Jesus Christ and allowing the Holy Spirit to live in and through us. Nothing can make us holy except through grace and mercy. Thankfully, Christ has made it possible! He saved us, cleansed us, washed us, and set us apart for righteousness for which we can be thankful. Thus, our holiness increases as we grow in spiritual maturity. This is the reason why our pursuit of righteousness has been made attainable through Christ. To be holy, we must pull away from old lifestyles of disobedience and uncontrolled passions of pleasure and allow the Holy Spirit to live through us, so we can be righteous.

D) Holiness has everything to do with our salvation. Holiness cultivates our intimacy with God and builds spiritual strength–**Psalm 15:1-4.** With holiness, we can have a good relationship with God and to experience His power. Therefore, connecting to God in holiness is vital. God requires holiness from us so we can have a relationship with Him. That is why in **Philippians 2:12,** we are urged to work out our salvation with fear and trembling. Without holiness, it will be impossible to see God's power working among us. For that matter, in **Leviticus 11:44–45**, we are told to consecrate ourselves and be holy. So then, we must pursue holiness in all aspects of our lives, always bearing in mind that without holiness, we cannot connect to the Father in His glory. A better understanding of this fact is that even though our God is Holy and pure, His Holiness is not automatically reflected in us. We must work toward it after we are saved, and Christ, through the power of the Holy Spirit, will help us live a holy life. Thus, we are responsible for asking the Holy Spirit to help us experience God's glory through being holy.

E) Sin is what makes us unholy. God is perfect and there is no imperfection in Him. He is love and harbors no hatred. He is genuine, and there is no dishonesty in Him. God is light, and in Him is no darkness. He is pure, and there is no iniquity in Him. He is righteous, and there is no unrighteousness in Him. He is good, and there is no evil in Him. In our quest to be holy, we must rid ourselves of all darkness and impurity. We must strive for holiness in a sin-filled world. be pure and righteous. This means that we must be kind to everyone; speak the truth without compromise; love without discrimination; never doubt what Christ has done for us, and what He can do to help us live a life that pleases Him. God's Holiness must affect our lives positively and entirely through love. **Philippians 2:14–16** states, "Do everything without grumbling or arguing, so that you may become blameless and pure, children of God without fault...Then you will shine like stars in the sky as you hold firmly to the Word of Life; then you will be able to boast on the day of Christ that you did not labor in vain." This means that our holy lives will guarantee our place in Heaven.

Though it is sometimes difficult to attain holiness in today's world, where everything around us appears to be polluted by sin and ungodliness, there is still a Holy God who is willing to help us through the power of His Holy Spirit. All things are possible with God. So, yes, He can help us overcome sin. Our goal must therefore be to imitate Christ and stay pure in a world filled with evil by always reading the Word of God, praying, and asking to be forgiven and giving forgiveness. And though the challenges of this world will make us realize our weaknesses, the Holiness of God will help us become dependent on God and take refuge in Him. Any unholy act brings shame to God's Name. In **Matthew 21:12–17**, we read that Jesus was angry with those who were trading in the temple. He said to them, "Take these things away. Do not make my Father's house a house of trade." Jesus acted this way because He wanted to maintain sacredness in the house of God. Our bodies are the temples of God. For this reason, we must do whatever it takes to flee from anything that may cause us to become unholy. With the help of the Holy Spirit, we can. Thus, by asking Him each day to teach us His ways, guide us to the truth, and direct our paths, we are requesting His help for purity and holiness.

F). Holiness can be attained by abstaining from sinful acts done by unbelievers. According to the word of God, we should not yoke ourselves together with unbelievers but separate ourselves from them and touch no unclean thing (**1 Corinthians 3:16**). Those who do not believe in the gospel of Christ have no spirituality; They are consumed by the pleasures of the world and live ungodly lives. For that matter, we can love them and tell them about Christ. Nevertheless, we cannot mingle with them and practice what they do. To maintain our purity, we must not engage in the things of the world orchestrated by ungodly people (**Psalm 1:1**). Since we want to have a good relationship with people, we also need to keep in mind that mingling with the wrong group of people could sway us from righteousness. We need to lead disciplined lives and focus on righteous living. The pursuit of wealth and fame, lust, money, sex, greed, lies, deception, and worldly desires will corrupt us and drift us away from righteousness. We must exercise faith in Christ, repent, and make a covenant with God daily.

If we know that we are set apart for holy things, then we must strive to live lives devoid of sin because profane acts are detestable to God. As stated in Psalm 1, we must stay away from sin. Thus, we must not: 1) walk in the counsel of the ungodly or the wicked; 2) stand in the way of sinners, nor 3) sit in the seat of mockers. On the contrary, we must delight in the law of the Lord, and meditate on His law always. In this way, the Holiness of God will be reflected in us, and His plans will materialize in our lives.

We need a good name. To make this possible, we must read what is written in **Proverbs 22:1** and to protect the image of our Father and His Kingdom by staying away from sin. When we live unholy lives, we tarnish His Holy Name, which gives the enemy the chance to mock us and blaspheme God. Therefore, we must strive for holiness in Christ and ask for forgiveness if when we fail. Although we are bound to make mistakes, these must not be willful. Staying away from sin, living according to God's Word, and living without compromising in righteousness will help us achieve holiness and prevent us from tarnishing the Name of God. It is because our holiness signifies true worship and utmost sincerity to God. **Romans 12:1** tells us to offer our bodies as living sacrifices, holy and pleasing to God because this act signifies true and proper worship.

G) Holiness can be achieved through love. Our love for God, ourselves, and others connects us to the Father and His Holiness. He is the one who first loved us and gave His Son to be sacrificed for our sake. Loving God makes it possible to extend love to ourselves and others. Therefore, to possess love, we must first have love for God. When we possess it, only then can we extend that love to our self and to others. In God, we have love and can give it. It is the only way. We cannot claim to be holy if our hearts are filled with hatred. **1 John 4:20** says, "Whoever claims to love God yet hates others is a liar." We can't hate people and claim to love God. We also cannot love just those who are good to us. We are being discriminative if we do that. It does not work that way. Therefore, we must show love to all because love is the fruit of the Spirit. In **Psalm 139:23–24,** David prays, "Search me, O God, and know my heart... and see if there is any wicked way in me and free me." This passage tells us that we can attain holiness when we ask Jesus to search our hearts, reveal to us any hidden evil, and help us rid ourselves of such evil.

I cannot believe how many years of my life I spent complaining about things that were unnecessary. For years, I grumbled over my mistakes, and the more I thought about my past, the more I reaped misery. Instead of forgiving those who had hurt me, love them, and repented from my sins, I allowed the devil to manipulate me to blame God for not honoring His promises. But does God lie? Absolutely not! He always keeps to His promises. God is not a man to lie–**Numbers 23:19**. Being conscious of the things that make us unholy and constantly asking God to search our hearts will help us lead holy lives. Just like David wrote in **Psalm 139,** so we must do likewise. You may wonder if David couldn't have identified the evil he had done. Well, the answer can be found in **Proverbs 21:2.** We may think our ways are right, but the Lord weighs the heart. For this reason, we must ask God to search our hearts because He alone knows our deepest secrets. David knew that God could search his heart better than he ever could. We can do the same by asking God to search our hearts. He can see any evil in us and can lead us in an everlasting way.

H) Holiness can be achieved by obeying the Word of God. **Psalm 119:9** tells us, "How can a young person stay on the path of purity? By living according to Your Word." This instruction is quite straightforward; that is to say, holiness comes with living according to the Word of God because His Word teaches us *His Will*. So, we must search the scriptures daily to help us stay away from anything detestable to God.

I) Holiness can be attained by being at peace with everyone. Again, **Hebrews 12:14** instructs us to "make every effort to be at peace with everyone." Living in peace reflects holiness because our Father Himself is filled with peace. The devil knows this. So, he causes divisions and quarrels. He tempts us to either despise peace or make others seek to fight us. Admittedly, living in peace and maintaining it is not easy, but again, because it is the work of the Holy Spirit to see to it that we are holy, He will give us the strength to do so when we ask Him. We must live in peace with all people, love them, and forgive them because, with love in our hearts, we can forgive without holding grudges. In **Matthew 5:47**, Jesus says we must show love to all. It does not mean does we should go about partying with those who hurt us. Rather, He wants us to let go and be at peace with ourselves and with them so that holiness can be achieved.

J) Holiness can also be achieved by having the mindset of Christ Jesus according to what is written in **Philippians 2:5**. Because all evil starts within the mind, by allowing the pure mind of Christ to be in us, we are imitating His Holiness. With the mind of Christ in us, no evil will sink into our hearts and hide, to entice us to act on it. This is why it is important to guard our minds and hearts against harboring evil thoughts. To prevent any orchestrated sin, we must remain in constant prayer and in the Word and meditate daily on Scripture to help us overcome any evil thoughts.

K) Holiness can be achieved in the church if we rid ourselves of any sin that pollutes and contaminates. The most prevalent sins are condemnation, unforgiveness, gossip, division, jealousy, and envy. These sins are mostly overlooked. Most of us talk about fornicating, idol worship, and adultery as the most prevalent sins. But the truth is when we talk about holiness, any, and all sin contaminates. Therefore, no evil is considered small or large in God's Eyes. In that case, we must stop judging others and pray for ourselves against any sin in our lives and in the church and let holiness reign in us. The devil's goal is to cause us to sin because he assumes that once we become polluted with sin, we will be separated from God and will not experience the power of the Holy Spirit in our lives. However, Scripture tells us that God is merciful and forgiving. Once we acknowledge that our goal is to live a righteous life, we will take holiness seriously. When God's Holiness becomes our desire, we shall confess our sins and repent; righteousness will be established, and sin in our own lives and in the church will be defeated.

The stories of Isaiah and Joshua show how relevant our holiness is to God. **Isaiah 6:4–6** narrates that when Isaiah saw the Lord, he cried out, "Woe to me! I am ruined! For I am a man of unclean lips, and I live among a people of unclean lips, and my eyes have seen the King, the Lord God Almighty." Then a seraph flew to him with a live coal in his hand, which he had taken with tongs from the altar, and with fire in His hand, he touched Isaiah's lips with it and said, "See, this coal has touched your lips. Now your guilt is removed, and your sins are forgiven." In **Zechariah 3:3-4**, what we read is that Joshua, the high priest was standing before the angel of the LORD with a dirty garment too; and Satan was ready to accuse him. Joshua's filthy garments, which represented his sins, were taken away, and he was clothed with a fine garment to symbolize that indeed, his sins were forgiven. Then the angel of the Lord said to Joshua, "This is what the Lord Almighty says: If you will walk in obedience to me and keep my commandments, then you will govern my house and ... I will give you a place among these standing here."

The touching of Isaiah's lips with coal and the changing of Joshua's garment represented God's cleansing and forgiveness. The stories of the two men were pure demonstrations of God's Power to cleanse and make us holy before Him. When Isaiah cried out, "Woe to me, for I am a man of unclean lips," he was declaring his sinfulness before God. He realized how unclean he was. The Biblical accounts prove that God is concerned about our holiness and is willing to pardon our sin and make us holy in His church. So, let's not listen to people who want to remind us of our past mistakes and sins. They are hired by the devil to cast stones. Ignore them because they are not in your best interest. Let them know that grace has done it all on your behalf. Jesus said, "It is finished" (John 19:30). Seek forgiveness and don't repeat the same mistakes. Be thankful to God and ask Him to help you overcome every weakness you may have, and He will help you.

L) Holiness can be achieved through forgiveness. Forgiveness is the best medicine, but have you ever wondered why? Unforgiveness entangles and pollutes human souls. Scientists have come up with something great about forgiveness. They say unforgiveness puts stress on the body and causes all kinds of sicknesses. On the other hand, forgiveness helps the body to release stress reducing hormones which promotes mental well-being. Their findings are fantastic, but Jesus has the best answer and solution to why it is important to forgive. These are His solutions to forgiveness; 1) Forgiveness is good for the body, soul, and spirit; 2) it helps us overcome feelings of anger, bitterness, or revenge which stresses the body; 3) it helps us not be enslaved by sin; 4) it helps us become more holy; 5) it draws us closer to God; 6) it helps us to see Him; 7) it enables us to come before the throne of grace with boldness without anything hindering our prayers; 8) it allows us to make good choices; 9) it brings the peace of God; 10) holiness brings us many blessings. For these reasons, it is vital to pay attention to forgiveness.

Chapter 8 – The Holy Names of God

Matthew 6:9

The name of the LORD is a strong tower; the righteous run to it and are saved (**Proverbs 18:10**).

God's Holiness makes His Name powerful; so, knowing about the Holiness of God and bearing His Name is important for every believer. In human lives, names exist for identification purposes. God required that all His creation be given a name. So, He created Adam, named him, and authorized him to name everything He made. As we know, a child's naming ceremony is very important. In the culture that I grew in, a man is expected to name his child. Any man who fails to name his child will be mocked in his neighborhood. A child must be given a name for identification. Whatever name is given to the child, it becomes his or her official name.

In every culture, names play a major role. They are not simply intended for identification. For instance, the Hebrew name Joseph means Jehovah shall add or God will give. This represents a blessing. Meaning you can claim it and Jehovah will bless you. The name Gabriel means God is my strength; Jude means the praised one; Eve means life; Hephzibah means my delight is in her, and Jennifer means praise. What am I trying to say? Every name has a meaning(s). Whether it is a first, middle, or last name, they all have meanings. For instance, my first name is Jennifer, and I have another nick names, Hephzibah. My birth name is Ama Safoah. Ama is my native first name which means a female born on Saturday. Safoah signifies that I have a key in my hand to open closed doors, and the ability to do greater things. This gives me the impression that I can do all things through Christ who strengthens me, no matter the obstacles – **Philippians 4:13.** The meaning of my name reminds me to never give up on anything, but it can never save me. Why am I adding these? I knew some friends who called God by only one name. Whenever I wanted to pray with them, they never allowed it, thinking I would mention the Name God, Adonai, or El Shaddai. To them, it is only one name, and nothing must be added to that. Of course, I know God is Yahweh (Jehovah). But does He have only one name? According to the Bible, God has other names, and they all have their meanings.

As a way of honoring our Heavenly Father, we must address Him by His titles. Jesus began His Prayer by teaching us how to properly address the Father through salutation by saying, Our Father. So, saying Father or God, is a sign of reverence. In my culture, I can never call any of my elders in the village or town by only their first or last names without a preceding title of respect (e.g., mister or misses), so why not God. Throughout the Bible, we are told of His various names in detail; so, we must call Him by His proper name(s) and use His titles to show respect to His Name. Example, the name Jehovah carries a meaning and power. But God has many names that, regardless of the language, all point to Almighty God – Yahweh. For instance, in my language, when we say Yehowah, I am calling on the Name of Jehovah. I can also use titles to reverence His Name. So, I can say: Asafo Yehowah (Great Jehovah); Onokwarefo Nyankopong (God of truth); Onwanwane (God of wonder or Wonderful God); Otumfuo (All-powerful God); Nyansa-Buakwa (All-wise God); Ahuntahunu Nyankopon (All-knowing God); Otumfuo Nyankopong (Almighty God); Abode Nyinaa Wura (God of all Creation); Onnimdifo Nyankopong (All-Wise God); and so on. All these help us to address God in a respectful manner. And with Jesus Christ, we can say Awurade Yesu Kristo – (Lord Jesus Christ) or Agyenkwa (The Savior).

A title or salutation comes before the name to show respect, just as Jesus said, "Our Father," (**Matthew 6:9**). The words God and Lord are mentioned countless times, but they are not names but titles. Throughout the Bible, God refers to Himself by different names, each revealing an aspect of His nature, power, and character. For example, when God called Moses, He identified Himself as "I Am (I Am Who I Am)" and we know what it means when someone says, "I AM WHO I AM," (**Exodus 3:14**). When we talk about the Savior, Redeemer, Mediator, Immanuel, King of kings, Lord of lords, Prince of Peace, Yeshua Hamashiach, we are referring to Christ Jesus. When we mention Jehovah, we identify the I Am God. He is Yahweh, El Roi, El Shaddai, Nissi, Alpha and Omega, Rapha, Mighty, Powerful, All-Knowing, Merciful, the God of Love, Peace and Joy, the Supreme Being, and many more. Each name has a meaning. When we talk about God's Holy Spirit, we are talking about our counselor, comforter, and helper.

The amazing thing I have discovered is that you and I can give God a title due to His power and might in our personal lives. Looking at the above names, we can see that some of the titles or names of God were given to Him by humans who had special or significant encounters with God. For example, El Roi is the Hebrew name for God meaning "the God who sees me." We discover this name of God in **Genesis 16:14–15** when Hagar, an Egyptian slave, encountered God in the desert and addressed Him as El Roi. In **Genesis 22:14,** we see that Abraham named the place Yahweh Jireh which means "the Lord will provide." To this day people use the Name Yahweh or Jehovah Jireh meaning "God provides." If we need healing, He is our Jehovah Rapha. If we need peace, He is Jehovah Shalom: "the Lord Is Peace," or God of peace. Despite all His Names and titles, He is still One God with the name, Jehovah/Yahweh or the I AM. As stated earlier, we can call His Name in every situation to help us. This is His mystery, and that makes Him exceptional.

In **Exodus 20:24**, God tells us that wherever He causes His name to be recorded through the revelation of His divine nature, He will bring His blessings. **Psalm 8:1** says, "O Lord, our Lord, how excellent is Your name in all the earth!" Yes, His name is excellent, and it is filled with the power to save, heal, and deliver. According to **Psalm 9:10–11**, He will never forsake those who call on His name. In times of trouble, they will be rescued." By His Name, no weapon formed against us shall prosper. We are surrounded by a wall of fire, and the devil cannot entangle us with cords of death. By His Name, we are set free from all harm, and no form of destruction can overwhelm us. By His Name, we are secured. These means if we call on His name in times of trouble, we shall be saved. According to **Isaiah 9:6**, Jesus is Wonderful, Counselor, the Mighty God, the Everlasting Father, and the Prince of Peace. He is the One whom we all adore. **Philippians 2:10–11** says, "At the mention of His name, every knee shall bow, and every tongue confesses Him as Lord."

The point I am trying to make is that I have 4 names and a nickname. So, if humans have the right to take as many names, then the One who gave names and gave power to humans to give names can have as many names and titles as possible for our sake. All His Names are for our advantage. We have His Names that we can apply to our every situation. My names are unique because each one has a significant meaning attached to it, but I can never call my own names for deliverance. However, I can call on God's Name(s). God's Names are exclusively special because they represent particular attributes of Himself. Petitioning and employing the Name of God releases power and blessings. The Name of God has the power to heal, deliver, save, give us victory, and bring us peace. All the names of God are there for our good, because in times of sickness, I can call on His Name, Rapha, for my healing, and it will bring miracles into my situation if I believe, or if it is *His Will*. Even if I am on medications, I can still call on the Name of Jehovah Rapha. Or I can call on His Name Jehovah Nissi for victory. It assures our triumph in God's Name. Moses gave this name to God when he built the altar to celebrate the defeat of the Amalekites (**Exodus 17:13–16**). **Psalm 20**, says, "Those who put their trust in chariots and horses are brought to their knees and fall, but we rise and stand firm because we have placed our hope in the Lord." The power in the Names of God does it all! That is why God commands us not to mention His Name in vain (**Exodus 20:7**).

The following are additional Names and titles of God:

• All-Powerful God: This means that all power and strength belong to God. The Lord is mighty and great, with the power to save, heal, and deliver us from all afflictions.

• All-Knowing God: God knows everything; nothing can be hidden from Him (**Isaiah 42:9**).

• Most High God: The Lord possesses power above all other powers. He can protect us from harm. **Philippians 2:9–10** says, "All power in Heaven and on earth belongs to God, and at the mention of the name Jesus, every knee shall bow."

• Immanuel: God is with us. In our walk with the Lord, He is with us every step of the way. He gives us the grace to serve Him. In **Matthew 28:20**, Jesus said to His disciples before ascending to Heaven, "I am with you always...."

• Jehovah Rapha: God, our Healer. He has the power to heal all kinds of diseases and free us from pains – **Psalm 143–11**.

• Adonai: The Lord God oversees all His creation. He is Omnipotent. He commanded all things into existence, and there is nothing He cannot do (**Jeremiah 32:17**).

• El Shaddai: Lord God Almighty – the eternal God. In Hebrew, Shaddai means to overpower or destroy. This describes God as the one who triumphs over every obstacle and all opposition. God is All-Powerful, All-Sufficient, and the Sustainer of Life. He will provide, supply, nourish, and satisfy all our needs despite apparent impossible circumstances.

• El Olam: Everlasting God; His existence is continuous. He is perpetual, everlasting, or eternal. He exists beyond time and space, and we can take comfort in knowing that our God was, is, and will always be (**Genesis 21:33**).

• Jehovah Mekoddishkem: The Lord our Sanctifier. In **Exodus 31:13**, it means Holy or set apart. The Lord has called, separated us from the rest of the world, and sanctified us. In **Leviticus 20:7–8**, it is written, "Consecrate yourselves and be holy. I am the Lord, who makes you holy." Due to our sinful nature, God takes us through His sanctification process to make us fit for His Name's sake.

• Jehovah Shalom: The Lord our Peace (**Judges 6:24**) When we are at peace, we receive the fullness of God. God's peace which surpasses all understanding, is what sustains us in difficult times. When we feel overwhelmed, when everything seems to come crashing down, and when we feel as if we cannot face a problem, we can turn to the God of peace and comfort to strengthen us because He is our refuge and our fortress (**Psalm 91:2**). So, no anxiety and depression then, can overpower us.

• Jehovah Shammah: The Lord is there. The Lord is with us, as stated in **Romans 8:31**; therefore, we have nothing to be afraid, regardless of our circumstances.

• God's Name, Elohim, or Yahweh emphasizes His role as the supreme creator. He created the heavens and the earth. This shows His power and sovereignty over all creation.

In **Psalm 18:1**, David says that God is our strength. He is our rock, fortress, deliverer, refuge, shield, the horn of our salvation, and our stronghold. God is our support, our defense, and the one who gives victory in every battle. He protects and keeps us safe in His love. Things can go bad, but God's Name has power to stabilize things. Nothing can ever separate us from His love because of His Name's sake. His Powerful Name saves us from all traps of the enemy. When the cords of death entangle us, when the torrents of destruction overwhelm us, and when the snare of death confronts us, we can always call on the Name of the Lord our God, through the powerful name of Jesus Christ, and all shall be well with us. "He will command His angels concerning us" (**Psalm 91:11**). He will cause the earth to tremble to destroy our enemies and will cause the foundations of the mountains to shake – all at the mention of His Name.

The Name of God is a refuge. **Psalm 46:1** says, "God is our refuge and strength, a very present help in trouble." Although there will be difficult times, God promises to be our refuge. When our enemies seek to devour us, the Lord will shield and rescue us because we know how to call upon His Name. **Psalm 9:9** states, "The Lord is a refuge for the oppressed, a refuge in times of trouble." If we seek the Lord, we will find Him because we know His Name; no good thing will be withheld from us – **Psalm 34:10**. We have a right to His Name, but first, we must establish a relationship with Him, keep His Name holy, and experience all the goodness that comes from calling upon His Name. Once God become the center of our lives, His Name shall be available as a refuge and a strong tower to shield all who take refuge in Him.

The Name of God is capable of healing. Sometimes, the challenges in life can be overwhelming. We could be sick, poor, depressed, afraid, or rejected by people, but God promises divine healing for the soul, body, and mind. Christ bore our sickness, pains, and sorrows on the cross because He is our healer. He heals the brokenhearted. So, He disclosed one of His Names as Jehovah Rapha (**Exodus 15:22–26**). Even if our situation is detestable like the waters at Marah, in His Name it can become sweet because He is Jehovah Rapha. God can demonstrate His power if we accept Him. If His power worked among the Israelites, it could also be manifested among us. The Name of the Lord Jesus saves, but those who feel self-sufficient will never find deliverance in His Name.

His name is above all because everything is embedded in His Name (**Philippians 2:9). John 16:23** says we can ask the Father in the Name of Jesus. In the Scripture, God reveals to us the path to salvation. That path is Jesus Christ. He shows us the way to peace, joy, and everlasting life, all because of His Name's sake. His Name does all the work. God's Name can change your situation. The powerful Name of Christ has power to do what you and I cannot do. It can turn things around and cause all things to work together for the good. His Name brings the lost into receiving salvation. His Name can guide us onto the right path. If we revere His Name, He will take care of our confusions and give us a sound mind. His Name can do what seems even impossible. There is nothing God's Powerful Name cannot do; Everything good is found in His Name. However, we must keep His Name Holy in everything we do before we can experience the power for which His Name stands. Amen!

Chapter 9 – Thy Kingdom Come

Matthew 6:10

***Thy Kingdom come* is one of my favorite phrases in the Lord's Prayer.** Do you want the Kingdom of God to come on earth? What will happen if the Kingdom comes? What must you then do? Romans 14:17 – For the kingdom of God is about righteousness and peace and joy in the Holy Spirit. God created the Heaven and the earth and instituted kingdoms on earth. In Heaven, He has His Kingdom. This Kingdom of God represents Heaven. There is also the kingdom of man, which represents earth. But among all the kingdoms, none can be compared to His. As Jesus said, "My kingdom is not in this world." The earthly kingdom was supposed to be for humans. We were to rule and bring glory to God in all we do, but again Satan took over when he saw what humans can do to bring glory to God. With this, he tried to make himself a king so that people can worship hm instead of worshiping God. The devil stole from humans because he hates to see humans glorifying the Name of the Father in Heaven. For that matter, he planned to destroy God's purpose for humanity. It was what he did in the garden of Eden. But thank God for His gift of salvation through Christ

In the Book of Genesis, we read that God created the Garden of Eden as human's kingdom on earth, but Satan deceived humans first and caused them to rebel against God. Since then, all of us choose to do as we pleased and rebel against God. However, is all about Satan's kingdom of darkness. The devil lies and deceives people. Some of these lies make people think they are serving themselves. What they don't realize is that serving themselves means serving the world, which is under Satan's control. Without God's Word through salvation, you are not operating from God's perspective, and you will end up destroying yourself through the pleasures of this life. That is the goal of Satan.

Jesus will reign forever and ever. Amen! Right now, we know about the Kingdom of God through Him. Through salvation, the kingdom of darkness becomes the Kingdom of light. God sent Jesus to earth to bring salvation, but the evil of this world crucified Him. Yet, God used His suffering to pay the penalty to save humanity. God raised Him from the dead, showing that Jesus has power and authority even over death and the kingdom of darkness. Today, He invites all of us to leave the kingdom of darkness and become part of His Kingdom of light through salvation. If we turn from our wicked ways, acknowledge that Jesus is our rightful King, then by God's mercy, on account of the cross, we will receive His forgiveness and escape from the kingdom of darkness into this marvelous Kingdom of light and reign with Him forever.

First, what is a kingdom? A kingdom is the throne of a king or a queen. It represents the glorious majesty of the monarch. I have categorized three kingdoms, namely:

Earthly kingdom and leaders: In **Psalm 115:16**, we are told that "the highest Heavens belong to the Lord, but the earth He has given to mankind." The earthly kingdom is mankind's kingdom. This kingdom covers a piece of land, territory, or domain governed by a king or queen. The king or queen exercises absolute authority and influence over the land and its people and has a responsibility to them. It is therefore a territory that no one must trespass. It is good, but it can sometimes also be bad and violent. This happens when a king or queen does not rule under God's power but under demonic influences. God anoints and appoints kings to protect the vulnerable, but they have limited authority. Historically, kings had complete dominion and power to make all decisions that modern-day governments make. However, in recent times, they don't exercise such absolute power. Their role is to rule a kingdom. In some cultures, the chief's linguist or the palace officials serve as palace advisors. A king or queen's most important duty is to establish order and keep peace within their borders by enforcing the necessary rules. This includes the duty to prevent intruders from entering. No kingdom can randomly seize the territory of another kingdom unless through wars of invasion. No earthly king could claim ownership over all lands or territories. Therefore, a king must respect other kings and their domains. So, this type of kingdom has its limits. There is also another kingdom which seeks to rules in the heart of every human being. We can call it 'the kingdom of lust or flesh. This is when we set up our own kingdoms in our hearts to rule over our own lives, just how we want it. Man's kingdom in the Garden of Eden was the perfect one, but the kingdom did not last for long. It was destroyed when humans obeyed Satan and rebelled against God. With this, people choose to serve Satan without realizing. In the heart of humans, the devil sets up his own kingdom, but God's salvation is for all humans to turn from their evil ways and surrender to Him so He can rule in our hearts.

Today, kings don't go to war; governments, through their militaries do. But sometimes, leaders take matters into their own hands without consulting God before they act. And this is dangerous because the devil works to hinder progress. Therefore, we must pray against his strategies. **Daniel 2:44** tells us that Daniel prayed, "The God of Heaven will set up a Kingdom which will never be destroyed. It will crush and put an end to all evil kingdoms, but it will endure forever." **Romans 13:1** tells us that "There is no authority except that which God has established...." Therefore, we must pray for the raising up of God-fearing leaders, who will choose to be under God's Kingdom and its authority. Yes, we need God-fearing leaders who will make decisions based on Godly principles; and not being enticed by evil.

The kingdom of the evil one. In **John 14:30**, Christ titled Satan as the prince or the ruler of this world. Satan is never a king; he is a prince or a ruler. Satan's ruling is what the Bible termed as the dark world. It is a place occupied by him and all his demons. They can be in the air, in the water, or anywhere, but humans can't see it even if it is in your neighborhood or home, church, or the government. It is the kingdom of spiritual darkness which is ruled by all kinds of wickedness. It is filled with hatred and confusions. This kingdom seeks to control, destroy, and rule within humans. It is called the illuminati in today's world, and it is what is written in **Ephesians 6:10-12.** This means there is another kingdom which seeks to rule over humans. It is the kingdom of darkness; we can only overcome it when we practice righteousness.

The Kingdom of God or Heaven: The Kingdom of God is the domain of God. This Kingdom is the Kingdom of all kingdoms. God's Kingdom is not visible to the eyes, yet it exists. It rules over all things and is ruled by His power. It is a Kingdom of Light and inside of it there is no darkness at all. This Kingdom is filled with Holiness, love, peace, and compassion. It is the perfect Kingdom that must rule in the hearts of humans. Just like earthly kingdoms are ruled by kings and queens, so God rules in His Kingdom as the King of all kings who reigns over His creation. Among these three kingdoms, only God's Kingdom is perfect. He is autonomous. In **Psalm 66:7**, we are told, "God rules forever by His might, and He keeps His eye on the nations." This means that He oversees all other kingdoms and that everyone, regardless of age or status, are under His authority. He is not subject to any other power, rather every kingdom is subject to Him. **Psalm 103:19** declares, "The Lord has established His throne in Heaven, and His Kingdom rules overall." Thus, when we talk about the Kingdom of God, we refer to the domain and reign of God. This means God's Kingdom is real. It comprises a multitude of angels and saints, which is also filled with purity and grace. **1 Chronicles 16:31** says, "Let the Heavens be glad, and the earth rejoice; and let them say among the nations, 'The Lord reigns.' God reigns. He reigns forever by His might." Just as kings and queens reign, so also does God reign. The difference is that God reigns as the King of all kings!

***God's* Kingdom is not an illusion**. He is the true King, and His Kingdom is the most powerful of all! In order to experience this amazing Kingdom of God, you must first believe that God exists. To understand this, you must know how God's Kingdom functions, which is through His love. We know this from **John 3:16**, "For God so loved the world..." What did He do out of love? He sent His Son, Jesus, as a sign of love to come and dwell among us. When Jesus came, He brought with Him the love, peace, joy, compassion, self-control, unity, and forgiveness of God into the world. He is righteous. Therefore, if we say that we are part of His Kingdom, then we must faithfully fulfil our part by making sure our lives are aligned to His Word.

What makes God's Kingdom exceptional? In **Matthew 13:44–46,** He says, "The Kingdom of Heaven is like a treasure hidden in the field, which a man found and hid again; and from joy over it he goes and sells everything that he has and buys that field." There are treasures hidden in God's Kingdom, and those treasures are only attainable through Jesus Christ and salvation. This means that the Kingdom of God is more precious than anything else; it is like a hidden treasure. If you find this treasure, you will let go of everything to seek what is in this Kingdom, just as King David did. In **John 18:36**, the Lord Jesus says, "The Kingdom of God is not of this world." Sadly, many have rejected this Kingdom, seeking Satan's kingdom of evil or worldly kingdom of fame and riches. Other than those who humble themselves under the rule of God, many people, including pastors, earthly kingships, and their subjects and citizens, are under the influence of the devil due to what they practice. Some earthly kings and pastors would do anything to retain power or whatever they want, even if they must kill. But thankfully, some have sold everything in exchange for this Heavenly treasure. Even if they are wealthy rulers, they give reverence to God and do not go against *His Will*. Today, my prayer is that we would sincerely pray for everyone to see the light, because God's salvation is the only one that brightens our world.

***The Kingdom of God as riddles*.** **Let's see how Christ describes the Kingdom.**

- **Matthew 13:** He compares the Kingdom to a merchant looking for fine pearls. When he found one of great value, he sold everything he had and bought it.

- **Matthew 25:** He compares the Kingdom to ten brides– the foolish and the wise. The wise were prepared but not the foolish ones. He also compares the Kingdom with a man going on a journey and entrusting his possessions to his servants. What happens when he returns is called loyalty in doing the work of God's Kingdom. How prepared are you? Can you be trusted?

• Matthew 18: He compares the Kingdom of God to forgiveness, meaning that unforgiveness will prevent you from entering the Kingdom of Heaven.

• **Matthew 22:** He says a king threw a wedding feast for his son, but the inviters refused the invitation: meaning, some will choose to reject the gift of salvation.

• **Matthew 13:** He compared the Kingdom of Heaven to a man who sows good seed in his field, and how his enemy also went and planted weeds among the wheat.

• **Matthew 20:** He tells us that the Kingdom of Heaven is like a man who goes out to hire laborers to work in his vineyard and pays them the same wages at the end of the day, even though they came to work at different times of the day.

• **Mark 4:** He tells us that the Kingdom of God can be likened to a mustard seed. Though smaller than all the seeds, it grows up and becomes larger than all the garden plants, which means that we need faith as little as a mustard seed.

• **Matthew 13:** The Kingdom is compared to fishing, where the bad ones are thrown away. So, at the end of the age, the angels will come and take out the wicked from among the righteous.

• Mark 10:15: The Kingdom of God is also compared to children. Jesus tells us to receive the Kingdom of God as little children. This means we need the humility and faith of children.

The Kingdom of God includes healing. **Luke 10:9** says Jesus healed those who were sick, and told them, "The kingdom of God has come near to you." In God's Kingdom, it is *His Will* that we are healed. Once we receive salvation, we have free access to His Divine Healing through the precious blood of Jesus. Physical, emotional, and spiritual healing are all included because the Kingdom of God is not constrained by weakness or infirmity. In **3 John 1:2,**

we are told, "Beloved, I pray that in every way you may prosper and enjoy good health, as your soul also prospers."

Did you know that we can visit God's Kingdom daily? Amazingly, we can! Just as we can visit a king or a queen's palace, so we can visit God. The difference is that earthly palaces are visible, but God's Kingdom is invisible. This is because God is a Spirit, and we worship Him in spirit and in truth. Jesus wants us to fully enjoy Him in His Kingdom one day, but that Kingdom starts right here on earth where we live. Then, how can we visit God's Kingdom daily? In this life, we must desire holiness. To achieve this, His Kingdom of righteousness must be established in us. With this, there must be no evil practices; we must desire to be in His presence, read the Bible, and pray each day. That is how we visit God daily.

What is done in the Kingdom of God? We can never talk about God's Kingdom without thinking about what He does in His Kingdom. In a worldly kingdom, it is said that a king reigns, but he does not rule. A king follows the government's laws. For instance, in the UK, the king is constitutionally obliged to follow the government's advice. His main function as Head of State is to appoint the Prime Minister and all other ministers, to open new sessions of the legislature, and to give royal assent or approval to bills passed by the government. In most countries, it is the same. Kings rule over their people but must abide under the leadership of the government. They reign over their citizens within their domain but with limited access and power. Contrarily, God's Kingdom is an autonomous Kingdom. His Kingdom is filled with His praise. Our praises must ascend to His throne for His Glory to descend. **Psalm 22:3** says, "God inhabits the praise of His people." Thus, worship of God is a must. Earthly kings are not being worshiped day and night as it is done in Heaven. In Heaven angels don't sleep. Instead, they sing a song day and night and praise God. The Bible gives an account of Heavenly beings who forever sing praises and worship the Name of God in Heaven. **Revelation 4:8** narrates that "...day and night, they sing Holy, Holy, Holy is the Lord God Almighty..." Once we ascend into Heaven, we will join the Heavenly choir in singing and praising the King of Glory. Until then, we can still take part in worship while residing here on earth. Ultimately, it is the reason why we are here. How can we do this? We must manage our lives, make time for the Lord by reading the Bible, praying, meditating, singing, praising, and worshipping in the beauty of His Holiness. This is how we visit the Kingdom of God each day. Although we may be busy with other things, we must make time for the Lord and His Kingdom in our heart anytime and anywhere.

God's Kingdom is Eternal, an everlasting Kingdom. The Kingdom of God has existed since time immemorial. It possesses everlasting power, holiness, glory, honor, wisdom, faithfulness, forgiveness, salvation, grace, and peace. In **Psalm 145:13**, we are told: "Your kingdom is an everlasting kingdom, and your dominion endures through all generations." In **Daniel 4:3**, King Nebuchadnezzar acknowledged the sovereignty of God and said, "His Kingdom is an eternal Kingdom." The king added, "I blessed the Most-High; I praised and honor Him who lives forever; for His dominion is an everlasting dominion, and His Kingdom endures from generation to generation" (**Daniel 4:34**). God's Kingdom is an everlasting one which will not be destroyed. (**Daniel 7:14**). God's Kingdom is transcendent. In God's Kingdom, He rules with autonomy because He is the King of all! God reigns and rules, and no one has power over Him. What He says is final. He displays His power everywhere. He deserves to be praised and worshipped for His power and glory. This Righteous Kingdom of Heaven is ruled only by God the Father, Son, and Holy Spirit. His angels are His messengers. God rules in His Kingdom as the King of all kings, and He rules forever by His might. In this Kingdom of God, the devil has no say. In Daniel 6:26, he gives a better understanding of God's Domain or Kingdom by saying, "In every part of my kingdom, people must fear and revere the God of Daniel as the living God who endures forever. His Kingdom will not be destroyed, and His dominion will never end."

It is essential for everyone to understand this given truth that heavens and the earth belong to God, it also means that He occupies all parts of them. The only problem that we are facing is Satan's rulership through humans with all kinds of evil. For that matter, it is imperative that we pray, Thy Kingdom come, and Thy Will be done on earth as it is done in Heaven. With this, we are asking God to reign in our lives, the lives of our families, all churches', and in the whole world in all aspect, so that evil cannot control us. If we pray for God's everlasting Kingdom to come into us, we shall be under His control. Therefore, we must pray for God's Kingdom to be established in our hearts, because it is how the Kingdom of Heaven will rule among us here on earth till Christ comes to establish His perfect Kingdom. With God's Kingdom in our still sinful hearts, we won't be perfect. Nevertheless, His righteousness will rule in our hearts to help us do the right thing instead of evil.

The Kingdom of God and the Church – In **Matthew 16:18**, Jesus said, "I tell you that you are Peter. I'll build my church on this rock, and the gates of hell shall not prevail against it." Sometimes, the most relevant things to be prayed for are overlooked, and that can be a problem. Believers have a responsibility to pray for God's Kingdom to rule in each day wherever we are. We can try to do God's work in the church and take the Gospel into the community or on the streets, but prayer must be the first thing we do. We must pray for the church if we want God to reign in the church. We must pray to receive the power of the Holy Spirit to do the work. We must also pray for our pastors, church leaders, and everyone to be protected, guided, and filled with the Holy Spirit to do the work with power and without compromising. Pray if you want to win souls and propagate the Good News of the Lord to everyone. Pray if you want God to choose spiritual leaders who are devoted. Pray if you need understanding, kindness, and compassion to do God's work. May we never set our careers, games, jobs, marriages, friendships, wealth, and all else as our kingdom. May nothing prevent us from seeking the Kingdom of Heaven. May our prayers reach to all for them to know God's Kingdom of Light and receive salvation. So, never cease praying until the Kingdom of God is fully established and *His Will* is done on earth as it is done in Heaven.

The Kingdom of God must come. Why must God's Kingdom come? God want to build His Kingdom in us. This can be done through salvation.

It is what salvation is about. This is because the Kingdom of God is pure and devoid of evil and ungodliness. It is established with righteousness. When salvation comes, God reigns in our hearts. With this, we develop love, kindness, compassion, faithfulness, joy, peace, gentleness, and self-control. In Isaiah 9:6, the prophet Isaiah prophesies of the divine birth of a child who will rule the world. It is written, "For a child will be born to us, and His government will rest upon His shoulders; and His Name will be called Wonderful Counselor, Mighty God, Eternal Father, and Prince of Peace." When He was on earth, Jesus was a representation of God's Kingdom. Jesus came to show us the way to God – salvation – and instructed us on what we must do to cause His Kingdom to come. When we pray for the Kingdom of God to come, we must also share the Good News to the world because salvation is the Kingdom's Business on earth. Therefore, when we pray, Your Kingdom come; Your Will be done, we are praying for souls to receive salvation, and for evil to be eradicated; Accordingly, we send the Good News for God to build His Kingdom on earth.

The Lord wants the inhabitants of the earth to be at peace and free from evil. However, because of the devil's schemes, the earth is filled with evil. This means without salvation, achieving peace on our own is impossible. Though the earth is extremely polluted with evil, the devil refuses to quit polluting it continually with sinfulness. The goal of Satan is to push humans as far away from the grace of God and His Righteous Kingdom as much as possible. Nonetheless, if we start praying each day, Your Kingdom come; Your Will be done in every way, then God's delivering power will guide us to the truth. He will also change the unbeliever's heart to accept the truth. Christ knows that prayer can make a tremendous difference. Praying for God's Kingdom to come means living our lives accordingly to *God's Will*. This brings God's love, kindness, and compassion to the world. When God's Kingdom comes, it will cause us to desire the things of God and not the things of the world. Thus, when I ask for God's righteous Kingdom to be established, I'm asking God to put an end to the devil's kingdom in me and in everyone. It means I desire God's ruling in everything I do. The secret is that when we pray with the Lord's

Prayer each day, in the powerful Name of Jesus, it will direct the world and its people in the direction of God, and even a notorious criminal can come to the full knowledge of God. Because when God's Kingdom comes into them, their lives will be changed.

*The Lord wants us to pray each day and ask for God's Kingdom to come to the world.

In his book, 'The Healing Path – How the Hurt in your past can lead you to a more abundant life', Dr. Dan B. Allender wrote, "We are powerless to escape living in a falling world, where our sinful flesh and the enemy of our souls work to destroy us" (p. 76). We live in a world where we desire to have our own kingdom in our hearts, where we will rule instead of God. However, this mentality is the work of the enemy who wants to destroy our souls. In this day and age, no one wants to be bothered or disturbed; we all wish people would leave us alone! One of the things the enemy uses to pull us away from doing God's work is making us feel like we are trespassing and intruding in other people's lives. When Jesus was on earth, He intruded; This was how He won souls for the Kingdom. He wouldn't have gotten one person to follow Him if He had quietly minded His own business. Jesus went out doing 'good' to all because He wanted the Kingdom to dwell in people. Accordingly, He took the time to interact with people – good and bad – everywhere He went.

True communication and having a personal touch are ceasing in our time! Today, it is about automated technology, emails, texting, and social media, which are all good, but we cannot become afraid or fed up with one another. People who try to trespass are sometimes killed or hurt; Therefore, we try to stay away from people. This should not be so. Unfortunately, this has become the norm. Why? It is because we are all afraid to get hurt. To see a change, we must pray for the Kingdom of God to come. If we do, the Holy Spirit will empower us, we shall become bold and courageous, and will have no fear of reaching out to the unsaved. It is our only solution because God's Kingdom is the only Kingdom ruled through Christ with the power of salvation. When the truth reigns, people will plan no evil against one another. They will live with peace in their soul. They will wake up thinking of what they must do to win souls to expand God's Kingdom on earth. They will think and do what is right, having no time to plan evil against anyone. Yes, I am aware that until Christ comes, the evil in this world will not be eradicated. But if we pray for God's Kingdom to rule in our midst each day, we will learn to do good and will enjoy life without being afraid of harm. There will be no evil of any kind because every evil will be under control. This is because God's Kingdom is a righteous Kingdom full of love.

Dr. Allender stated, "The world is a maw open wide, waiting for us to slip. Our flesh sings a siren song, calling us to loosen the bonds of wisdom and abandon ourselves to debt, food, alcohol, TV /social media, noise, busyness, or any other form of numbness. As if we have not had enough; we have a personal enemy committed to destroying us. Evil works to delude and destroy. It wants dominion. Satan, as the ruler of this world's kingdom, seeks all of us as servants, whether as intentional slaves of darkness or unwitting sycophants" (p.75). Yes, it is the devil's goal to rule this world, dominate people, and use humans as his slaves. In that case, what can we do? The only thing that can bring us freedom is when Satan's evil kingdom is destroyed completely! But how? The Lord has set a time for his destruction; until then, we can do our part, which is to pray and show people the only way to God; so, let's do what is right and acceptable unto God. This is how we tear the evil kingdom down on earth.

If more and more people get to know the truth, evil will be minimized. Each day as we spend time praying for the saved to continue in their faith and the unsaved to know the right way, we are building the Kingdom of God on earth. Once God's righteous Kingdom reigns, we will see love also ruling. In this way, we can weaken the devil and his evil kingdom. There will not be too many sins ruling among us, because we will ask for forgiveness each day. For example, the more I ask for forgiveness for myself, for my children, their children, the church of God in Christ, and for people all over the world, and learn to forgive others, the more kindness and empathy shall rule. We will think and act right. This means that it is only in God's Kingdom that we can overcome evil. Thus, to destroy the devil's kingdom, we must plan to reach out to people with the Good News of Salvation wherever we are. Today, my sincerest request is that we shall pray so that the message of Jesus Christ shall reach beyond our communities. Many missionaries are out to preach the good news, and with our prayer support, God will protect and use them for the reason why they were sent. This is vital because anytime we pray for God's Kingdom to come, it means we are inviting God to have His rightful place and reign in the hearts of people each day with the power of His Holy Spirit. May Kingdom of God rule.

Peace comes when God's Kingdom comes into us. **If** Jesus if the Prince of Peace, then we need His Kingdom. As Jesus said in John 14:27, "My peace I leave with you..." The most important thing is to know that it is God's Kingdom that can bring us peace. The Kingdom helps us to have a heart of repentance. Praying, "Thy Kingdom come" helps us walk in obedience to God. We are all aware that if Satan keeps ruling among humans, there will be no peace on earth. But the righteousness we have in Christ can help us each day to overcome any evil that seeks to trouble our minds. Thus, the evil kingdom must be destroyed through salvation for humans to be set free. Until then, there will be no peace on earth.

The warfare in this life is not carnal. The spiritual forces of evil that we deal with are demonic entities fighting against our welfare, and we see this from **Ephesians 6**. This means that reaching the goal of salvation is not about condemning; but it is about love, peace, kindness, which involves prayer and God's Word. These will destroy the works of the principalities and powers of the dark world which seek to fight against the work of the Kingdom on earth. Without true love, we cannot do away with the enemy who makes lawlessness increase; causes the love of many to grow cold, and makes wickedness continues. Because the powers of the dark world are spiritual, we cannot fight against them in the flesh; but there is hope through Christ. In His Word, there is victory. God's Word can set us free; it can show the way, give us light, and reveal the truth in us, as we see written in **John 8:32**. The truth is what sets us free. With the Word of God, Satan will get no chance to deceive people with his lies. When

God's Kingdom comes into them, they will not be conformed to this world, but they too shall be transformed according to *God's Will*, and their minds will be renewed. This means we defeat the devil and his allies with the Word of God. When we ask God's Kingdom to come into people through the Word, they will know the Truth. With the Truth, their chains shall be broken, and they shall be set free.

God's Kingdom is based only on righteousness. In choosing to follow Christ, we must pursue **righteousness. Isaiah 32:**1 declares that God's Kingdom cannot be separated from His righteousness because He reigns in His Holiness. **Galatians 5:19–21** tells us about all kinds of sins that cause unholiness, which the doers thereof can never be found in God's Kingdom. These sins mentioned in the above scripture are as follows: sexual immorality, debauchery, idolatry, witchcraft, hatred, jealousy, rage, selfish ambition, dissension, drunkenness, murder, rape, division, power struggles, boastfulness, hypocrisy, covetousness, deceitfulness drunkenness, scamming, and the love of money, among others. All these come from the dark kingdom of the evil one. But God's Kingdom of righteousness comes to transform us and fill us with hope because God's Kingdom is love not to hate; acceptance not condemnation; peace not war; joy not sorrow; and humility not haughtiness. For us to live in God's Kingdom while on earth, we can choose to display the fruit of the Holy Spirit, which make us pure before God: love, peace, joy, forgiveness, forbearance, kindness, goodness, faithfulness, gentleness, humility, and self-control. Therefore, if we truly desire the righteous Kingdom of God, then our prayer must be, Lord, may Thy Kingdom come.

This is God's plan for us. God's Kingdom will redirect us to *His Will*, which will in turn lead us to His plans. His plans will take us to a good ending; There is no way around that. We cannot separate God's Salvation from His Plans for us. They are intertwined. **1Peter 4:2** says, "We should no longer live the rest of our life in the flesh for the lust of this world but to the Will of God." Each day, as we pray and commit ourselves to the Father, we renew our vow, and He secures our faith in Him. This does not mean that our lives will always be perfect, but since He is eternally perfect, He will give us a firm foundation to stand on through the Holy Spirit.

God's Kingdom on earth is salvation. The Kingdom of God on earth means salvation through Jesus. Without Jesus, there is no salvation; without salvation, there is no righteousness. As **John 14:6 and John 8:12** say, Jesus is the Way, the Truth, the Life, and the Light of the world. In **Matthew 4:17**, He preached the message of repentance to the people, warning them that the Kingdom of Heaven was near. "The coming of the Kingdom of God cannot be observed, and no one will announce, 'Look, here it is,' or 'there it is.' For behold, the Kingdom of God is among you" (**Luke 17:20–21**). This makes it very clear that in this case, the Kingdom of God is about salvation through Jesus Christ. Christ said, "If you open the door of your heart, I will come in and dine with you" (**Revelation 3:20**). Christ is our hope (**Colossians 1:27**). When we talk about the Kingdom of God on earth, we imply that God's Heaven has come to preside over us through righteousness. Salvation then becomes our goal. So, do you want to know more about God's Kingdom? And as stated earlier, do you want to visit God's Kingdom? Accordingly, every time you read His Word, pray, and fast in faith, you visit God in His Kingdom. Therefore, we must plan and work towards it for ourselves and help others to know the truth. We can plan to do many things: travel to many places, make money, acquire knowledge, have many achievements, or make a name for ourselves. These are all good, but they are insufficient because true life only comes from God and salvation for the soul. So, after all is accomplished, we will pass from this life. However, life doesn't end here on earth because *we are mere travelers on this earth*. **Like pilgrims on a visit, we shall return to where we came from when the time is over.** The question then is this: to where will you return? Heaven/the New Jerusalem, or Hell? Christ is our only way. Once He establishes Himself in us, we will live on earth as though living in Heaven. So, this is why we pray, 'Thy Kingdom come into us.'

We need the Kingdom of God and salvation. Sin separated us from the Father. To mend and restore the broken relationship between us and God,

Jesus was sent as a Savior. In **John 8:28,** Jesus said, "I do nothing on My own initiative, but I speak these things as the Father taught Me." Although sin severs the relationship between us and the Father, Jesus' sacrifice has made a way for us to return to Him through repentance. If we confess our sins, accept Jesus Christ as our Savior, and invite Him into our hearts, we will be restored. **Romans 10:9** tells us to confess with our mouths that Jesus is Lord and believe in our hearts that God raised His Son from the dead that we might have eternal life.

Once we accept Jesus and repent of our sin, we receive salvation and become born again. This new birth in Christ is our ticket to the Kingdom. As Jesus says, salvation means being born again. Unless one is born again, one cannot see the Kingdom of God. In **John 3:3–17**, the followers of Christ didn't quite understand what He meant about salvation. Nicodemus asked, "how can someone be born again when he is old? Surely, he cannot enter a second time into his mother's womb to be born again! Jesus answered, ...no one can enter the Kingdom of God unless he is born of water and the Spirit." To receive salvation, we must first repent and then accept Jesus as our Savior, receiving the Holy Spirit at that point. Receiving salvation and getting baptized are both a step of faith. **Romans 10:10** says, "For it is with your heart that you believe and are justified, and it is with your mouth that you profess your faith and are saved." We may have plenty of time to accept Jesus as our Savior, however, because we do not know how long our lives will be, it is best to view each day as the day of salvation. Until God's Kingdom is established on earth, the news of the Kingdom of Salvation must be spread to everyone.

So, again, since entry into the Kingdom of God revolves around salvation through repentance, the Gospel of Christ must continue to be spread everywhere. Jesus began spreading the Word about the Kingdom because it was part of His earthly mission. It has been over 2,000 years since His death and resurrection, yet the message of the Kingdom is still being spread around the world with the belief that many will come to believe and be saved before the end times . In **Matthew 24:14**, Jesus tells us that "this Gospel of the Kingdom shall be preached to the whole world as a testimony to all the nations, and then the end will come." Today, that promise is nearly fulfilled, even if not yet. Missionaries, along with devoted translators, have gone to remote villages, where no one had been able to reach before with the good news. There are also numerous Bible translations, and advances in technology have made it even easier to print Bibles in various languages. Now, we are getting closer! So, in my opinion, the gospel of salvation is fast spreading, which means the end is near. The conclusion is this: just as Jesus travelled to towns and cities, taught in the synagogues, and proclaimed the Gospel of the Kingdom, so we must also do. Until Christ returns, we shall not stop proclaiming the Good News, so that there will be no excuse for anyone – **Romans 1:20**.

Prayer – Dear Heavenly Father, let Your Kingdom come. Let Your Kingdom of righteousness be built in us, in our children, in their children, and in the world. Let Your Kingdom destroys any kingdom of evil that tries to find its way in us. May each one of us be consumed with Kingdom mindset. I pray for each person on the face of the earth that any evil kingdom aiming for destruction will be destroyed. Lord, open our hearts to receive Your Kingdom. Let our whole being, be consumed with the fire of the Holy Spirit; establish in us your Kingdom to bring love and peace on earth. We want Your Holy Kingdom of salvation which bring the Truth and Your Light in us, so that there will be no lies and darkness found in us. With Your Kingdom of love, there will be no more hatred. Our hearts will be filled with joy; because the goodness of Your Kingdom brings healing to the mind, the soul, and the body. Father, we open the gates of our hearts, enter as the King of Glory and reign: **Psalm 24.** May Your *Kingdom of Light* shine through us, so that Your Will, will be established in us. Amen!

Chapter 10 – Thy Will Be Done on Earth as It Is in Heaven

Matthew 6:10

Are you living according to *God's Will* for your life? It is important to seek *God's Will* in everything we do. **Jeremiah 29:11** says, "For I know the plans I have for you..." People seldom seek the Lord's guidance before going about their daily activities: making a move, doing business, pursuing an education or career, establishing friendships, getting married, traveling, etc. I know this because before my encounter with the Lord, I was in the same category. I thought I was seeking the Lord's guidance, but not really. On many occasions, I planned things before I invited God into the situation without even realizing it. As humans, we, by nature, take matters into our own hands. We ask God for something and expect to instantly receive that for which we asked. We are unwilling to wait. According to **Ecclesiastes 3:1**, God has a timing for everything; therefore, it is important to prioritize seeking God's direction in everything we do.

It is written in **Matthew 7:21**, "Not everyone who says, 'Lord, Lord,' will enter the kingdom of Heaven, but the one who does the Will of my Father." Think of the Will of God this way: if I build a house, I will organize things to ensure its safety. Therefore, there should be rules. I would require whoever wishes to stay in the house to abide by the rules established in the house. There will be rules: the stove must never be left unattended; it must be turned off immediately after cooking to prevent a fire. The tap must not be left on running; and doors must be locked at night; lights must be turned off when not in use; the house always stays clean. The idea is that in order to keep the house safe, I will make sure things are in good order. Anything that will likely cause damage must be prevented from occurring. God takes *His Will* seriously; therefore, we cannot enter the Kingdom of God without living according to *His Will* right here on earth. *His Will* is what guides us. Doing *God's Will* or walking on His path is what brings peace of mind and many blessings. On many occasions, we get ourselves into trouble and become miserable when we go our own ways.

God's Will, the Kingdom, and His Holiness are indivisible; they are intertwined. God's Kingdom will always require holiness; holiness comes when we are living according to *His Will*. Thus, when we live in *God's Will*, we become His Holy nation. As **1 Peter 2:9** declares: "But you are a chosen race, a royal priesthood, a holy nation, a people for His possession, that you may proclaim the excellencies of Him who called you out of darkness into His marvelous light." This means we must stay away from that which is unholy. For example, God wants us to avoid evil deeds. This means if we find ourselves committing sin, then we are not living according to *His Will*. So, we must lean on God, trust Him in all our ways and not on our own understanding – **Proverbs 3:5**. We must love the Lord our God with all our heart, soul, and strength, and not the things of the world..." (**Mark 12:30**). This is because the love of the world will put our love for God in danger. Another example is this: we are instructed to love our enemies and pray for those who persecute us; contrastingly, by choosing to hate and bear grudges, we are acting against the Will of God.

The Will of God is revealed in His Word. 1 **Corinthians 10:13** states that we are at liberty to do all things, but not all things benefit us. In **Joshua 1:8**, the Lord also tells us to meditate on His word day and night and not to behave as unbelievers. In **Psalm 1**, we are told to not sit, walk, or stand in the ways of sinners, but to meditate on the Word of God, day, and night. If we decide to do what we please, we will tread an ungodly path, and go against His Word. God has given us the freedom of choice, but there are always consequences for both good and bad choices. Once we receive salvation, the Kingdom of God is established in us to help us live according to *God's Will*. **Psalm 25:4–5** says, "Show me Your ways, teach me Your path, guide me to the truth, and teach me. For You are God my Savior..." We notice that the psalmist speaks in complete submission to the Will of God. In his prayer, David asks that he be led in a way that pleases God. A life that pleases God mean that we are conformed to His standards. To be able to live by God's rules, we must submit to Him. By doing so, we allow *His Will* to rule in our lives.

Jesus knew how important it was to let go of *His Will* to sacrifice Himself for the good of humanity. During His time on earth, He lived in total submission to the Will of God. Jesus understood that His purpose was to do *God's Will* of preaching the gospel and sacrificing Himself to save humanity. Thus, everywhere He went, He directed people's attention to the Kingdom of God through salvation. Jesus never sought to please or exalt Himself above the Will of the Father (**John 5:30**). In **Hebrews 10:9**, He says, "I have come to do Your Will." **Matthew 26:39** tells us that in Gethsemane, Jesus said, "My Father, if it is possible, let this cup pass from Me; nevertheless, not as I Will, but as You Will." Jesus said this prayer even when He knew that His death was imminent. He asked for nothing but for the Father's Will to be done. This act of submission sums up Jesus' commitment to do the Will of God, regardless of the situation in which He was. Jesus submitted because He trusted in God and His divine plan. He had to save humanity from sin. We also must follow Jesus' example because it is worthy of emulation. We must learn to submit our will to God and trust that His ways are perfect and will lead us to a desirable outcome.

When we become believers, the Holy Spirit comes to live in us and suppresses our will if we give in to His desires. Once the Holy Spirit suppresses our will, He guides us to make the right decisions because He is a counselor and teacher. Thus, the Holy Spirit comes to break, mold, and transform us into the likeness of God's Son Jesus through His teachings, guidance, and directions; and we are not to go back and take the old will again because God does not want us to be conformed to this world; rather, He want us to preserve our bodies from the pleasures of the flesh that we may appear holy and acceptable to Him. God commands us in **Romans 12:1–2** to present our bodies as living sacrifices, holy and acceptable to Him, so that we may prove what is good and acceptable and the perfect Will of God. It is *God's Will* that must take place over every facet of our lives. Thus, in choosing a career or a partner, moving to a new place, making business plans, choosing friends, or making decisions about anything, our prayer should be Lord, 'Your Will be done.' Let's ask for heavenly wisdom to guide us to make the right choices.

There is also a permissive Will of God that we must keep in mind. The permissive Will of God is manifested in a situation where He allows us to make our own choices, rebel against Him, make mistakes, learn from our mistakes, and become submissive to Him. In this, God puts up with our mistakes even though we pursue our desires contrary to *His Will*. The Lord does not force us to do *His Will* because He has given us freewill. However, there are consequences to choosing to live how we please. For instance, *God's Will* commands us to live in obedience to Him. If we choose not to do so, the spirit of rebellion will take over and cause us to do things our way, which will likely lead to destructive results. In such destructive circumstances, the Lord will draw our attention back to Him to surrender to *His Will*; we always suffer unnecessarily for our mistakes. When we sin against God, He allows us to go through the wilderness or challenges, which may seem too harsh sometimes. However, it is the only way for us to learn. After that, if we return to Him, God will prepare us for even greater things. **1 Peter 5:10** states that after we have suffered a little while, the God of all grace will restore us and make us strong, firm, and steadfast.

A perfect example of the permissive Will of God is seen in the story of Jonah. In the book of Jonah, we are told that the Lord commanded him to go to the city of Nineveh and preach repentance to the people. Jonah refused because he believed that the people of Nineveh were enemies of Israel who were not worthy of God's forgiveness. As a result, he got on a boat and headed in the opposite direction, hoping to get as far as he could from Nineveh. While he was in the boat, the Lord sent a storm. Jonah blamed himself for the storm and told the men on the boat to throw him into the sea, and everything would be calm. Immediately, they tossed him into the sea and the storm stopped. Jonah was swallowed by a whale and stayed in its belly for 3 days. However, while he was there, he repented, prayed, and asked God to save Him. The Lord heard Jonah's plea and caused the whale to throw him up onto the shores of Nineveh. Jonah preached to the people of Nineveh and warned them to repent; otherwise, the city would be destroyed. The people believed what Jonah said and turned from their wickedness. Therefore, God had mercy on them. Like the story of Jonah, it is important to know *God's Will* and stay in *His Will* because it is the best for us. It is also crucial to repent and ask for forgiveness when we go astray. **1 John 1:9** states, "if you confess your sins, God is faithful to forgive your sins and cleanse you of all unrighteousness." The Lord's mercy was displayed after Jonah prayed, repented, and sought forgiveness once he acknowledged that he had sinned. This story demonstrates the 'Permissive Will' of God. It reminds us that God knows exactly what to do to help us return to Him and submit to *His Will*. Sometimes, He allows circumstances to make us realize our need for Him and His power to save. For this reason, we must abide by His commands to help us do *His Will* so that we do not have to face unnecessary pain.

Rejecting the Will of God is not wise. When it comes to decisions concerning our lives, we tend to think that because these are personal matters, the decisions lie in our hands. Let's consider marriage, for instance. When we decide to get married, the best thing is to wait on the Lord in prayer until He approves of the person whom we desire to marry. We should believe that through prayer, the Lord will guide us in choosing the right partner because marriage is part of God's plans for us. He wants His children to have long-lasting marriages filled with happiness; that is why He created holy matrimony. He knows what is best for us. Even though all marriages go through difficult phases, a marriage ordained by God will weather every storm and grow stronger. Yes, a marriage with God's Word as the basis will survive, no matter what. On the contrary, if we get married in pursuit of our desire, it will fade with time. When we fail to seek God's approval of our choice of a partner, God still allows the marriage, but there will certainly be so much trouble. Many become hurt, damaged, or even die due to bad marriages. If we marry out of lust or a desire for money, fame, or anything other than what God has planned, we will encounter difficulties, which may be impossible to fix until we turn to God for His mercy. Many are deeply troubled as a result of abusive relationships. Others become addicted to drugs, while some have been married multiple times. A good number of people have also ended up in mental institutions due to bad marriages. So yes, we are all have our right to choose whom we want as a spouse, but we should always remember that God intends marriage to be a journey of a lifetime; thus, whomever we choose as a companion on that journey makes all the difference.

What about making a move, travelling, choosing a career, etc.? They all must be according to the Will of God. There was a time in my life when I pursued my desires outside the Will of the Lord and its outcome. Many years ago, my husband and I traveled to the US as missionaries. Because we didn't come to make money, I had no idea what the American dream was. I only knew about my work as a missionary. But while in college, I overheard my colleagues talk about how they arrived from all parts of the world to pursue their American dream. When I came home from school, the phrase "the American dream," was still ringing in my ears. When the Holy Spirit deepened my understanding of what the American dream meant, I was not worried because that was never my intention. In fact, besides their studies, some of the students whom I met in college were working twice as hard as the average American and pushing themselves to extreme limits. I always said in that case that my American dream is my mission work. Despite that, I thought I also needed money to do the Lord's work, so I tried to work hard. But I was wrong because it pulled me away from reality and I lost track of my American dream. Thankfully, the Holy Spirit pulled me back to my true American dream. Today, I am thankful to the Lord for putting me back on the right track. My American dream was 'the Kingdom's Work.' People work two or three jobs and sleep less; I must also do the same to win souls for the Kingdom. I am not saying that they shouldn't aspire for a comfortable life, but pursuing riches should not be at the expense of God's purpose for our lives. My advice is that you should know your calling before you pursue anything. Whatever you are doing today, is fine; just make sure you are in *God's Will* for your life to bring glory to His Name.

I think the main reason why my focus was diverted was that while working as a missionary, I faced several challenges, which caused me so much pain. Instead of surrendering my problems to God, I bore the burden and tried to handle it all by myself and regretted in many ways, even coming to America. My pain, anguish, and regret went on for years because I was upset. For years, my prayers were more like questioning God than as communicating with Him as a Father, until surrendered my will to Him. We all have a purpose on earth, and everything that happens to us can be a blessing or a curse, depending on how we handle each situation. The most important thing to do in all our struggles is to ask the Lord to guide us to our purpose. This reminds me of one of Dr. Charles Stanley's quotes. He said, You can't always avoid adversity. But you can choose how you respond to it. This is so true. *The time has come for each one of us to bear our own cross, because hard days are ahead. When I compare my trials to that of Joseph's in **Genesis 37,** I see that I handled mine wrongly. The Lord has a purpose in every situation just like what happened when I got locked out of my house. When Joseph's brothers persecuted him, he learned to quickly forgive them. Joseph knew that God could cause all things to work together for his good (**Romans 8:28**). God did not cause what I endured, but He planned to use my adversity for His glory; however, I missed the point through my negative reaction.

The Lord made this point so clear to me when He restored my ability to do *His Will*. For some time, I worked with a company that took care of sick people in the comfort of their own homes. On one occasion, I was scheduled to work with a woman with a chronic cough. She told me that her doctors could neither identify the cause of her illness nor provide a cure. One night, after assisting her with bedtime routines, I asked the Lord if I could pray for her. I knew that it was against the company's policy to pray for a client, but after I was prompted by the Holy Spirit, I could not resist doing the Kingdom's Business in her home. That was the night when she received her miracle. She slept so peacefully without coughing. I was speechless. Early the next morning, she got up, and when she saw me, she looked at me and said, "You healed me." I immediately replied and said, "Ms., I simply did what the Lord directed me to do. To Him be the glory.' Then she said, "I guess we receive not because we ask not." I said, you are right, as it is written in **James 4:2**. It was at that moment that I was able to talk with her about salvation. Our conversation went on so well. Coming to find out, she and her husband were missionaries many years ago. They also faced many challenges that broke her heart; for years, she lived with regret. In the end, I realized that the assignment to her home was a divine purpose because I learned many valuable things from her. She called to tell her family what happened. Her son came and said to me, "I think you have direct contact with God." I answered, "We all do," and we all laughed. I was filled with wonder. Today, it is not a surprise to see many people visiting their doctor's office before they seek God's divine healing. Some tend to trust in medications more than God's healing power because of modern medicines. There is nothing wrong with medications but make sure you ask God's blessings upon any medication you take. That same week, the job ended; I was not disappointed at all. Rather, I was happy because I knew God sent me there on a mission.

Sometime later, I ministered to a homosexual man who repented through our short conversation and prayer and gave his life to Jesus. Not only that, but a suicidal lady also came to her senses. After that, I was sent to a Satan worshiper's home. What happened right after getting to his home was beyond my imagination! Truly, we serve a Mighty God, and yes, there is power in the Name of Jesus Christ! What I did not know was that the Lord had sent two believers to warn him earlier, and it was his final chance. A few months later, he died in his sin because he chose death instead of God's gift of life. God never intends for anyone to die in their sins. The encounter with that demonic guy also taught me many lessons of how to live for God and do what He has called us to do without compromising, because what I did while in his house was completely the Will of God.

The Lord has anointed us to proclaim His good news to the poor, to mend the brokenhearted, to proclaim freedom for the captives, to comfort all who mourn, and to speak of His goodness, part of which is healing. This means that being on the wrong track and trying to win the race is impossible! My freewill caused me to mistrust and doubt God's power. Even though I was aware of what He could do, I still doubted. I thought God had failed me. But I was my own enemy. One day, the Lord showed me the heavy burdens I was carrying. They were rejection, betrayal, and unforgiveness. Then the Holy Spirit gave me **Psalm 1.** Today, a day doesn't go by without prioritizing the Lord's Will. Thankfully, the encounter with the Lord concerning His Prayer has brought me complete healing. Now I live my life in total submission to the Will of God. I believe in *His Will* and trust in His plans for my life. I don't question Him, I don't argue, and I don't doubt. I just trust and obey because I know it is the only way. Not only that, but *God's Will* is perfect.

Today, I am happy that the Lord has given me the courage to pursue my American dream, and this has brought me thus far on my journey to becoming a Christian Counselor and the writer. Glory to God! I was on the wrong track, but the Lord put me on the right track when I learned to let go of my will and surrender. I ran away many times as Jonah did and suffered for years. Today, I am all for the good work of Christ!

Nothing works for our benefit if we continue to act outside the Will of God. We cannot pursue our own desires and always expect to achieve good results. To be in the Will of God, we must ask the Lord to reveal to us His plans for our lives, our purpose, and why we are here. I struggled unnecessarily because I was trying in my own will, but that was not what I was called for. God has power over everything; therefore, He will provide if He calls. I now believe that all the frustrations were God's way of trying to bring me back to my senses. He did it to reaffirm my trust in Him till I could humbly say, "Not my will, but Yours be done."

This reminds me of a time when I was moving around in search of a job. One day, I had a terrible accident that almost took the lives of an entire family. Thankfully, no one was hurt, but when my license was suspended for months, I realized that if we are not careful serving the Lord, certain privileges can be taken away to make life even more miserable. After this incident, my car was towed from a no-parking zone. After the police traced my car to an impound yard, it cost me my entire savings to retrieve it. But after I came back to the Lord's Will for my life, He took care of all my needs. For example, one morning, I was just about to get on the freeway to go meet with someone for salvation, when I suddenly got a flat tire. Thankfully, God sent an angel in human form to assist me. Not only that, but the cost of the new tire was also paid in full by a stranger. What an amazing God we serve! All this time, my troubles had become like a mountain before I finally realized what was wrong. My will was in His way. I fasted, prayed, and asked for forgiveness, forgave all those who hurt me and surrendered my life to God. This was how I became completely healed. The Lord must have His way. If you are called like Jonah, don't try to run from Him; run to Him, because you will never win by going your own way.

What I was missing was the Will of God. I acted faithlessly. After submitting to God, things have become stabilized. The Lord has me under His control. Today, *God's Will'* is my passion. I have been sent to tell everyone *God's Will* that there is a difference between simply knowing about the Father and living in *His Will*. Do not get me wrong. I lived in *God's Will* when I became a believer, but I lost it when I faced the biggest giant. So please don't think you are okay. Always depend on God and ask for *His Will* each day. As **1 Corinthians 10:12** says, "If you think you are standing strong, be careful not to fall." Praying to submit to the Will of God is not an easy task but it's worth it. Being able to pray and personalize your prayers for *God's Will* in your life means nailing your will to the cross daily. I believe this is our greatest sacrifice. I encourage you to stop running from God. Instead, you must run to Him, give Him your will, and you will never regret it.

I once read a story about a young evangelist who died on an island in India while on a mission to preach the gospel. His last words were, "Lord, is this island Satan's last stronghold where none have heard or even had the chance to hear your name?" "I think I could be more useful alive...but to you God, I give all the glory for whatever happens. Forgive the people on this island who will try to kill me especially if they succeed." Although the young man died, I strongly believe that forgiving his enemies and asking God to let *His Will* be done was a blessing. Taking matters into our own hands is not a blessing. This story is something that we can learn from to help us wholeheartedly forgive those who are trying to hurt us. It is the Lord's Will for us to forgive so we can live in His Kingdom and *His Will*. "**Matthew 5:44** tells us to love our enemies and pray for those who persecute us. This was exactly what the young man did. As I reflected on the story of this young missionary, I wondered if it was the Will of God for him to travel to that island in the first place, or if he went there on his own. Then it dawned on me that praying and asking for forgiveness for his enemies was *God's Will*. It was the same thing Jesus did on the cross. So, he acted according to *God's Will* because it is only in *God's Will* that we can forgive. I believe that he died knowing that he did what was right.

Once we accept Jesus as our Lord and Savior, God bestows on us the power to trample over the enemy, just as it says in **Luke 10:19.** However, we are bound to be tempted, just as Jesus was tempted because the devil's main goal is to destroy our faith and relationship with God. Nonetheless, the Lord says that He will not allow temptations we cannot handle to come our way. So, if you become upset in times of trial, it means that you still have not learned to submit to *God's Will*, and you are giving the enemy a chance. You need to evaluate your life and completely surrender your will to God.

In all these, what I learned is that when we have a true encounter with the Lord, we realize that the Lord loves us very much and wants us to understand anything that confuses us. In my most difficult times, I asked God, "Why? Why me?" This was before I sacrificed my will to the Lord and learned why God allows us to face trials. One morning when I was alone in my room folding clothes, I had real encounter with the Lord. I did not realize that my prayers were not pleasing to the Lord because they were always in the form of questions. This continued for a while until I encountered the Lord. It felt as if someone had entered the room, put his hand around my shoulder, and was saying, "Who else, if not you? Everything in life happens for a reason. Someone must suffer in My Name, but if not you, then who else?"

It felt so real that I thought there was someone in the room, but after checking every room in the house and finding no one, I knew it was the Lord. In fact, on that day, I wept bitterly for disappointing the Lord. When we fail to accept our trials as part of *God's Will'*, we make Him sad. But if we learn to surrender, we learn from our mistakes, and it makes things easy on us. It does not allow the devil to manipulate the situation. **James 4:7–10** says, "Submit yourselves therefore to God. Resist the devil, and he will flee from you. Draw near to God, and He will draw near to you. Cleanse your hands, you sinners, and purify your hearts, you double-minded." When we submit to God, the enemy cannot have any power to control us. It is very essential to live and pray according to the Will of God. It is *God's Will* that we are guided through the power of the Holy Spirit. He is the One who guides us to the precise assignments for us. With that, we shall never be diverted to something unimportant. Therefore, let's be in tune with the voice of the Holy Spirit.

Praying each day is also the Will of God because we are commanded to pray. Prayers align our will to *God's Will*. A friend once said, "God can do everything; therefore, He does not need our prayers. True, God doesn't need our prayers. Our prayers are for our own good because we cannot do the Kingdom's Assignments without prayers and the *Will of God*, because prayer keeps us in *God's Will*. So, let's align our will to His as Christ ambassadors.

God's Will is a key passage for setting the stage for all that follows. Satan is roaming about finding faults. God boasts about Job's, whom He considers to be pure, but Satan takes that to make an argument because he was jealous. Satan said, "It is no wonder that he serves You; but if you take all away from him, he will turn against You." Satan believes that the only reason anyone, including

Job, worships God and obeying God's laws is for the rewards. As interesting as this may seem, do we see any truth in this? Why do people choose to serve God? Is it for prosperity? Eternal life? Or both? Is it possible to love God for salvation without worrying about any worldly stuff? Can we still serve God, be happy, rejoice even when all outward signs and prosperity are no more? Answer this honestly. Be true to yourself. God knows what is in your heart. I have my answer as well.

Matthew 4, explains that Jesus was led to be tempted by who? Satan! Can we stop the devil from tempting us? No, this is because his every attempt is ordered by God. No believer is exempt from temptation. As Jesus was tempted, so shall we. God allows temptation for a purpose, but what we choose to do towards that is a choice to make. This is because we all have been given 'a free will,' and that allows us to choose. **John 10:10** says, the devil comes to destroy, but Christ came to give us abundance life. What can we do to stop the enemy? **1Peter 5:8** says, "Your enemy the devil is like a roaring lion. He prowls around looking for someone to devour..." We can win if we resist him. This is if we live according to God's Word and ask the Father to lead us not into temptation; help us to overcome temptation and deliver us if we fall into temptations.

In *God's Will*, we can submit to Him. In so doing, the enemy will have no power over our daily activities. Once he sees that he has no chance over us, he will ward off. Yes, living according to *God's Will*, we can resist him. And though, he will target another person, but asking the Father to "Lead us not into temptation and to deliver us from evil" each day, and asking the same for all people will give us victory over evil. Therefore, learn to exchange your will for *God's Will*; pray for yourself and for all people; and submit 'your will,' to God if you are tired of 'your will' getting on His way. Pray for the Kingdom of Heaven to come into you each day, so you can do what is right and acceptable unto God. With these, salvation will take place in many lives, God's power will rule over humans' lives, and the devil's work will become less and less devalued.

Prayer: Dear Heavenly Father, let Your Will be done in my life, in my family, and in this world around me. Lord, have Your way and rule here on earth as You rule in Heaven. I pray for Your Will to sanctify and mold me into the image of Your Son Jesus Christ. Give me the strength to live a pure life. I cannot accomplish this so, I need You. Lord, help me to surrender as I yield my will to You, for Yours. I pray that You will help each one of us to live for you. Help us to love You with all our hearts, souls, minds. Father, we pray against evil. May Your grace abound and overflow so we can do Your Will, in Jesus' Name, Amen!

Chapter 11 – Give Us This Day Our Daily Bread

Matthew 6:11

As human as we are, our needs and wants are limitless; our limited ability makes it impossible for us to meet all those needs. Therefore, we are constantly finding ways to be able to do so. So, from where do you get your needs? Today, worldly pleasures are compelling people to go the extra mile. **Psalm 23** says, "The Lord is my Shepherd; I shall not want." In **Matthew 6:11**, the Lord Jesus says, "When you pray, say, 'Give us this day our daily bread'...." Why does the Lord want us to pray in such manner? Because He is the true provider. In **Genesis 22:8**, Abraham answered his son Isaac saying, "God Himself will provide the lamb for the burnt offering." After He did, Abraham called God, Jehovah Jireh—God my Provider.

In **John 16:23,** Jesus promised, "Whatever you ask the Father in My Name, He will give to you." Then in **Mark 11:24** He says, "Therefore I tell you, whatever you ask in prayer, believe that you have received it." and it will be yours. **Philippians 4:19**, "My God shall supply all your needs according to His glorious riches in Christ Jesus." God is without limitations. He is rich in His glory. He is the One who holds all power to do it all! He does it all because of His promise, and He will never fail us if we keep our hope in Him. Knowing this should help you agree with David. Since the beginning of time, the Lord has been a provider to His people.

Here are a few examples:

• In the Garden of Eden, Adam and Eve had everything at their disposal (**Genesis 1:28–31**).

• **Exodus 14:21** says, God opened a path through the sea while the Egyptians were pursuing the Israelites.

• At every point throughout their 40-year journey to the Promised Land, the Lord provided food and water for the Israelites. During the day, He led them by a pillar of cloud and during the night, by a pillar of fire, so they could travel both day and night (**Exodus 13:21**).

• The Lord sent ravens to feed bread to Elijah while he was in the desert (**1 Kings 17:2–5**).

• **Daniel 3:16–30 says** God sent angels to protect Shadrach, Meshach, and Abednego when they were thrown into the furnace for refusing to bow to King Nebuchadnezzar's gods.

From the above occurrences, notice that the Lord has proven Himself to be a provider. Let's not wait until we are desperately in need before we pray. He has promised to supply our needs, but we must have a relationship with Him and know how to communicate with Him daily. The cited verses are God's way of reassuring us that He is our provider and that no amount of worrying will solve our problems, but God can. Thus, we must rely on Him and pray. The daily bread promised by the Lord is not limited. We have **physical**, **spiritual**, and **emotional** needs. To live a fulfilled life, all three types of needs must be met. But we must know how to ask for our needs. The Lord is our eternal hope.

Our physical needs: Our physical needs are all the things we need each day such as: food, water, rain, sunshine, good air, etc. They are just as important as our emotional, psychological, and spiritual needs. With God as our Provider, we need not worry about what we shall eat, drink, or wear because our Heavenly Father knows what we need and has promised to provide – **Matthew 6:25**. If our needs are not met, it may be because we fail to ask. In my entire walk with the Lord, I never knew how to ask God to provide for my needs until after the secret of the Lord's Prayer was revealed to me. I am sure that during all my years of struggles, part of them was because I failed to include God in my physical needs. The only things I remember asking from God were spiritual needs (health, salvation, love, faith, and divine healing). It took a long time for me to know how to request material things from God. I think my inability to ask God for material things can be attributed to my childhood. I never lacked anything growing up. My parents made sure that our needs were met without having to ask. Although they were not millionaires, they had enough to provide food, clothing, and shelter. Another reason could be that my family was not Christian at that time; therefore, I never quite learned that God was my provider of physical needs.

When I became a young adult living on my own, I was able to support myself without depending on anyone. Long after I became a believer, I still depended on myself for the things I needed. When I was sick, I prayed. When I learned about the gifts of the Holy Spirit, I prayed for, but never material stuff (food, a car, a house, clothes, etc.). This continued until I got married, worked in the ministry in Africa, and moved to the US with my family as missionaries. Here, life became difficult after the mission work. They say, "It is a land of plenty," but my shelves were empty. I began struggling to provide for myself. Sometimes, our struggles were a part of God's purpose, but sometimes they were because we had chosen our own path or because we failed to ask. It was after I learned the secret of the Lord's Prayer that I learned to ask. The privilege to know how to ask for all my needs was awesome! As humans, although our ability to meet all our needs is limited, we always seem to want more. In that case, we should turn to God as our great provider because His provisions exceed health, marriage, relationships, peace of mind, good jobs, good homes, lasting friendships, and so on. The Lord can provide everything and more because He is our Great Provider! And we must wait patiently on Him because He has time for everything; in His time, He will make all things beautiful! So, we can ask, seek, and knock daily. It means a lot to God because He wants us to depend on Him.

Thankfully, the Lord used His prayer to teach me to depend on Him. He increased my faith to solidify my dependence on Him without having to depend on my strength. It hasn't always been easy, but I never give up. I lean on Christ, and I ask God to meet my needs; I trust Him for who He is, and what He can do. Just like the Israelites' journey through the desert, through His constant miracles, the Lord provided for them. Today, my faith is grounded, and so is my reliance on Him. With thanksgiving, I ask and receive in faith. So, with confidence, I can say that the Lord is my Shepherd. I also pray for everyone; both the saved and the unsaved. For those who are saved, I pray that they overcome any challenges and continue their journey trusting the Lord for all their needs. For the unbelievers, I pray that God will show them the way.

When Paul and Silas were imprisoned and needed to be free, they called out to the One whom they knew could meet all their needs. In their case, they needed both faith and freedom. It was their faith that set them free. God supplied their needs of faith and made them strong (**Acts 16**). While in prison, Paul and Silas were held down in shackles so they could not escape, but through praise, God caused something to happen. Their shackles were broken, the prison gate was opened, and they were set free. In this, we can see that their physical, emotional, and spiritual needs were all met. May their story encourage us to put our trust in God, give thanks and praise to Him in good times and bad times, because He is a Great Provider!

We must ask according to *God's Will* because He has promised to meet all our needs according to His glorious riches in Christ Jesus. He has granted us the freedom to ask whatever we want in His Name and according to *His Will* (**John 14:13**). However, we cannot be greedy. All we need is faith and trust in God to receive what we have asked of Him.

Our needs are not limited to clean air, water, food, shelter, rain, and sunshine. These things are all vital for good health. Poor air quality causes all kinds of health issues, so we pray for good air, so that what we drink, eat, and breathe into our lungs will not have any negative impacts on our health. We also pray that He grants us wisdom to know how to protect our environment from pollution, as this is equally detrimental to our health. To be physically healthy, we need all these. According to The National Institute of Environmental Health Science: "poor air causes all kinds of sicknesses and diseases, and so do GMO foods and an ineffective water sanitation system. Anything bad we put into our systems becomes toxic to the body. So, we pray for a healthy lifestyle. Maintaining a healthy lifestyle and clean environment can lead to longevity. And putting good things into our bodies can keep us healthy. In effect, when we pray for rain and sunshine in due time, we are praying against global warming, because God provides rain to wash our polluted air and refresh the environment. Therefore, our everyday prayer must be, Lord, protect and give us the wisdom to know how to care for our bodies and environments.

Physical healing as a daily bread. We all need healing in our bodies sometimes. In those situations, it is a good idea to ask for healing as part of our daily bread. We ask God for good health and a strong immune system that can fight against all kinds of diseases. May God grant us healing. Medical innovations are also important and are needed for breakthroughs. Consequently, we ask God to provide successful medical innovations that can stand the test of time.

We need physical protection. We need to be protected in all aspects. We ask God for our physical and spiritual protection. We need God's divine protection against spiritual forces. We ask the Lord to keep us safe in everything we do: driving to school or work; walking in our neighborhoods or local parks; hiking; and traveling by bike, by plane, or by sea. In all things, may God's protection be around us to keep us safe from all harm. We also ask for wisdom to know how to be watchful of our surroundings.

Our daily need of protection and against natural disasters. The feedback I received about praying against natural disasters differed. While some said we could pray against it, others said we cannot, because they had to happen. I believe that if we pray, *God's Will*, will be done. God can prevent natural disasters, and if they come, they will not come near our tent, as **Psalm 91** declares. Through His power, God can stop any danger from coming near our borders because He has promised to keep us safe. **Matthew 18:18**–20 states, "We have been given the keys of the Kingdom of Heaven; whatever we loosen on earth will be loosed in Heaven, and whatsoever we bind on earth shall be bound in Heaven." As stated in **Matthew 7:7** – *we must ask, knock, and seek.* In **1 King 17,** Elijah was able to control the rain through faith and prayer. In **Genesis 18:22–33**, Abraham interceded for Sodom and Gomorrah. In **Joshua 10:1–15,** the sun stood still, and the moon stopped until the Israelites won the battle. **1King 17:18** and **James 5:17** tell us that Elijah prayed and stopped the rain. In the book of Esther, we learned that Haman has already put in motion his genocide plot against the Jews and seems like he was winning, but through prayer, Esther was able to stop that from happening. Yes, God has given us the ability to pray until something happens!

Spiritual needs of our daily bread include divine healing and gifts of the Holy Spirit. We cannot ignore our spiritual needs because they are as vital as our physical needs. One vital daily bread we cannot ignore is divine healing; so, we can ask the Lord. This is a very important because when all medical hope is gone, God can display His power through divine healing, as according to *His Will*. Unfortunately, some believers do not know or believe in divine healing. Today, due to the advent of modern medicine, people tend to believe in medicine more than they do in divine intervention. But that is okay if it is what they believe. However, I believe divine healing is God's way of displaying His power, mercy, and kindness to people when all hope is gone. The Bible tells us in **Hebrews 13:8** that "Jesus Christ of yesterday is the same today and forever." What He did yesterday, He can also do today, if it is *His Will*. There is nothing wrong with that. They are all God's perfect gift to humanity. I know miracles still exist. I believe that God can use medicine to heal us, but He can also heal us through divine power. I have heard many testimonies of the Lord's divine healing; but I am also a living testimony of the incredible healing power of God. To receive your divine healing, you must first believe that the Word God and all His promises are true. (This is not to say that you should not seek medical help). Pray if doctors' think there is no hope for you. God's divine healing is His free-gift for all who believes. He will touch you if your time is not yet.

God is the Great Physician. He can heal you through the power of His Holy Spirit, but it takes faith. He has the power to heal us and free us from any affliction. **Isaiah 53:5** says, "He was wounded for our transgressions. He was bruised for our iniquities; the chastisement for our peace was upon Him, and by His stripes, we are healed." Likewise, **1 Peter 2:24** says, "He bore our sins in His body on the cross, so that we might die to sin and live for righteousness; by His wounds, we have been healed." This is both physical and spiritual healing. In **Psalm 103:1–3**, David says, "...He forgives all your sins and heals all your diseases." The above verses teach us that Jesus Christ paid for our sins on the cross. As a result, we have been freed from all afflictions by His blood.

According to Regina E. Herzlinger, in her article 'Why Innovation in Health Care Is So Hard,' drug discovery, biotechnology, digital health services, and medical devices that potentially provide new and improved treatments for some of the leading causes of death are helping in the cure of many diseases. I believe it. But we must keep in mind that God's healing power can be through medicine and divine healing if we believe. Because all things are possible if we believe. These innovations make a huge difference in human diagnoses. Yet there are always medical errors, but there are no errors when God stretches out His healing touch. So, we can ask for divine healing by faith just as we would seek medical interventions and just as we ask for our daily bread. The Bible gives accounts of several instances where the Lord healed people. Read **Mark 7:24–30**, which recounts the story of a desperate woman who wanted Jesus to heal her daughter. **Mark 5:24–34** also talks about a woman with the issue of bleeding who was healed instantly after touching the hem of Jesus' garment.

Not only that; there are many more scriptures that tell of how Jesus healed the sick. Matthew 9:35 – Jesus was going through all the cities and villages, teaching in their synagogues, proclaiming the gospel of the kingdom, and healing every kind of disease and illness. **Matthew 14:14** – when He saw a large crowd, He felt compassion for them and healed their sick. **Matthew 15:30** says large crowds came to Jesus. They brought with them those who were lame, crippled, blind, mute, and many others. And they laid them down at His feet, and He healed them all. Also, in **Matthew 19:2,** large crowds followed Him, and He healed them there. Whenever Jesus went, they brought the sick before Him, imploring Him that they might just touch the fringe of His cloak; and as many as touched it were healed. Therefore, I believe divine healing is God's way of showing mercy to the oppressed. We can take medications, but we can also believe in divine healing, because sometimes, some of the sicknesses and the diseases that attack humans are nothing but the work of the enemy who comes to steal, kill, destroy. And for those, no amount of medication can save the person's life unless we pray. In my opinion, the reason why sometimes, we don't receive healing is because we have come to trust in medical innovations more than divine healing. But God can use either way for His glory. So, let's continue believing in the power of the divine healing because Jesus Christ of yesterday is the same today. His power through His Word is still working.

Spiritual protection is equally important. We ask God for our spiritual needs of daily protection. We need God's divine protection against spiritual forces. Wherever we may, we can trust God's divine protection for our safety. It is only God who can protect us against witchcraft and demonic powers in Jesus Name. In terms of our spiritual protection, we can always read **Psalm 91**; and we must not be afraid when troubles arise because the One in us is Greater and Mightier.

Since we do not wrestle against flesh and blood, we must put our hope in God for His divine protection power for us and our families. We need God's supernatural power to protect us against the evil one. Therefore, we must pray against evil spiritual attackers. In today's world, many people have come to see that there are all kinds of witchcraft practices; for that reason, everyone wants to protect themselves against evil, but instead of finding protection in the Lord, some seek protection elsewhere, but for us, as David said in **Psalm 23**, "The Lord is our Shepherd." So, let us agree with King David in **Psalm 34:7**, which states that "The angels of the Lord encamp around those that fear Him." In **Psalm 18:2**, he says, "The Lord is my rock, my fortress, and my deliverer, my stronghold, in Him will I trust." God is our protector; therefore, we are not to be afraid.

The Word of God is our daily bread. Use Scripture for daily protection. You can add these Scriptures to the above ones and memorize them for protection. **Psalms 1, 35, 100, 116, 118, 119, and 121**, are all good. Memorizing God's Word is extremely useful. The Word is our weapon against evil. Other relevant verses include **Psalm 16:8, Psalm 121:7–8, Malachi 3:6, Genesis 28:15, Deuteronomy 31:6, Psalm 3:3, Isaiah 46:4,** and **2 Thessalonians 3:3.** Sometimes the enemy will try to bring trouble, but God has the final say. When Moses performed wonders before him, Pharaoh also tried his best to have his own way, but he was overpowered by God's wonders. God's Word and prayer are very important. God's Word connects us to God. It is our daily bread. Before we can grow in the Lord, we must read, pray, and meditate on the Word daily. Just as we need food to maintain the body, so we also need God's Word to make the spirit in us grow. Though the spirit in us does not age, it grows spiritually and stays strong to do God's Kingdom Work with spiritual food. Here is how: **John 1:1** says, "In the beginning was the Word. The Word was with God, and the Word was God. Through Him, all things were made, and nothing was made without Him." The Word is a lamp unto our feet and the light onto our path (**Psalm 119:105**). We can never survive without the word of God. In Him is life.

Once we are connected to God, the Holy Spirit becomes our helper as the One who quickens, empowers, and fills us. Lastly, God's Word is sharper than any two-edged sword (**Hebrews 4:12**). It builds us in faith, helps us put our trust in God, and helps us grow stronger in the Lord. The Word helps us practice true love, make us become self-control, have humility, and live with compassion. It makes us kind and gentle with more patience. The Word of God also sanctifies, purifies, nourishes, and purges us so we can continue to live and bear good fruit. God's Word is everything we need live according to God's rules. As King David wrote in **Psalm 1:1**, God's Word helps us to live and grow in righteousness.

The Lord's Prayer has helped me to see the importance of the Word and prayer. What makes the Lord Prayer more powerful is that it is the Word of God. As John 1 states, there was nothing made without God's Word. Through Him all things were made. This means that we will make it if we pray through The Lord's Prayer. Every day that you spend time in prayer through the Word, you are building your hope and endurance based on the foundation of Christ. This is the solid ground on which we all must stand. God's Word is very powerful when we use it to pray, meditate, and apply to our lives. When we spend time in the word of God, we are feeding our inner spirits with the power of the Holy Spirit. Though, with His Word, He rebukes, He also encourages, edifies, builds, empowers, strengthens, and fills our minds with His peace that surpasses all understanding. And through the Word, we will receive the promises of God and are empowered by the Holy Spirit for what we are called to do. With the Word, we abound in hope, become faithful, have compassion, and the confidence to do His Work as He recommends. According to **Romans 15:13**, we must operate according to His Word and remain in it without giving up, because through the Word of God, nothing is impossible.

As the Word of God was to **Joshua 1:8**, so it is with us. It says, may this "book of the law never departs from your mouth. You shall meditate on it day and night, so that you may be careful to do according to all that is written in it; that will make your way prosperous and successful." The Word is our source of power for victory. It is in the Word that we receive answers to our prayers. Thus, each day my prayers are that the Holy Spirit helps me read, meditate, and carefully follow the instructions found in the Word.

In my personal life, I have come to realize this truth: regardless of what I face in this life, it is only the Word that I can truly depend on. With the Word, it won't matter what comes my way, I can make it through any storm. I can make it because God has a better solution in His Word. In the Word, I can find strength and courage, even in the mist of challenges; I will be content, and if the enemy tries to bring anything that will divert my course, the Word will bring it to my attention before I become trapped by discourage. In the Bible, I can read that the Name of the Lord is a strong tower that I can run to in times of trouble.

God's Word is everything. It is the only thing that brings life. It is all that we need to make it to the end successfully. The Word is our source of strength. It encourages and empowers us so we will not be stressed out. Because The Lord's Prayer is also part of the Word of God, which teaches us to pray according to *God's Will*, it makes a perfect sense to pray with it daily; therefore, we cannot ignore it. The Word plants a living seed in our hearts and causes us to grow and bear good fruits. The Word has power to keep us pure and alert. It also has power to help us keep our focus on God. The Word directs our path to keep us from sinning and helps us to pursue holiness; therefore, our heart will remain pure if we read and meditate on God's Word. If we keep the Word, treasure it in our hearts, and adore it, then we shall become more productive. Because the Word is living and sharper than any two-edged sword, it gives us the resources we need to overcome the enemy. When you pray with God's Word, you are speaking life into your prayer, which causes your situation to change in *God's Will*. Your prayer becomes more effective when you use God's Word to pray. Thus, if you want to know how your prayer will be answered, use God's Word, and you will see the difference. So, take the Word seriously because it has power to transform your life. According to **1 Corinthians 3:16–17**, God's Word can teach us, correct us, train us, and equip us for every good work. The Word is powerful!

The anointing of God's Holy Spirit is important. If you are unsure of the power of His Spirit, please ask God to help you understand the works of the Holy Spirit. There is some confusion surrounding the Christian community and the Power of God's Holy Spirit. Please, ask God if you are confused. He is the One who can help you in your Christian Walk. He helps us to understand what we read and teaches us God's ways. He also helps us to have strength to accomplish our goals in life. Above all, He helps us to pray, and intercedes for us with groanings. He helps us in so many ways. Read **Romans 8; John 16; 1 Timothy 3,** and other cross references. Jesus said in **John 14,** "I will ask the

Father, and He will give you another comforter." The Lord's Prayer has it all to guide you to more Scriptures.

God's Heavenly Ruling is like no other. It is the perfect government! He has Jesus as the Savior and mediator, and the Holy Spirit as our helper, comforter, and teacher. Take it as this: God is the President; Vice President – the Lord Jesus Christ; the Holy Spirit – the Secretary, and the angels are His soldiers – the messengers. Isn't that beautiful? You can ask God if you are still confused. God's system of operations is excellent! He will teach you because you are His child. You deserve to know all that concerns your salvation. And you must know before it is too late. Everything you must know will be revealed if you spend time with the Lord in prayer and bring before Him all your concerns or confusions. God works with His team. It is not as humans who are filled with power struggles, like Satan. God is United. He is not a divided God and He is not three Gods, but One God.

There is no way we can understand anything about God with the limited minds we have without the help of the Holy Spirit. But through the help of the Holy Spirit, the eyes of our understanding will be opened to know the truths of God and His system of operation. So, in your pursuit of holiness, never think you can make it to the end without the Spirit of God. It is the Holy Spirit that convicts, strengthens, and helps us to face the storms of life and all the challenges we face each day. He gives us an enduring spirit to overcome every obstacle.

My dear one, I cannot go on any more about the works of the Holy Spirit, because they are too deep. So, I will wait till the Lord gives me an assignment on that subject to help you with any answers you may be searching for. With the help of the Holy Spirit, you will get to see how and why spending time in the Word each day can help you face challenges peacefully. So, bring your confusions before God.

Everything in the physical realm is temporary, whereas everything in the spiritual realm is eternal. Spiritual growth brings maturity. It brings freedom and restoration. It helps us become like trees planted by streams of water, so we can bear fruit in good seasons. Through spiritual growth, we can be fearless. When life's difficulties arise, we can face them with confidence because our hope is built on nothing less, but Christ Jesus and His righteousness. He is our solid rock. These requires reading and meditating upon God's Word. The Word helps us to learn from Jesus' experience, become like Him, and overcome the devil's trickery. If Jesus said to Satan, "It is written...," in **Matthew 4**, then we shall also have victory over Satan if we follow His examples. God's Word can help us to stand strong in all we do.

The fruit of the Spirit is our daily bread. It is for our spiritual growth. In **Galatians 5:22–23**, the Apostle Paul offers a profound yet simple list of nine Christian personalities: love, joy, peace, patience, kindness, goodness, faithfulness, gentleness, and self-control. These fruits of the Spirit are very important. They are our daily bread. We must pray for them daily. This is because loving one another as children of God is vital. God commands us to love our neighbors as we love ourselves – **Mark 12:31.1 Corinthians 13:13** declares, "Three things remain: faith, hope, and love. But the greatest of these is love." For this reason, we must love genuinely because it will bring healing into this world. Our prayer should be that God will grant us hearts big enough to love one another, have compassion, patient, self-control, and be gentle.

The gifts of the Spirit. We need spiritual gifts to do God's work. The spiritual gifts are for the growth. In 1 **Corinthians 12:31**, Paul encourages Christians to "eagerly desire the greater gifts." So, visions, dreams, discernment, the ability to teach and counsel, knowledge, prophecy, etc., are all God's daily bread which we need to help us do God's work.

We also need wisdom as our daily bread. According to **James 1:5,** we must ask God for wisdom if we lack wisdom. We need wisdom; without it, we can act unwisely, make bad decisions, and don't live uprightly. Therefore, we need wisdom in all aspects of life: choosing to serve the Lord, go to school, get married, pursue a career, and so on. Wisdom brings discernment; without it, we can make bad choices. Making the right choice means living a life that pleases God. Unwise choices are detrimental to life. For instance, excessive smoking and alcohol intake weakens the body and causes lung and heart diseases; sexual immorality destroys good marriage; stealing puts one in jail; lying, gossiping, hatred, anger, jealousy, and envy destroy reputations and relationships. On the other hand, Godly wisdom makes us think logically and make good decisions. The wisdom of God helps us stay away from things that could damage us. With this newly acquired wisdom, we can make the right choices, abstain from all acts of ungodliness, and live according to God's purpose. Each day, we must pray for God's wisdom to make good decisions. May we have God's wisdom to manage life.

Faith is our daily bread. **Hebrews 11:6** says, "Without faith, it is impossible to please God." Faith helps us to know that God exists and that He listens when we pray. It helps us to receive from God. Read **Matthew 17:21–21** and **Hebrews 11**

The daily bread of holiness is important. We must keep in mind that without holiness, we cannot see God, as **Hebrews 12:14** explains. Therefore, the pursuit of holiness should be a priority. If we want to experience the presence of God, then we must be holy. When God leads us on the path of righteousness, we can bear many spiritual fruits and make our service to God a meaningful one.

Emotional needs as our daily bread are important. We have three major emotional needs: peace of mind, good relations, and forgiveness. These are what the soul requires for its sustainability. Some of these needs hold the key to emotional well-being, life satisfaction, and success.

Peace of mind as a daily bread: We need peace of mind, so, the *pursuit of peace* is more important. Therefore, asking God's peace as our daily bread is very vital; it helps us to function well. One of **James Allen** quote says, "The more tranquil a man becomes, the greater is his success and his influence." A mind without peace causes a person's life to be in chaos. Jesus knew how relevant peace was to our earthly existence; therefore, in **John 14:27,** He promised us His peace. Peace is what helps us to function as normal humans. Peace helps us to remain calm when we are faced with opposition. When we face challenges, unpleasant feelings and tensions that cause distress can disturb our peace. Feelings of anxiety, worry, and depression can take control of your inner peace. Without peace of mind, you will eventually notice symptoms of anxiousness, which will affect your mood. It can even cause headaches; it can also disturb your sleeping pattern and the way you function. The truth is that peace of mind can be attained and enjoyed right here and now, even while you are facing life's challenges. With a daily dose of peace, we can function well. Peace of mind offers countless benefits. With peace of mind, you will be able to easily focus no matter the obstacles. It brings a sense of wholeness, completeness, and well-being.

We cannot thrive in chaos; that is why peace of mind and serenity must be sought from God daily. **Philippians 4:7** states: "And the peace of God, which transcends all understanding, will guard your hearts and your minds in Christ Jesus." **Psalm 119:165** says, "Great peace have they that you're your law..." With the peace of God, nothing can cause us to stumble. Without peace, our education, money/wealth, power, fame, and talent would be meaningless. In their anxiousness, some people have tried using alcohol and drugs as a means of escape. However, these substances only make them forget their worries for a short period. Once they become sober, they realize their problems were never solved. While some of our problems are due to medical reasons, others are caused by unhealthy relationships or a lack of love and peace. For these reasons, we should rely on God to fulfill our physical, spiritual, and emotional needs, which include peace of mind. A person could also be stressed out when confronted with uncertainty, shame, or failure. As believers, we can have assurance that trials are not intended to harm us but draw us close to God; and believing that they will soon pass will help us. That way, they will not have the power to drag us down due into over-anxiousness.

Here are a few benefits of peace that I have come to personally enjoy: 1). The ability to concentrate and dwell on better things. 2). No stress, worries, and anxiety will not rule over me. 3). The competence to handle my daily activities. 4). I can focus on what I must achieve for His Kingdom. 5). The patience and endurance I need for tolerance. 6). I have happiness and joy as my portion. 7). Mental freedom, any evil thoughts which might cause me to think incorrectly or become restless, will be prevented, so I can do important things for the day. 8). Naturally falling asleep at night because of the peace of God in me.

All these benefits help me to focus, read God's Word, pray, and meditate. Peace of mind will enable you to understand things from God's perspective and help improve your lives. I have already stated about peace of mind. Now, let's check into good relationships.

Daily bread of good relationships ***is also important.*** Many of the emotional difficulties we struggle with have something to do with unfulfilled needs. When emotional needs of a good relationship are met, the soul is refreshed. Fulfilled emotional needs bring about safety and assurance. For this reason, God fills our lives with good relationships so that our emotional needs can be satisfied. Good relationships bring happiness, love, and peace. Their absence causes sorrow, which goes a long way to harm a person's emotional state. A good relationship should be able to uplift and encourage you. For instance, you know that you are in a good relationship with your spouse when he or she is willing to stand by you and encourage you, even at your lowest state. In contrast, when you are in an unhealthy relationship with someone, you will be despised and neglected by that person. Your partner or friend will make you feel worthless, especially at a time when you need their support. To avoid situations like these, our prayers should constantly be filled with supplications to God, asking Him to bring good people our way and into our lives, who will offer us genuine care, love, respect, and support.

Unhealthy relationship is toxic. In this, there is a persistence jealousy, lack of support, control, and poor communication. According to **Psalm 139:14**, I am fearfully and wonderfully made. But unhealthy relationship will bring the worst out of me. So, I must keep in mind that I am very special. And you must do the same. Do not allow anybody to belittle you. Declare positive things over your lives during times of chaos and adversity, and through the power of God, they shall come to pass.

Please make the following affirmations:

I'm a child of the Most-High God; I am fearfully and wonderfully made.

I'm beautiful and amazing.

I'm favored, loved, forgiven, healed, and have been made whole.

I'm unwavering, gifted, strong, anointed, confident, courageous, determined, unstoppable, and victorious.

I'm positive, enlightened, and untangled.

I'm powerful, intelligent, important, authentic, true, reliable, and good.

I'm prosperous and blessed!

Do not allow anyone, be it your spouse, parent, sibling, child, friend, or pastor make you feel worthless. Be who you are and how God created you because you are unique. There are no two of you, and there never will be! If you sin, ask God for forgiveness. Do not allow anyone to humiliate or ridicule you, and don't put yourself down. Encourage yourself. Do not allow anyone to victimize you or make you feel terrible. Always keep in mind that people are unforgiven, but God is a forgiving God. 'He is compassionate and gracious, slow to anger, and abounding in love.'

Forgiveness is emotional daily bread. I believe that forgiveness is one of the most important types of daily bread that God gives. It is the most important gift you can give to yourself. For this reason, learn to forgive yourself and others. We all need a daily dose of forgiveness in order to forgive the way God wants us to, without grudges. Unforgiveness can disrupt your peace of mind; so, learn to forgive and let go. Since forgiveness is a step toward holiness, we experience the presence of God in our lives when we learn to forgive daily. "Do not be overcome by evil but overcome evil with good" (**Romans 12:21**). Forgiveness helps us overcome evil with good. Therefore, it is important to ask God to give us a forgiving heart. Harboring grudges only worsens things and makes us more disturbed. With unforgiveness, you will become bitter. So, don't become bitter; become better. Don't retaliate; learn to give it to God. Before we can wholeheartedly forgive the wrongs done to us, the anger we feel must be dealt with appropriately. Once you forgive, your mind and heart will be at peace. Bear in mind that you may find it difficult to forgive if you fail to seek God's help. So, learn to forgive. Keep in mind that people may fail to forgive, but God always will. So, ask God to pardon you if you sin, and learn to forgive as well. God is a forgiving Father; ask Him for help if you find it difficult to forgive. He will forgive you without holding it against you. He will also help teach you how to genuinely forgive. Find genuine people who can pray with you so that you can have the freedom and peace of mind to serve the Lord.

Gratitude of a thankful heart. A heart of gratitude is another daily bread. We will forever appreciate the Lord and all His goodness to us. We are grateful for all He has done, so we give Him thanks each day for all His provisions. Sometimes we take things for granted, but that should not be if we count all our blessings as not by might nor by power, but by the Spirit of the Lord (**Zechariah 4:6**). Here is a little story that was sent to me by a friend long ago. There was once an 80-year-old man who collapsed and was rushed to the hospital. On his arrival, he was given oxygen to sustain him for 24 hours. After spending some time at the hospital, he was discharged and asked to pay his bill. When he saw the bill, he started crying. The doctors told him not to worry because he could pay the bill in installments. However, the old man explained that he was crying not because he couldn't afford the bill but because 24 hours' worth of oxygen was costing him so much, yet the Lord had supplied him with oxygen all his life and never asked him to pay for anything. I completely agree with the man. I will never forget when the Lord told me to start counting all my blessings. I then realized how good the Lord has been to me. From that time, I never complained about anything again. After seeing all the Lord had done for me, I now live with a heart of gratitude.

I conclude by saying that God is our Great Provider. Each day, I can enjoy God's blessings of good health, food, water, air, shelter, money, well-being, faith, love, peace, joy, happiness, righteousness, holiness, gentleness, self-control, compassion, wisdom, and everything I need without limiting my request. He has the power to provide them all. He can supply our physical, emotional, and spiritual needs if we ask Him in prayer. We cannot depend on money, power, or fame to meet these needs; but we can always depend on God's providential care. With Him, all things are possible! Unquestionably, we are aware that *lacking* is a part of life, but we pray that God helps us to overcome every obstacle of sickness and troubles of any kind. We pray for His wisdom to help us make good decisions and for His empowerment to dwell in us so that we may do greater things. May the Lord supply all our needs according to His glorious riches in Christ Jesus.

Prayer – Dear Heavenly Father, for the many blessings and opportunities that come our way each day through Your love, we ask that You maintain our faith and fill us with Your Light always. In asking for all our needs, we ask that You help us to fix our eyes on You and Your Kingdom and give thanks in advance because we know all things shall be added to that in Jesus' Name. Amen!

Chapter 12 – Forgive Our Sins as We Forgive Those Who Sin Against Us

Matthew 6:12

What is **forgiveness? Romans 12:17** – Don't repay evil for evil but give thought to do what is honorable in the sight of all. Forgiveness means letting go of wrongs done to you. But have you ever struggled to forgive someone? Today in our world, forgiveness has become a major issue affecting us in every way. And it is not surprising to know that it is affecting the church as well. Unforgiveness is overburdening numerous people, and vengeance is turning into retribution. Everyone wants their own brand of justice. When people take matters into their own hands, they find it hard to forgive, but it is important to forgive because forgiveness is a command from the Lord. It is an act of submitting in obedience to God and His word. God forgives us even if we don't deserve His forgiveness. He shows us mercy, even if we don't deserve mercy. He does that so that we can forgive and show mercy to others as well.

What is **forgiveness? Romans 12:17** – Don't repay evil for evil but give thought to do what is honorable in the sight of all. *Have you ever struggled to forgive someone?* Forgiveness means letting go of wrongs done to you. Today in our world, forgiveness has become a major issue affecting the church of God in Christ, as well as the whole world. Unforgiveness is overburdening numerous people, and vengeance is turning into retribution. Everyone wants their own brand of justice. When people take matters into their own hands, they find it hard to forgive, but it is important to forgive because forgiveness is a command from the Lord. It is an act of submitting in obedience to God and His word.

God forgives us even if we don't deserve His forgiveness. He shows us mercy, even if we don't deserve mercy. He does that so that we can forgive and show mercy to others as well.

In this way, vengeance will not have its power to take root and rule over humanity. When we forgive, we make a conscious effort not to hold anything against another person. We release feelings of anger, bitterness, and vengeance we had toward a person who hurt us, regardless of whether that person deserves our forgiveness or not. **Ephesians 4:26–27** tells us that we shouldn't let the "sun go down on our anger or give the devil any foothold or opportunity."

If you are commanded to not allow the sun to go down on your anger and you refuse to forgive, it means that you have given the devil a chance to rule your life. This is why the Lord commands us to forgive. It is because He does not want the devil, our enemy, to rule over us. Therefore, forgiveness is for your own good. It is not to harm you but to prosper you. Forgiveness brings healing to your souls and frees you from bondage. Lastly, forgiveness brings many blessings. Unforgiveness puts you in bondage; it rips you away from everything good. It rips you from your joy, your peace of mind, and freedom. It can also destroy everything you have and render you hopeless. There is no blessing in unforgiveness! So, learn to forgive if you want God's blessings. This is because forgiveness is a command and an act of obedience to God, and obedience is a blessing. That means refusing to forgive is a curse.

For that matter, you must think again if you refuse to forgive others as you too have been forgiven by God. **Matthew 6:14–15** reminds us that, if we forgive other people, God will also forgive us, and our prayers will not be hindered. In verse 15, Jesus clearly shows the consequences failure to forgive; in the same manner as we forgive is the same manner in which we will receive God's forgiveness. **Matthew 5:24** tells us to "leave your gift in front of the altar. First go and be reconciled to your brother; then come and offer your gift." This means forgiveness is a serious matter. If we forgive, we lose nothing; on the contrary, we gain so much more. "Give, and it will be given to you. A good measure, pressed down, shaken together, and running over, will be poured into your lap. For with the measure you use, it will be measured to you" (**Luke 6:38**).

What are some steps toward forgiveness? Here are a few steps to guide you toward forgiveness if you have become disappointed with yourself or someone and you are still struggling to forgive. First, admit that you are hurt. Once you do, you will be able to seek help from the Holy Spirit. It can be likened to seeing a doctor. When you believe that you are sick, you don't hesitate to seek help from a physician. Second, be obedient to God. Knowing what Jesus teaches about forgiveness will help you know how to forgive as an act of obedience to God. When you obey, you resist the devil's advances in trying to poison your mind and heart with anger and thoughts of bitterness. Third, know God's promise concerning forgiveness, think about it, and consider it deeply. Jesus not only said we should forgive but we must also forgive, and you shall be forgiven – **Matthew 6:14.** This means that God will forgive us when we forgive others. God will, in turn, forgive you if you forgive others who has done you wrong. Fourth, depend on the power of the Holy Spirit to help you forgive. The Holy Spirit is the One who can help you forgive and forget. **Psalm 103:8** says, "The Lord is compassionate and gracious, slow to anger, abounding in love." Learn to depend on God, knowing that He is a faithful Father, and if you trust Him, He will let the Holy Spirit teach you how to forgive without holding back.

Unforgiveness and health crisis are real. Unforgiveness affects our health more than we know because it is detrimental to good health. In explaining '3 Big Ways Forgiveness Is Good for Your Health', Kaitlin Sullivan wrote: "Whether you're working on forgiving yourself or others, forgiveness is imperative for mental and physical health." This means that holding on to any wrong done to you can affect every part of your life in many ways. It can affect the following: your cardiovascular system; your brain; your immune system, leading to many other chronic health problems.

Now, let's delve into the subject of repentance. An unforgiving heart needs repentance. Unforgiveness must be treated like treating an incurable disease. For it to be treated well, repentance is a must. It takes only God's Word to cure it, which derives from repentance. In **Exodus 23:25**, God promised the Israelites that "He would bless their food and water, heal their land and remove sickness from their midst." I was once a victim of unforgiveness, but thankfully, today, I am healed. Although I am not perfect, but the spirit of unforgiveness has no control over me. So, when I pray for myself, I also pray for people who are still ensnared and struggling to be set free, because unforgiveness can be a burden.

Self-forgiveness: Why is self-forgiveness important? Self-forgiveness brings us inner peace and healing. So, please, do not let a day go by without asking for forgiveness and forgiving yourself. It is the best gift you can ever give to yourself. There is a secret to forgiveness that brings total healing to the body, soul, and spirit, and it is this: you cannot give forgiveness until you have forgiven yourself. This means it is impossible to be forgiven without showing forgiveness to others and forgiving ourselves. We can have faith to move mountains, but without forgiveness, the mountain won't move. If without faith, our prayers are ineffective, and if without forgiveness, our prayers remain unanswered, then faith and forgiveness give us something to think about. We need both for our prayers to be accepted.

How many times must we forgive? In **Matthew 18:21–22**, Peter asked the Lord, how often he should forgive, "As many as seven times?" Jesus answered, "Not seven times, but 77 times 7." This simply means forgiving without counting. There is no shortcut to forgiveness. It must be given wholeheartedly. **Romans 12:17** tells us to "never repay evil for evil." When we forgive, the love of God is witnessed in us. In **Ephesians 4:31–32,** we are encouraged to "put away all bitterness, wrath, anger, clamor, and slander. Be kind and compassionate to one another, forgiving each other, just as in Christ God forgave you." It is easy to judge and condemn because we live in a world where everyone is quick to do so, ignoring the fact that, we have all sinned and fallen short of the glory of God. **Luke 6:37–38** says, "Do not condemn, and you will not be condemned; do not judge, and you will not be judged; forgive, and you will be forgiven. Give, and it will be given to you, a good measure, pressed down, shaken together, and running over, will be poured into your lap. For, the measure you use will be measured to you." This verse is not only about wealth but forgiveness as well. It is not only directed at the poor or the church; it is also about forgiving those who need your forgiveness. If you give forgiveness, your peace of mind, healing, and blessings will be in plentiful for you.

After my encounter with the Lord regarding His prayer and gaining more insights about forgiveness and why the church is suffering from unforgiveness, I have now come to understand why many people refuse to join a church. The enemy has infested the church with unforgiveness to a point where we sometimes don't pay much attention to it. Sometimes, this is due to jealousy and envy. Even among church leaders and pastors, there is unforgiveness. In **Romans 12:10**, the Apostle Paul exhorts believers to "be kind and affectionate toward one another with brotherly love." **1 John 4:20** further states, "If anyone says I love God and hates a brother, that person is a liar; for he who loves not his brother whom he can see, cannot love God whom he has not seen." We cannot choose whom to love and whom to hate (**Matthew 5:43–48**). We all need acceptance, love, comfort, and forgiveness from one another, just as Jesus loves us equally. Even if we think that they don't deserve it at all, we should do it as a requirement for blessings. I pray that the Lord gives each one of us a forgiving heart.

What happens when we fail to forgive? Forgiveness is not only for the other person but for yourself. Many people, including myself, have been set free from the bondage of unforgiveness, but there are still many believers struggling to forgive. Each day that you walk with a load of unforgiveness, you destroy your own self. Forgiveness cannot be faked. It must be genuine. God's forgiveness depends on how we forgive others. Jesus is not talking about the eternal fate of another person, for He has the power to forgive and save. He knows the heart of everyone and knows if you and I forgive wholeheartedly. If **Luke 6:38** tells us to give to be given, in good measure, pressed down, shaken together, and running over, the same will be given to us if we forgive. In **Luke**

2:52, we are told, "Jesus increased in wisdom, stature, and favor with God and men." You cannot grow in wisdom, stature, and favor if you are still dealing with unforgiveness and bitterness. The spirit of unforgiveness will make you sink in faith, your prayers will go unanswered, and you will be miserable. **Mark 11:24** tells us that whatever we desire when we pray and believe that we have received it, we shall have it. But guess what? Unforgiveness blocks your blessings from God and prevents you from receiving the best from Him. Your prayers will go unanswered if you refuse to obey the Lord's command regarding forgiveness.

Unforgiveness makes us look down on others. We gossip, backbite, and destroy reputations. On the other hand, forgiveness brings emotional, mental, and spiritual healing. If you want to be healed, then you must learn to forgive. Harboring grudges will not bring healing because it does not reflect the love of Christ. We abide in Christ by keeping His commandments, which include forgiveness. So, the bottom line is that forgiveness is an emergency. It is a 911 call, because when we fail to forgive, we become toxic, get sick, and die spiritually. There is no way out; learn to forgive before the sun goes down, and by that, I mean ASAP!!!

Understand that sometimes, God allows us to go through something to help us grow. Here is the story of what I went through when I first came to the United States as a missionary. My story of unforgiveness started this way, just as Joseph suffered at the hands of his brothers but became a blessing because he learned to forgive. **Matthew 10:36** says, "A man's enemies will be the members of his household." From the story of Joseph, we see that as painful as his tragedy was, he overcame it with forgiveness. The brothers feared what he would become if they let him live. So, they planned to get rid of him.

Years ago, when my husband and I came to America as missionaries from our home church in Africa, we suffered greatly. Just like Joseph, our church brothers and sisters thought we wanted to become famous; therefore, they try to stop us from leaving and becoming missionaries. What we did not know was that there was so much jealousy surrounding us for us having been chosen to come to America. One day, we were getting ready to go to Canada for a weekend church program. The elder who was going to drive us was a very nice person, and we loved his personality. On that evening while sitting in the living room waiting for my husband to get ready, that elder said something. Though it is long gone, I have never forgotten what he said, "Mama, I envy you." I said, "What did you mean by that?" He explained it very clearly. I took it as a joke, smiled, and forgot about it. Little did I realize that what he did not say it jokingly.

In **Luke 6:45,** we are told, "For out of the abundance of the heart the mouth speaks." How did I know? Well, it did not take long after he said that before the worse thing happened; they were debating among themselves. While some of them were praying for us, some were jealous because of our position. They thought we had become famous. For that reason, they tried anything they could to prevent us from progressing. It was just like the brothers of Joseph, my dear elders in the church planned to destroy us. They did not put us in a physical ditch. Rather, they accused us of some things we knew nothing about and wrote character assassination letters against us.

See, God never allows anything to come out for no reason. He wanted to tell me what the people were thinking about us behind our backs, so I could pray against it, but I took it lightly. For that reason, I failed to pray against it. This was because it never dawned on me that the church members who I dearly loved would think of planning any evil against my family and me. I am sure Joseph never thought for a minute that his dear brothers would ever plan any evil against him. But, yes, it happened. It happened because the devil is not a respecter of anyone. Whoever makes him/herself available, Satan can use them for destruction. What made it even sadder was when my husband was told that there were even some pastors who were instigators because they thought they were the ones who deserved to come to America. This means they were somehow poisoning the minds of the people about us just like what we see in politics. It was unfortunate, but it happens sometimes. When a church operates from a political arena, jealousy and envy can be produced because they are the parents of hatred.

Today, I don't blame them. The devil's plans succeeded because we didn't act wisely and forgive, but rather allowed unforgiveness to take control. The devil wouldn't have had a chance if we would had prayed, taken a biblical approach, and forgiven those elders. The Bible says in Matthew 5:11 that "Blessed are you when people insult you, persecute you and falsely say or write all kinds of evil things against you because of me." It was because of Christ that we came to America. Whatever we faced, was for His Name's sake. This means, there was nothing for us to worry about. Whether we were hated, insulted, or persecuted, it was okay for Christ's sake. It was not a big deal. But we were angry, and for years, we couldn't let go of the pain of humiliation. Why? It was because we gave in, to the lies of the devil. I was deeply hurt, and my reason was that it seemed to me as if the church was operating from a political standpoint. I thought something was not right. There was a lot of division, and many groups of people unintentionally made it difficult to work without offending others. Because we were new in the church, we found out later about these divisions. We had just started getting to know the people. So, I was deeply hurt, which was okay. What was not okay was the fact that our anger went on for so long. It wasn't for a day, a week, or months, but for years.

Forgiveness must be instantaneous! Jealousy and envy triggered the brothers of Joseph to hate him and sell him into slavery. And it was the same jealousy that triggered the church leaders to betray us. Joseph handled his tragedy well, but my husband and I did not. God moved through these heartbreaking trials in Joseph's life for His glory and Joseph's blessings, but we suffered for too long. Joseph was taken and moved far away from his family. So, I am sure he was hurt, but he did not allow that to cause him to sin against God. Even seeing his brothers for the first time after years and taking time out to weep shows that he was deeply hurt. But the way he handled them, shows that he forgave them. Otherwise, he would have ordered their execution or imprisonment. Once our dear Dr. Charles Stanley said, "The issue of trial is not how we are treated but how we respond."

Do whatever it takes to overcome unforgiveness before it overcomes you. So, here are some more steps to help you conquer unforgiveness. When someone hurts you, you can either hold on to anger and resentment or forgive the person and move on with your life. But, because unforgiveness brings nothing but a curse, it is a blessing to conquer it. To do so, the following steps are recommended:

- Understand what unforgiveness is about.
- Identify what happened to make you upset.
- Know why you are having a hard time forgiving.
- Know what the Bible says about forgiveness.
- Understand the benefits of forgiveness and the consequences of failing to forgive.

You can use these facts to help you overcome unforgiveness effectively.

*The Lord says unforgiveness is weakening the church. And the time has come for God's people to know how to forgive genuinely before it is too late. So, let's keep in mind that forgiveness is an everyday affair. You will need forgiveness for yourself and for others; therefore, always let forgiveness be in your pantry to readily give to someone who needs it.

Prayer – Dear Heavenly Father, thank You for Your gift of forgiveness. Please help us to know how to forgive without holding any grudges in Jesus Name. Amen.

Chapter 13 – Lead Us Not into Temptation, but Deliver Us from Evil

Matthew 6:13

Have you ever found yourself trapped in temptation, and did not know how to free yourself from that bandage? Temptation and evil are running rampage, but **James 4:7** tells us to "Submit to God. Resist the devil, and he will flee from you. Really? How? They are everywhere and are very destructive. But what is temptation and evil? Temptation is the desire to do something that is considered immoral, and it can cause us to do evil. So then, evil becomes the fruit of the temptation when we fall into it. This means temptation itself is not a sin, but giving in to temptation is sin. Temptation becomes sin when we surrender to our evil desires. This means we have refused God and His law.

Evil has become rooted in every aspect of life due to our inability to overcome temptation. The devil's main goal is to plot and trigger humans to sin against God, and he uses temptations, but Christ has given us power to overcome. As **Revelation 12:7–12** declares, the devil, who deceives the whole world, along with his angels are cast down, and they are here for real nasty business. There are those that come about through people, things, and even our self. But as I stated earlier, Jesus knew that temptation is unavoidable. As He was led to the wilderness to be tempted, so shall we be. Therefore, He is aware that overcoming temptation is possible; so, He teaches us how to overcome it. They are the cause of all evil, so it is our responsibility to be conscious of God's provisions for defeating the devil. To defeat him, you must first know all his diplomacies and strategies. So, keep **James 4:7** in your heart, mind, and **allow it to sink deep within your soul.**

Temptations and trials that come to you are not hidden from God. He permits them. Understand this to know how to resist the devil in times of temptations and trials. God knows you before He allows you to face temptation. He protects you from being tempted above your capability. He does not allow us to be tempted beyond our level of competence and always **provides a way to escape and overcome that temptation.** God is faithful; He will not let you be tempted beyond what you can bear. But when you are tempted, He will also provide a way out so that you can endure it. God uses His Word to prepare and equip us ahead of time. So, let's prepare ourselves and be strong to stand against any test. If we fail, it means we were not fully prepared. **Proverbs 11:14** declares that "Where there is no guidance, the people perish."

From the beginning of Creation, the devil, and his desire to destroy humankind has not changed. It is his goal that humans are against humans. After he was expelled from Heaven for rebelling, that became his target. So, surround yourself with good people to avoid being used by the enemy. **John 10:10** says, "The devil comes to steal, kill, and destroy.

*He deceived Adam and Eve to disobey the Lord's command.

*He instigated Cain to kill his brother, whose offering was more pleasing to God.

*Abraham thought it was okay to go against *God's Will* by having a baby out of wedlock, all because they were deceived by Satan.

*The devil sowed seeds of discontent in Joseph's brothers and drove them to sell him into slavery.

*While Joseph was in slavery, Potiphar's wife tempted him to sin against God.

*The devil tempted David to have Bathsheba's husband, Uriah, sent to the frontlines to die so that David could marry Bathsheba.

*King Saul was tempted to have David killed.

*Elisha's servant, Gehazi, was tempted to be greedy.

*Peter was tempted to deny Jesus when he was identified as one of Jesus' disciples.

*Ananias and Sapphira were tempted to lie. They had promised to bring all the proceeds as offerings to God. Instead, they lied and died instantly.

*It was the same devil that tempted our Lord Jesus Christ; but thankfully, the Lord defeated him.

*In our time, he can use anyone: brothers, sisters, fathers, mothers, husband, wife, friends, neighbors, children, pastors, etc., because the devil is only a user. Therefore, he couldn't care less of whom he could use.

I could go on and on with the list of Bible characters who were tempted by the devil to sin against God. In all the above cases, except Jesus, these people fell victim to the devil's manipulations.

In **Mark 3:27**, Jesus said something very serious about the kingdom of Satan that many don't know. Jesus speaks about the concept of a strong man and said, "No man can enter into the strong man house and take from him unless he first binds the strong man, then he can raid his house. The domain of evil was what Jesus was talking about. This statement implies that Satan is the strong man guiding his house. The enemy, Satan, has put many into his spiritual prison using them as he pleases; but Jesus came to destroy the power of Satan and free humanity from his captivation; that is why Jesus came. He came to free us from the power of sin. It is written in **John 10:10**, "The thief comes not, but to steal, kill, and destroy. But I have come that you might have abundant life. While Jesus is the Father of all goodness, Satan is the father of all evil. While Jesus tells us about the truth of the Father and leads us to life eternal, Satan lies about God; misleads people, pollute the minds of the weak, and turn them away from knowing about the true nature of God the Father.

Today, across the globe, temptation, and evil rule. They rule in the hearts, minds, and the lives of humans. Consequently, we see evil on our streets, in our homes, in our neighborhoods, in schools, in hospitals, in government sectors, and even in the church of God. There is too much cruelty. Our world today is filled with all kinds of evil, more than ever. Around the world, we hear of terrorism attacks, wars, and rumors of war, envy, jealousy, greediness, love of money, power struggles, drug abuse, violence, murder, unnecessary killings, prejudice, racism, political issues, attacks on religion, mass shootings, kidnappings, witchcraft practices, hatred, rape, sexual immoralities, idol worship, proudness, boastfulness, etc.! All these are evil that steal human minds and cause us to sin against God. They are temptations that led humans to sin against God. Our only way to defeat all these evils is when we pray each day and ask the Father to lead us not into temptation but deliver us from evil. It may seem as if our world and its troubles are too much, but God has power over every evil. Though, the devil's aim is to steal, kill, and destroy, we will overcome through the word of God, Prayer, and Faith. The mere thinking of these things consumes energy, but God has power over them all with prayer because with Him nothing is too hard. So, know what is tempting you, and do what God's Word commands you to do, and the Lord will help you overcome your trials and temptations. But not only that, but after you are out, He will get you to make a difference.

- Is anything pushing you to do the wrong thing?
- What is it? Can you name it?
- Do you know how to rid yourself off evil?

We must know how to overcome temptation and evil in our everyday life. Is there any way? Can we defeat temptation and evil? If so, then how? We can if we submit to God. Thus, the first solution to victory over temptation is 'submitting to God. Be watchful or alert. Pay attention to who or what the enemy is trying to use to tempt or entice you. Don't be blindfolded. You must keep the word of God in your heart so you can compare it with whatever you are tempted to do and see what God's Word says. Keep doing this each time you are being tempted, and you will overcome the devil.

Living an exemplary life demands a lot of responsibility. It pays to live by a high moral and spiritual standard. However, temptation often draws us away from such upright living. In that case, it is your responsibility to not allow sin to overrule you. Find a way out of every temptation that comes your way by connecting and tapping into the resources that God has provided for overcoming the evil one. Never assume that you are not well equipped. You must be conscious so you can overcome every tempting situation you face.

The Word of God, Prayer, and Faith are your powerful tools to help you build up strength and resistance against any temptation. Do not miss these important measures. Study and meditate upon the Word; pray over the Word and have Faith. Be conscious of these weapons; they are your strength. Always keep in mind that you are not wrestling against flesh and blood, but against the powers of the dark world. But you are an overcomer because your preparation in the Word can help you build strength to resist temptation. *Be alert and sober* **(1 Peter 5:8)**. **2 Samuel 11** tells us about David and Bathsheba. David fell into temptation because he couldn't resist it. In David's mind, Bathsheba was too beautiful to let go. That is how the devil seeks to entice. For that reason, do whatever you can to resist him. Do not give him a chance. Do not entertain him. Do not make him feel comfortable. Make his life miserable with the Word of God, prayer, and he will run away fast. Do not allow or tolerate his ideas and proposals; let him know that you are not interested in anything he sells or does. Flee from dangerous places. Read **1 Thessalonians 5:22** which says to "abstain from all appearance of evil." If you find yourself in a situation that may threaten your faith, run for your life.

Let's surround ourselves with good people. Surrounding yourself with people of faith is very important. Why this is so important is that evil communication and association corrupts good personality or character. Associating with people who believe in what you believe is safe. In times of trouble, they will be a positive influence, but bad people will corrupt you. Follow that which is written in **Psalm 1**, and delight in the ways of the Lord. In **2 Samuel 13**, we read that Amnon had an exorbitant desire to have sexual relations with his own sister Diana, but he could not carry out his plans. However, when he told Jonadab, his friend, he was able to help him plot schemes to commit this outrageous sin against Israel. So also, was Zeresh, the wife of Haman and his friend able to help him. In **Esther 5:15**, what we read is that they advised Haman to build high gallows of 75 feet high to hang Mordecai on it. So, again, we must submit ourselves to God. The devil will flee from us if we do that.

We cannot fight temptation, but God's Word can. God's Word teaches us how we should live our lives. In the Book of Zechariah 4:6, we are told, "It is not by might nor by power, but by my spirit says the Lord." This means it is not by our strength. If we fight evil and temptation in the flesh, we will fail. According to **Ephesians 6:12**, we do not wrestle against flesh and blood but against principalities and powers in the dark world; therefore, we need to put on the full armor of God. Relying only on our strength to overcome temptation will be an exercise in futility because our victory is in Christ Jesus and His name. Read in **Matthew 4:4–6** how the Lord overcame evil.

Keep in mind that our opponent, the devil, is always prowling around like a roaring lion looking to devour someone. We must stand firm in faith and resist him. Pray for strength because if you do, you will **grow into spiritual maturity. Matthew 26:41** *says, "Watch and pray, that you enter not into temptation; the spirit indeed is willing, but the flesh is* weak." Ask God for strength and grace to ward off temptations when they come. **Romans 13:14** says, "Clothe yourself with the presence of the Lord Jesus Christ. Don't indulge in any evil desires. Be sober; have discernment, repentance, be watchful, and have faith." In other words:

- Know whom you are dealing with.
- Learn how to rely on God and His power.
- Learn to cast all your cares upon Jesus (**1 Peter 5:8**).

In **Luke 10:19**, it is written, "I have given you authority to trample on snakes and scorpions and to overcome all the power of the enemy; nothing will harm you." The Lord has given us the power to trample over the works of the enemy, and may this power never be diminished in us. Let's pray for holiness daily, so our prayers will be answered, and confess our sins daily so we may be healed. The prayer of a righteous person is powerful and effective" (**James**

5:16). May the Lord keep us under His shadow, deliver us from evil, and set our feet on the right path.

In conclusion, keep in mind that the main key to overcome temptation is prayer and being watchful. And the word of God makes these possible. So, read the Word, watch, pray, and keep in mind that you are never alone. Pray when you are being tempted instead of giving in to temptation. Because just as angels were sent to strengthen Jesus in time of temptation, so we too would be strengthened if we pray – **Matthew 26:41**.

Prayer: As **Ephesians 6:10–12** says, we need to put on the full armor of God. So, Father, please, help us arm ourselves as good soldiers. I know that the trials and temptations of this world I face come from the devil. Therefore, I pray that You give me Your armor and protection against his ways and tricks. Father, help all my sisters and brothers out there to be stand strong and firmly rooted in Christ Jesus to the end. We rely on Your strength and not on our own. Help us not to be wise in our own eyes. As Your Word tells us in **James 4:7–8**, we must submit ourselves to You and resist the evil one, and he will run away. Help us to draw closer to You. Create in us a pure heart, renew a steadfast spirit within us, and help us to wash our hands and be clean. Father, You cannot be tempted by evil; so, help us.

I pray against temptation. Please, help us to overcome any bad habit. Please, help me to stay awake spiritually so that temptation won't take hold of me, my children, their children's children by surprise. And I ask the same for all Your people elsewhere. I thank You Father for helping us overcome the evil that tries to lure us, in Jesus Mighty Name. Lord, our God, may Your power keep us safe from all evil. Protect us against the devil and his schemes. Break away his chains and help us to overcome all his temptations. Give us the power to overcome all evil practices. I pray that we shall be holy for Your Name.

May every evil of sickness and disease be removed from our bodies. I command all inherited illnesses to leave our bodies in Jesus Mighty Name. May our family lines be blessed. I pray that the Lord's Kingdom of humility may dwell in us so that no evil can establish itself in us. May any boastfulness and prideful spirit be cast out. I pray against every curse of arrogance that was inherited from our ancestors. Let them be broken in the name of Jesus Christ. Lord, destroy every kingdom sent to hinder our progress through temptation. By the powerful Name of Jesus, we are delivered from all evil, in Jesus Name I pray with thanksgiving, Amen!

Chapter 14 – For Thine Is the Kingdom, the Power, and the Glory, Forever

Matthew 6:13

Do you really know what belongs to God the Father, Jehovah? **Psalm 62:11** – God hath spoken once; twice have I heard this that power belongs to God. At this point, Jesus tells us what belongs to the Father, what He deserves, and what we must give to Him. When we say, "For Thine is the Kingdom, the power, and the glory, forever and ever," we refer to God and His reign. This part is straightforward, because after knowing who God is, you should also know what He deserves. The Kingdom, the Power, Glory, and Dominion belong to Him. **Revelation 4:11** says, "You are worthy, our Lord and God, to receive glory and honor and power, for you created all things, and by your will they were created and have their being." This means our worship to God who reigns and rules with power.

This is why we give thanks, praise, and worship God. He has power and authority over all things. God has plenty of power to execute everything and to do what He pleases. Both in Heaven and earth, He is not bound by anything. God is the Sovereign Creator of all things, that He is the One who rules over all things, and that nothing can happen without His knowledge. He is worthy of all praise and adoration. He alone deserves to be worshipped.

All our songs of praise, thanksgiving, and adorations are all directed to the Lord for His supremacy and goodness. In **Psalm 29**, we are told, "Ascribe to the Lord the glory due His Name; worship Him in the splendor of His Holiness." Just as angels exalt God in Heaven, so the Lord teaches us to exalt

Him. And in this final part of His Prayer, the Lord helps us to know how to acknowledge His kingship, supremacy, kingdom, reign, and rule, so we too, can worship God. The earthly kingship depicts God's Kingdom, yet they are not what we must worship. Though they are only reflections, it shows us how we should honor and respect and adore God. In other words, the Lord instituted earthly kingdoms for us to learn what it means to exalt Him. The Lord will always remain supreme, and His Kingdom is unlike any other. He is the King who the kings with all their splendor must worship.

Read **Psalm 145:3; Psalm 148; Psalm 150:6;2 Chronicles 16:31; 2 Chronicles 20:6; Colossians 1:16–17;** and **Revelation 19:6.** With this, we can attribute all glory and honor to the Holy Name of God our Father.

For a better understanding, read **Genesis 4** about the offerings of Cain and Abel. It will help you when you come before the Lord in prayer to offer to Him your sacrifice of praise. Keep in mind that God does not delight in bent offerings anymore. He requires a pure heart.

Psalm 100 – Give praise to God.

"Shout for joy to the Lord, all the earth. Worship the Lord with gladness; come before Him with joyful songs...Enter His gates with thanksgiving and His courts with praise; give thanks to Him and praise Him." Amen!

Chapter 15 – Amen

Amen is a biblical term. It is a Heavenly language with its origin from the Hebrew word ah-MANE. It means to confirm, support, or establish. We end The Lord's Prayer with "Amen," which means that whatever the Lord has said in His word is true and shall be confirmed. When we say Amen, we are affirming or agreeing to what was said. It means 'let it be done as according to God's Word'. Amen will become voluntary if we are really listening to the message, because it is an indication of acceptance or belief in what has been said, if it is according to the word of God, and your spirit agrees to the prayer or the preaching, then, you can agree by saying, Amen. Keep in mind that some churches do not mind. There are many biblical instances to support saying Amen to a message or a prayer. Below are some examples:

1 Chronicles 16:36 "Blessed be the Lord, the God of Israel, from everlasting even to everlasting. Then all the people said Amen and praised the Lord."

Psalm 41:13 "Blessed be the Lord, the God of Israel, from everlasting to everlasting, Amen."

Psalm 106:48; Psalm 89:52 "Blessed be the Lord forever! Or from everlasting to everlasting; and let all the people say, Amen!"

Nehemiah 8:6 "Then Ezra blessed the Lord, the great God. And all the people answered, Amen, while lifting up their hands; then they bowed low and worshipped the Lord with their faces to the ground."

Romans 11:36 "For from Him and through Him and to Him are all things. To Him be the glory forever. Amen."

Ephesians 3:20–21 "Now to Him who is able to do immeasurably more than all we ask or imagine, according to His power that is at work within us, to Him be glory in the church and in Christ Jesus throughout all generations, forever and ever! Amen."

Philippians 4:20 "Now to our God and Father be the glory forever and ever. Amen."

Philippians 4:23 "The grace of the Lord Jesus Christ be with you all. Amen."

1 Timothy 1:17 "Now to the King eternal, immortal, invisible, the only God, be honor and glory forever and ever. Amen."

1 Peter 5:10–11 "After you have suffered for a little while, the God of all grace, who called you to His eternal glory in Christ, will Himself perfect, confirm, strengthen, and establish you. To Him be dominion forever and ever. Amen."

Revelation 1:7 "Behold, He is coming with the clouds, and every eye will see Him, even those who pierced Him, and all the tribes of the earth will mourn over Him... Amen."

Revelation 5:14 "And the four living creatures kept saying, Amen. And the elders fell down and worshipped."

Revelation 7:11–12 "And all the angels were standing around the throne and around the elders and the four living creatures, and they fell on their faces before the throne and worshipped God, saying, "Amen, blessing and glory and wisdom and thanksgiving and honor and power and might, be to our God forever and ever."

Now that you know about Amen, I am sure you will love to say, Amen!

If you believe this simple yet powerful prayer of the Lord can bring a tremendous change on earth, then say, Amen!

If you believe that you are a child of God, then say, Amen!

If you believe in the Kingdom of God, then say, Amen!

If you want the Kingdom of God to come on earth, then say, Amen!

If you want *God's Will* to be done on earth, then say, Amen!

If you believe you are in the will of God for your life, then say, Amen!

If you believe your sins are forgiven, then say, Amen!

If you trust the Lord to supply all your needs, then say, Amen!

If you agree that the Lord will answer you when you call out to Him, then say, Amen!

If you believe the Lord has already answered you, say, Amen!

If you trust the Lord to keep you and family safe through all difficulties, then say, Amen!

We believe there is nothing impossible with God, so, we say, Amen!

Several aspects of God and His power have been revealed, and we are going to see a change. If you believe it, then give thanks, bless the Name of the Lord, and say, Amen!

Chapter 16 – Who Benefits from the Lord's Prayer?

In **Matthew 21:22** Jesus states, "*And whatever you ask in prayer, you will receive, if you have faith.*" *The Lord's Prayer* is a prayer for all believers, but also for unbelievers to know we have a Father in Heaven. It tells us everything about the Father, the Son, and the Holy Spirit. The Father has a Kingdom, a Holy Name, a will, protection, and gifts to give. *The Lord's Prayer* also tells us about the love, grace, and mercy that He bestows on us. It also tells us about Christ Jesus as the One who made a way for us to become part of God's Kingdom or God's Family. It helps us to pray in a way that covers every area of life. As I already stated, there is no area in life that the depths of His prayer do not cover. This is what makes it the most amazing prayer. It should not be a surprise because Jesus Christ is God. He knows everything and can do everything because He comes from the place where prayer rules – Heaven. All other places can have prayer meetings, but it is not necessarily a prayer if it is not directed to Jehovah through Jesus Christ with the help of the Holy Spirit. They can meditate, chant, and do all kinds of rituals, but a prayer to God is different. Through *the Lord's Prayer*, we can gain a greater understanding of the truth about prayer, because the Holy Spirit will reveal everything in detail to us.

The amazing thing about *the Lord's Prayer* is that everyone can benefit from using it. More importantly, true believers are the ones who benefit the most. However, a believer must also know that being a believer of the gospel does not guarantee automatic benefits from *the Lord's Prayer* until one understands it in detail and uses it accordingly. For instance, a person who has accepted Christ and still lives in sin will not receive the benefits that come with praying *the Lord's Prayer.* It demands holiness, so we can pray and cover everything in life. If we put it into practice, we can pray to bring the Lord's Kingdom on earth just by praying each day for ourselves to live according to the *Will of God* and praying for lost souls to see the light. We can pray *the Lord's Prayer* to shift things in the spiritual realm. We can use it to pray to tear down the walls of the evil kingdom on earth.

According to **Ephesians 5:8,** "For at one time you were in darkness, but now you are light in the Lord." Walk as children of light. Also, in **John 8:12,** Jesus says, "I am the light of the world. Whoever follows me will not walk in darkness but will have the light of life." In these verses, we are reminded that before Jesus' sacrifice, we were sinners who lived in the dark. However, the death of Christ brought about salvation and through it, we are cleansed from sin and made to walk in the light.

Living holy lives reflects the light we have received. Therefore, continuing living in sin is a clear indication that a person does not abide in the *Will of God*. At that point, the person becomes of the world and like those of the world, and for that, the things of God have little or no relevance to that person's life. So, let us come to an understanding of the *Lord's Prayer, use it* to pray, and help draw us closer to the Father and build a personal relationship with Him by praying it each day. because if we do, God's holiness will clothe us like a garment. **1 John 5:14–15** says, "And this is the confidence that we have in Him, that if we ask anything according to *His Will*, He hears us. And if we know that He hears us in whatever we ask, we know that we have the requests that we have asked of Him." Therefore, let us use *the Lord's Prayer* as a guide, and establish a prayer foundation with the help of the Holy Spirit.

Chapter 17 – What Unbelievers Must Know

Romans 3:23

Romans 3:23 "For all have sinned and fall short of the glory of God...."

It is important to pray for unbelievers!

The **devil is a rat-trapping expect**, and unbelievers are his targets. Nevertheless, through prayer, God will work wonders in the unsaved for their salvation.

Even though the Lord's Prayer is primarily for believers, this book encourages unbelievers as well. It allows unbelievers to know about God the Father through salvation, if they decide to take a step of faith. If you have not yet believed in the gospel of Christ, you will need to be saved to fill that void in your soul. Salvation puts the soul at peace; so, without it, there can only be dissatisfaction and emptiness. Perhaps you attend church regularly, yet you do not have a deep understanding of what it means to be a child of God. Or perhaps you attended a Christian school, where going to church was a daily routine or a formality. Regardless, be rest assured that you can always find your way to God because He is right where you are.

The Bible says in **Psalm 145:18**, "The Lord is near to all who call on Him, to all who call on Him in truth." Draw close to God, and He will draw close to you. Maybe, you are pretending to be happy and to be living your best life, but deep within your soul, you may be hurting. True happiness is found only in Christ. Listen to your soul, and you can hear it yearning for a deep sense of satisfaction that can only be found in Jesus Christ. Respond to your soul's cry, for salvation through Christ has come and is near you. Open your heart and allow all that you've read in the pages of this book about God, His holiness, kingdom, will, forgiveness, provision, protection, and His glory minister to you. The Holy Spirit will direct you to salvation.

Unbelievers and repentance. Acts 3:19 says, "Repent and turn to God so that your sins may be wiped out, or converted, so that your sins may be blotted out." If you are an unbeliever, then it is time to confess your sins, accept Jesus into your heart, and be born again. After you have declared your faith in Christ, have repented, and have received your water baptism, the Holy Spirit will start His training in you, you can believe that your sins are cleansed, and that you are no longer under the control of sin, your soul is delivered from hell, and you have been set free. After all these, you will become a child of God and part of His family.

If you are a non-believer, I pray that this book will help you come to the full knowledge of the gift of salvation through Jesus, your understanding of the Lord be broadened, and your faith in Him be deepened as you build a relationship with Him and become part of His Heavenly Kingdom. At the end of this chapter, you will have the opportunity to accept Jesus into your heart. Make Him your Lord and Savior and pray the prayer of salvation to surrender your life to Jesus. I assure you that Jesus will come into your heart, and His Holy Spirit will dwell within you. He will make your heart His home; He will teach you many things, and I assure you, your life will never be the same.

Here are some verses to help you with why your soul needs to be delivered.

Romans 6:23 "*For the wages of sin is death, but the free gift of God is eternal life in Christ Jesus our Lord. We are* assured of eternal life, but those do not believe will die both physically and eternally. Wages of sin means that the punishment for sin is what one has earned and deserves."

John 3:16-17 "For God so loved the world, that he gave his only Son, that whoever believes in him should not perish but have eternal life. For God did not send his Son into the world to condemn the world, but in order that the world might be saved through him."

Philippians 2:12–13 "Therefore, my beloved, as you have always obeyed, so now, not only as in my presence but much more in my absence, work out your own salvation with fear and trembling, for it is God who works in you, both to will and to work for his good pleasur*e.*"

Mark 10:45 "For even the Son of Man came not to be served but to serve, and to give his life as a ransom for many."

Luke 19:10 "For the Son of Man came to seek and to save the lost."

John 10:9-10 "I am the door. If anyone enters by me, he will be saved and will go in and out and find pasture. The thief comes only to steal and kill and destroy. I came that they may have life and have it abundantly."

Romans 5:10 "For if while we were enemies we were reconciled to God by the death of his Son, much more, now that we are reconciled, shall we be saved by his life."

Now, pray this prayer and allow the Lord Jesus to come into your heart and rule your life with His holiness.

Prayer of Confession: Dear Lord Jesus, I ask You today to come into my heart and forgive me of all my sins. Wash and cleanse me. I make You my Lord and my Savior. I surrender to You my life and my will from this day forward. Please, forgive all the evil things I have committed against You, anyone else, and myself. Father, cleanse me from any evil doings that may have brought a curse upon my life. Cleanse me from any generational curse. Dear Lord, make me a new person from today. Let me be a new creation. Let the old me be gone and let everything become new so I can have a good relationship with You. **Read 2 Corinthians 5:17.** Help me to love You, love myself, and others. Father, let Your Holy Spirit teach me Your ways and help me know more about You—Your Holy Name, Your Holy Kingdom, and Your Perfect Will for my life in the world I live in, so I can work for Your Kingdom and bring about a change in my home, community, churches, and everywhere.

Father, help me to forgive others and myself as You have forgiven me. Help me to rely on You, as my great provider, for all my needs. Protect me from all evil and temptation, so I can live a righteous life. Lord, plant in me the fruits of the Spirit to show love and kindness to all so that my family members who do not know You will come to know You through my actions and words. Lord, give me the spiritual gifts to work toward building Your Kingdom and tear down the kingdom of darkness. In Your precious name, Jesus, I give You thanks, I praise You and honor Your Holy Name, now and forever. May Your gift of salvation to me today be also for all that needs it! In Jesus Christ's Name, I Pray with thanksgiving. Amen!

Chapter 18 – A New Believer's Salvation Journey

Salvation journey is beautiful! But it can also be tough sometimes.

The following is what you must know as a new believer. You have now overcome the devil and on your way to eternity through Christ Jesus. However, there are more lessons to learn on this new journey. You will now be hated by the devil because you are no longer part of him, but a child of God. For this reason, he will do anything to distract you from being attentive to God. For that matter, you must always stay close to God; this can only be done through prayer and the Word of God through faith. With these, a new believer, like you, would be guided by the Holy Spirit.

Allow me to compare the standards of a new convert's journey to that of a school system. The school system has set up three basic levels of education: primary, secondary, and tertiary. It is set up in a way that is well structured. After completing kindergarten, a child will go on to the first grade. The truth is, going from no formal education to kindergarten could be a shock to a child. For that reason, it is essential to enable the child to become accustomed to the school system and be prepared. In every way, the skills they receive in their early school year, will help build their thinking skills and enhance their problem-solving skills to give them confidence. Children need all the preparations to reach their full potential. Whether it is preschool, pre-kindergarten, or transitional kindergarten, they will undeniably gain immense skill sets for years to come throughout their education.

As you can see, quite a bit goes into school preparations. Since every child learns and develops at one's own pace, parents need to strongly consider the emotional, physical, and educational needs of their children to determine the best option for them. Regardless of what parents decide, there are options for children to learn and grow in the classroom. If the environment is safe and the children feel comfortable, they will have excellent building blocks to attain their full potential and flourish. It is from here that they can climb the academic ladder to the highest level.

Now, let us analyze a road map for new believers. In the preceding paragraphs, the various levels of education have been explained. The same applies to the Christian journey. New converts also need a road map or a set of guidelines to help them find their way to spiritual growth. I am sure everyone comes to Christ desiring to be firmly rooted in Him. Nevertheless, Christianity can sometimes be tough. So, new believers need a firm foundation based on Biblical principles to help them become firmly rooted. In **Matthew 13:1–23**, Jesus tells a parable about seeds scattered on a roadside, rocks, and good soil. The ones that fell on good soil were able to overcome all obstacles and grow.

The church has a responsibility. It is the church's responsibility to help a new believer/new convert grow spiritually. There must be good Bible Study and prayer guide structures. There should also be a group who can do follow-ups. Sometimes, the Christian structure can be complex. I am sure you will agree with me if you know about how the Christian system is structured. You will need time to understand how Christianity works. Many distractions can easily pull a new believer here and there, but whether old or new, a believer's strongest weapons are the Bible, fasting, and prayer. The attacks and the temptations hurled against new believers are immense because the devil hates to see anyone escaping his influence. Therefore, it is never easy when a person first becomes or decides to be a believer. Yes, one that has started attending church may think that it is just a church, but there can be more to it. To prevent a new believer to become confused in the church's system of operation, they must be properly guided.

It is the work of the Holy Spirit to draw new converts to God. However, the church can also set up a system to provide support and comfort. Like strangers in a foreign land, new believers in Christ need to be guided and taught the ways of God. Without guidance and instruction, they will most likely backslide. They need to know about the *Word of God* and prayer. They must know about meditation and waiting upon the Lord. They need in-depth knowledge about salvation, faith, holiness, and everything regarding salvation, which includes the Holy Trinity—God the Father – the Son – and the Holy Spirit. They must know about the Kingdom of God, and *His Will*, among others.

Like a seed planted in good soil, every new believer will have the opportunity to grow if they are planted in good soil. Because there are many distractions, new converts will need to be mentally capable of handling things they hear or see. They need to be physically prepared to fellowship with other believers. They need emotional stability and spiritual balance. Christian walk can be a challenging, new converts need help navigating through the Christian life. They need spiritual development, coupled with emotional intelligence to help them understand Christianity. They need to be taught the true nature of God (His Character and Personality), which include His Love, Grace, Kindness, Compassion, Forgiveness, and most importantly, *His Will.*

As Jesus said in *His Prayer,* it will be helpful for new converts to know that they are now part of God's Family on earth. They must have the understanding that upon accepting Christ, they have become children of God. There must be a conscious effort to build a relationship with God. They must know about God's Holiness and how He expects us to be holy. Therefore, if you are a believer who needs to renew your vow, then do so now.

If a new believer is guided, they will know the importance of Bible study, prayers, and fasting. So, they must be well informed about the doctrines and the principles of Christianity to help them fit in well. They must know about God's Fatherly Love right from the beginning, His Protection and Forgiveness. They must be willing to completely let go of their past and live according to the rules of God's Kingdom and *His Will*. They must be ready to pray daily, just like we all do because prayers and the word of God are the main key to becoming a strong believer. Both new and old, we all need to know the importance of prayer because prayer draws us closer to God.

This is so because when we read from **Isaiah 40:31**, we are told, "They that wait upon the Lord shall renew their strength; they shall mount up with wings like eagles; they shall run and not be weary, walk and will not faint." Only prayer and the *Word of God* can strengthen us all. So, as a new believer, you must have the desire to pray; if you do, the Holy Spirit will empower and equip you. He will form a formidable wall around you to ensure your protection and growth and anointing.

Without prayer and the *Word of God*, your new life in Christ will never become well organized. So, as a new believer, you must be organized by tapping into the church's setup systems for your connectedness and growth. Why? This is because **we are all like batteries in the Lord: without charging, we will surely die**; **just like flashlights, without good batteries we cannot function**. **We are like cars, without gas; we cannot move**. Imperatively, we all need prayer and the Word. Whether new or old, we all need a recharge to keep us growing stronger in our Christian journey.

When we are ready to pray, we need a place to be alone with God. In **Matthew 6:6,** "Jesus says *you must go to your room, shut the door, and pray to your Father in secret, and He will hear and reward you*." There should be no distractions. It must be a place of quietness. Wherever we may be, it must be a serenity of the mind and heart – peace within our souls. No matter where we are, the heart, mind, and spirit must be involved. **Mark 1:35** tells us that Jesus usually went to isolated places to pray. Thus, wherever we may be, in the farm, in the kitchen, bedroom, bathroom, on a walk, in school, at work, in the store, driving, on a plane, or whatever we may be doing, we must keep in mind that we are spending time in prayer. That is what **1 Thessalonians 5:17,** telling us about praying continually means. This means there must be no distractions in our minds, and our hearts must be opened for the Lord.

Prayer is always needed in all circumstances. Morning prayer is particularly important because a good start of the day begins with prayer. Once we commit our activities into God's hands, we are good to go! Throughout the day, we are likely to face circumstances that are tempting and require the grace of God to overcome them. However, Prayer and the Word ahead of the day will give us a good balance. It will keep our desires and focuses on God. You will need the goodness and mercy of the Lord to be guided because you do not wrestle against flesh and blood throughout the day, but against principalities and powers. Nevertheless, the Lord will smooth your ways if you pray. Of course, you may still face challenges even if you pray, but God will grant you the grace and wisdom to persevere. As you begin your day with prayer and acknowledgment of the Lord, surrender, give thanks, and commit to Him. He will ensure your protection.

Prayer: Pray this simple daily prayer. Father God, I thank You for Your saving grace. My life is in Your hand. Please, answer me when I call. Help me to carry Your Word everywhere I go. Give me strength when I need, and grace to take me to the next level. Take the thrones of my hearts and reign over my hearts and emotions. Lord, please control my minds and teach me Your way and guide me and my family to the truth. I pray the blood of Jesus continually washes me and my family each day. Let Your protection be as a wall of fire around us always. Lord, let our every step of faith be guided by You. And may Your grace, peace, and love be upon us all in Jesus' Mighty Name. Amen

Chapter 19 – Coming Before the Throne of God

Enter into His gates with thanksgiving... (Psalm 100:4)

How do you prepare to come into the presence of the Lord? When we come before God in prayer or worship, the Bible does not tell us to adopt a particular position during prayer. It only recommends some positions. But there is one specific thing that is required, and it is recorded in **1John 3:21**. Do you know? **It is about your heart.**

In *the Lord's Prayer*, there is no mention of how we should position ourselves in prayer, but as we know, human beings communicate verbally and non-verbally, and postures demonstrate expressions of the heart. Therefore, we can read people's postures and tell if they are being courteous. Although there is no requirement to be in a certain position in prayer, we can position ourselves in ways that honor God. In our various churches and homes, we can choose a position that is fit for the King of all kings – the Almighty God. We can sit, stretch out our hands, lift them, lie down flat, bow, kneel, face down, before the Lord. All these are good, but the most important thing is to be able to connect to the Lord with our hearts. If our hearts do not condemn us, we have confidence to come before God. Jesus said in **Matthew 4:24,** "*God is spirit, and His worshipers must worship Him in spirit and truth.*" It is always imperative to involve the body, the soul, and the spirit. Whether praising, giving thanks, or making a request, our whole being must be involved.

Let's check some recommended postures for prayer found in the Bible.

Kneeling – Psalm 95:6 "O come, let us worship and bow down; let us kneel...."

Outstretched hands – 1 Kings 8:22–23 "Solomon spread out his hands toward Heaven."

Walking – 2 Kings 4:35 records Elisha walking back and forth.

Lying prostrate before God – Genesis 17:3 tells us that Abraham fell on his face, and God spoke with him. No position symbolizes humility better than being on our faces before the Lord God. It is a recognition of the need for God's Mercy.

Lifted hands – Psalm 63:4 "...I will lift my hands."

Standing – Nehemiah 9:5 tells us that the Levites told the people to stand up and bless the Lord!

Looking up or lifted eyes toward Heaven – Luke 9:16 tells us about when Jesus blessed the five loaves and two fish before breaking them for the multitudes.

Bowing – Exodus 34:8; Psalm 72:11– Bowing signifies honor and gratitude to God. It is also an expression of worship. We pledge our complete loyalty to God when we bow to His Majesty. In **Exodus 34:8**, Moses bowed down to the ground and worshipped the Lord.

Sitting – Judges 20:26 and 1 Chronicles 17:16 both indicate that this position signifies giving and receiving mercy.

Lying prostrate – Revelation 1:17 shows us that this position demonstrates a recognition of unworthiness on our part.

Genesis 17:3, 17:17 records Abraham falling face down before God. Lifted voices – Along with lifted hands and lifted eyes, the Bible also encourages us to lift our voices to the Lord in prayer. "Give ear to my voice when I call to You," David prayed in **Psalm 141:1**. "My voice rises to God, and He will hear me" (**Psalm 77:1**).

Crying out – In **1 Samuel 30:4**, David and his men wept aloud until they had no strength. King David cried out many times before the Lord. Sometimes, people do not want to see you crying. But weeping before the Lord is okay. He understands. It is okay to pray silently for the person if you want to bear with him or her. But it is better to not interrupt. You will quench their spirit if you do. Do not tap and do not try to rub their backs. Let them weep until they are done. Just pray silently on their behalf if you are concerned. Everyone has a special way of communicating with the Lord in prayer.

I have heard someone saying that do not want their members to come before the altar and flood it with tears because it is against God. No, God is not against the cries of His children. He cries when we cry. He feels our pains and wants to help us because He cares. It can be dangerous to stop people from crying in prayer. An example of the danger of interference is found in **2 Samuel 6:7**. When Uzzah tried to reach out to offer help by straightening the *Ark of the Covenant*, he was struck down. So, please, let's not interrupt people when they are praying in the spirit. In **John 11:35** and **Hebrews 5:7**, we are told that Jesus wept. Listen to what David said in **Psalm 55:17**, "Evening, and morning, and at noon, will I pray, and cry aloud: and He shall hear my voice." It did not matter the day and time, David prayed, cried aloud, and offered his supplications with loud cries and tears.

Silence – Habakkuk 2:20 "The LORD is in His Holy temple; let all the earth be silent before Him." This is when we are in complete silence before the Lord; it is usually during meditation or worship. In silence, we can hear God's voice when He speaks.

Praise and Worship: When it is time for worship, we give thanks, praise, and adore Him. Here are some powerful blessings. The Lord is in His *Holy Temple*, let the whole earth be silent before Him. O Lord, You sit majestically in Your Holy place, surrounded by Your Holy angels who sing: "Holy, Holy, Holy is the Lord God Almighty!" You are our Lord and Savior, and we offer to You our sacrifices of praise. Lord, it is only You who deserve to be praised! Your Kingdom is everlasting, and Your dominion endures throughout all generations. We give glory and honor to You. *You have established Your Throne. We shall speak of the glory of Your Kingdom, Your power, Your wonderful acts, and we shall talk of Your Power and Might. We will make known Your glory and the majesty of Your Kingdom.* You are our Savior, our Redeemer, and King. We worship You as the King of all. We bless and magnify Your Holy Name. For Your Name is great!

Lord, the works of Your Hands are mighty, and Your Greatness is unsearchable. One generation shall say of Your Works to another, we shall meditate on Your Wonderful Works and talk about Your Mighty Deeds. You are the Lord who is enthroned as the righteous judge. We declare Your Greatness and Your Wonderful Love to all. Oh, Most High Lord, You are great and awesome, and we praise Your Holy Name. Great God, You uphold all who fall and raise all those who are bowed down. You open Your Hand and satisfy the desire of every living thing, those who fear You. You are righteous in all Your Ways, and You are gracious in all You do. Year our cries, preserve, and save all those who love You. Let all that has breath bless Your Holy Name forever, **Amen!**

Chapter 20 – How the Lord's Prayer Connects to Our World Today

Involve yourself in the Kingdom's Work today. We live in a broken world. All around us, we see dejection, and pain. And for that matter, we ought to pray. **Ephesians 6:10–12** "...Be strong in the Lord and in His mighty power. Put on the full armor of God... For our struggle is not against flesh and blood...." **Psalm 122:6** – Pray for the peace of Jerusalem. Pray for the world.

Both John the Baptist and Jesus Christ began their ministries focusing on the Kingdom of Heaven. This shows the importance of the Kingdom's Work—**Matthew 3; 4;** and **5**. So, involve yourself in the Kingdom's Work and make a difference today! If you want to get involved, you can contact us, check our website, or find a support group at your local church.

Before you continue, please take some few minutes to answer these questions: What do you know about God? Do you know about His Love? Do you have a personal relationship with our Father in Heaven? Do you know about God's Holiness? Are you living a Holy life? How? What about His Kingdom, *His Will*, and His Purpose for you? How do you explain God's Kingdom? (with money, power, fame, or *His Will*) Do you know God's gift of forgiveness? How does He teach you to forgive someone? How do you resist temptation and evil that comes your way? Do you know how? Do you know the importance of thanksgiving, praise, and worship to the Lord? How do you know these things?

Your answer to the above questions will determine your need for a Savior, Jesus Christ, or your appreciation of the Father. Confess your sins and accept Jesus as your Lord if you don't have answers or if your answers were mostly unfavorable. You can change your lifestyle to reflect God's plan for your life if you are a Christian and not living by His standard. But if you were able to answer these questions mostly in an agreeing manner, that's great! If you want the Lord to use you, then follow these steps just as I did. I hope that you will not take these as repetitions but as ways to remind you of how important the Lord's Prayer is and the need to use it daily.

The Holy Spirit has unfolded the secret within the Prayer of the Lord and how it connects to the world today. We have gotten to know about the Father, His Kingdom, *His Will*, His Holiness, His thanksgiving, praises, power and glory, forgiveness, temptations and trials, and our needs. In these, we see how we must live our lives and interact with one another and pray. I have also explained why there is so much evil in this world, and what we must do to bring God's Kingdom down. You have read everything you need to know to get you ready to pray and intercede. However, it is not over yet because the rest of the information you are about to read will add more views about the time in which we live in today to get you prepared. We are commissioned as it is written in **Matthew 28:19.** This means we must do the Will of God. Jesus knew the power of prayer, so, He has given us unrestricted access to prayer.

All praise and glory to His Mighty Name. He has made it possible! Let what you have read from this book connects you to prayer. Let it deepen your love and faith as it has filled my heart with the zeal for prayer. Know the importance of prayer, God's Kingdom, and salvation and prepare your heart for intersessions. Pray for yourself, others, and for the world. It is my prayer that everyone shall have the same zeal. It is the main reason for this book. We can pray on our own, and we can also pray as the Lord commands. We can pray on our own but can also join prayer groups to pray for ourselves and to intercede for the church and for people to turn to God. You are going to see more of this urgency and why there is a need to pray with the Lord's Prayer. This part of the book provides a step-by-step guide to help us.

The secrets in this book about the Lord's Prayer and Our World Today have never been explained to this extent. From all that has been stated, you have now seen in detailed of the Lord's Prayer and its connection to us and our world today. The Prayer of the Lord has everything needed to help you love the Lord, love yourself, love others, and pray for His Kingdom to come. I am certain this will help you have the desire to pray and intercede for the world. So, take a closer look because the few things we are about to unveil will prepare your mind as to what this little and short prayer of the Lord can do.

The troublesome world of today: I don't have to tell you of the world in which we live. I am sure you already know. Not long ago, I heard some stories that made me cry for the world. Here are few of them. There was a man who had a wife. The wife and the housekeeper were lesbians; the man was aware of it but pretended not to know. He set up a camera in the room so he could record their secrets and sell it to the entertainment industry for money. One day the housekeeper offended the wife. From then on, they became enemies in secret, and each planned to kill the other. While the man was busy making money out of them, the girls were planning on killing one another. The wife said she would kill both the man and the housekeeper so that the estate and business would become hers. The housekeeper said she would kill the wife, so she could marry the man. Here is the question: did the man record the girls' intentions but didn't care? Don't be surprised. This is how the devil uses humans.

Here is another story: An abusive man kidnapped his children from their mother and ran away with the kids, leaving the mother helpless. Though the judges were aware of the abuse, they still gave the kids to the father. In another story, a woman was walking at the park one evening when she was attacked and beaten to death. Another tragedy occurred during a church service, when a man just walked in and started shooting everyone. At a school, students were in class when a gunman opened fire, killing as many kids as he could. Yet another disaster involved a young girl at the park with her two children, when one was kidnapped. Moreover, 2 neighbors went out on their appointments. When they returned, their homes had been raided. In another story, a teacher went to use the bathroom before going home. What she did not know was that a 14-year-old boy was preying on her. While in the bathroom, he came inside, stubbed her to death, put her in a trash can, and buried her right behind the school. In another case, a pregnant girl decided not to keep the baby any longer; therefore, she made appointment, went into a clinic and terminated the pregnancy. She left home with a baby inside her, but she returned with an empty stomach. In another incident, children left to school and never return home because someone came to school with a gun with the intention to murder all the children in a class. One day, while pregnant women and families were living in peace, the Russians invaded their country and destroyed the innocence of Ukraine. We live in a strange world, don't we? The troubles of this world will go on and on if I continue, because they are endless. Here are some questions to consider: Why do people hate each other? Why do people kill the innocent, rob, and rape? Why are many families being broken? All this evil in our world is not what God had intended for humanity.

Evil exists in our *world* because humanity continues to rebel against God. We have lost sight of the true importance of our existence; we have chosen our own ways, and that has corrupted us. I am sure you would agree with me that something is not right in our world. but who is to fix it? Some even delight in serving Satan than serving God Almighty. But the question is this: what can Satan offer those that serve him? Can people make it on their own without Christ? No! Thankfully, the Lord has saved and delivered us from the same evil practices and has prepared us to stand in the gap with the good news. In **1 Peter 2:9,** we are told, "But you are a chosen generation, a royal priesthood, a holy nation, a people called to proclaim the goodness of Him who called you out of darkness into His marvelous light." We are called to proclaim the goodness of God, but praying for ourselves, for others, and applying the Word of God must be our focus, so we won't be used by the evil one in any way. If we place our lives in the hand of Jesus, pray seriously according to the Will of the Father, and put the Kingdom's Work above all, our lives, as well as many lives will be transformed.

The World must know the Father in Heaven. God is an All-loving God. He is kind and full of compassion. He is the One who we can always trust and call on at any time. This means that everyone must hear the gospel. What is sad about salvation for others is that instead of them looking to God, they have chosen to look to other gods, people, and things. Today, many are still in doubt about this specific Father whose Name is Jehovah. They would rather believe in many gods than God the Father. Some are confused about who they should choose to serve. This means they don't know what to believe. According to Wikipedia, the world's population today is about 7.9 billion. But out of this, only 31.11% (or approximately 2.4 billion people) are Christians. So, where are the rest? What do they believe? What kind of a god are they serving? Are they serving idols, practicing witchcrafts, the world and its fame, beauty, money? Even among those who say they are believers; I am sure not all can be counted as true believers. Just as Jesus said in **Matthew 7:21–23**, "Not everyone who says Lord, Lord will enter the Kingdom of Heaven...." The question then is this: for what are they waiting?

In **Matthew 24,** Jesus told us of the many signs of the end times. When the disciples asked Him about what they should look for before the end comes, He gave them many signs to watch for so they would not be deceived, and those signs are also for us. Today, things that are happening are clearly warnings, but still, people are not thinking about eternity. There are many people whose mindset is completely different from what is ahead of humanity. For believers, everything tells us that now is the preparation period. In college, I did my internship at the senior center. One day, I had the chance to speak with one of the seniors about salvation: a 70-year-old lady, who thought she could still have fun, and I will never forget her response to salvation. She said, "I want to wait till when I am 80 to think of going to church so I can go to Heaven." First, attending church is not a way to Heaven. According to the senior, there is no need to serve God while we are young and beautiful because it is a waste. She wanted to be very old and feeble, possibly in a wheelchair, then she would think about the afterlife and going to church. This mentality has caused many young people to want to have nothing to do with God. They think their beauty is for the world because God does not deserve anything beautiful.

In **Ecclesiastes 12:1**, Solomon gives critical guidance for the worldview he assumes was the truth about life by saying, "Remember your Creator in the days of your youth before the days of your trouble comes." When are the days of your trouble? They are when you find no pleasure in doing things. In this case, why are people waiting until they are too old? Seek God today. Life is about remembering your Creator and serving Him now with your youth, beauty, fame, money, strength, and knowledge. Salvation is about getting to know the One True God and His Kingdom, and why He brought you here. What can you do for the Kingdom of Heaven when you are old and feeble? Not much or maybe nothing! Yes, God is merciful. The 70-year-old woman can be saved at any age, but her mentality for serving God was wrong.

Right now, we have no more time to waste. Any little amount of time we get, we are to talk about the Savior and brag about Him and His Salvation to the world. We must campaign and broadcast salvation. We must tell the world that Jesus is the Way, the Truth, and Life, and the Light of this world. God's Word tells us that without Christ, we walk in total darkness. Many are still wandering. They are confused and being deceived about who to serve. They are lost; they need someone to show them where to go. Some have bangles on their waist as their gods to show them the way; some have a chain on their neck, wrist, or ankle; some have a sign on their forehead, nose, or cheeks; some have theirs in a form of a tattoo. To some, their gods are mountains or hills, trees, animals. Some are deeply into witchcraft, and they cannot get out. Some will travel far away in search of God, whereas He is already near to them. To some, it is making money: they would do anything even if they must sell their body and souls to get rich overnight. Some even prefer to get rich and die young. As far as riches are concerned, to some it doesn't matter what they indulge themselves in to become rich. Is there anything we can do to help such people find the way to the Truth? What are people's conceptions for attending church? What things do people talk about the most? What matters the most to them? Is God and salvation their priority? Is it wealth, happiness, fame, relationships, or the love of God? This is the time for people to come to the true knowledge of God.

As far as I know, a house without a father is like a man without a head, and a man without a head is a dead man. The world without a savior has no life. The Lord says, "When you pray, say, 'Our Father.'" This speaks volumes. It tells us that the world needs a Father (God). Think of it this way: what happens when a father is not involved in a child's life? According to the US Census Bureau (2022), the absence of a father figure at home affects children. They are at higher risk for many childhood issues such as emotional and behavioral problems, neglect, abuse, obesity, poor school performance and dropping out. Others include teen pregnancy, incarceration as juveniles, alcohol and substance abuse, criminal activity, and suicide. They are more likely to: get in trouble at school or with the law, get put into prison, have behavioral problems, use drugs and alcohol. This is what happens without God in a person's life. Just like a house without a father suffers, so is a world of souls without God. But it is why the enemy is doing anything possible to break up families or pollute people's mind of the existence of God.

A father's absence is not ideal. Because children grow up to become parents, it becomes a problem if this cycle repeats itself. There are many homes without God as the head of the family, and there are many lives without the reign of God and His Kingdom. Many people are still trying to find the truth from different sources. They are confused and misled, and they don't know what to do. Even if there are many good fathers, none of them can take the place of God the Father. So, people must make changes to their current situation. They must turn their lives over to God. He is the God of the universe, the Great Father. He is the One that every family, school, government, king, queen, president, police officer, military man/woman, judge, lawyer, priest, and everything that has breath needs. He is unavoidable!

If we agree to US Census Bureau, then we can see there is much evil in our world today than ever. Some of these evils include: violence, war, murder, rape, kidnapping, sexual immorality, anger, gossip, hatred, infant mortality, abortion, gun proliferation and weapons of mass destruction, criminal activity, incarceration (including that of juveniles), racism, robbery, high teen pregnancy rates, and all kinds of abuse (e.g., domestic, neglect, alcohol and substance), poor school performance and dropping out of school, depression, suicidal thoughts, and suicide, rejection, greed, lack of contentment, jealousy, envy, and emotional and behavioral problems, and on and on it goes. These show that the world we live in has too many problems that are beyond humans' capability, all because God has been left behind. We have neglected the Father and His laws. If you are in doubt about this, sit down for a moment and ponder what you just read. We as humans must come back to God, revere His Holy Name, and make His Kingdom and *His Will* our priority.

Christ is our hope. Nothing will be perfect in our lives without Him. There will be no peace in our individual lives, homes, school, neighborhoods, communities, hospitals, and government. We need the mercy of God to intervene because leaving God behind is worse than a home without a father figure. Therefore, we can never leave God behind and think we can make it; we simply can't survive without Him. He is our only hope because He created us to depend on Him and need Him. John 3:16 says, "For God so loved the world...." God is a loving Father whose love is incomparable. He is One True God.

Our dear Dr. Charles Stanley once said, "Idolatry takes place in our life when a thing, person, or practice is more important than the relationship we have with the Lord Jesus Christ." When we are more dedicated, devoted, or committed to a person, a thing, or practice, then we are committing idolatry, which also means we have gone against God. So, let's ask the Holy Spirit to help us remain loyal and be equipped so we can spread the good news to all who are still confused about God, so they too will come to know the truth or have a good understanding of salvation.

People must know the Holy Name of God in their own lives. With a better understanding of the Holy Name of God, they will be saved because there is salvation in that Name Jesus. It is through His Name that we all can be saved. The simple truth is that our names can never save, only the Holy Name of Jesus Christ can save us. Until people learn what salvation and God's Holiness is about, they cannot think of living a holy life. We worry about different types of pollution that are destroying our planet, but what we never stop to think about is how we are polluting our souls. Thus, we must know the evil that pollutes the human heart and ask the Lord to save the world from evil doings. Just as we worry about physical pollution, we must not ignore spiritual pollution.

During Covid 19, we used many prevention strategies such as practicing washing of hands, consistently wearing mask, improving ventilation, and keeping our distances. These were because we wanted to avoid the virus. Let's do the same the Biblical way to protect ourselves from getting ourselves attached to sin. So, let's fight against sinful behaviors just as we fight physical elements that pollute the body. This will happen when Jesus reigns in human hearts. Jesus wants the humans' heart that is why He taught us about the Holiness of the Father. The basic element of theLord's Prayer is so, we can get rid of the effects of sin. This means we must pray "Hallowed be Thy name" and ask the Father to help us all overcome evil by depending on Jesus Christ. God's Name is Holy regardless. He comes to help people so they can overcome sin and live according to *His Will*. The world must know this simple truth because God loves us all! Our holiness is nothing compared to God. Nevertheless, His love for the world will do anything on humans' behalf and helps people to overcome sin, because our righteousness comes from Him. He will cleanse us from all evil, so we will choose holiness over evil.

The Kingdom of God must come to people. You cannot choose your own kingdom and survive. God and His righteous Kingdom is what you need. If people believe in earthly monarchies, then they must believe that there is a King who rules over all kingdoms, and that king wants to rule in the heart. If we believe in worldly kingdoms, then we cannot ignore God's Kingdom. Read Daniel 3 to see what happened to king Nebuchadnezzar. God's Kingdom must come to put an end to evil. The evil in the world will have no control over humans if we are praying for people and living our lives according to God's Kingdom and *His Will*. So, we need the Kingdom of God to rule.

Today many things are happening and causing our attention to be driven away from the Kingdom's Practices. May the Lord help us! Many are still behind the barn because they have chosen to live their way. They are carrying heavy loads and are struggling with all kinds of issues that are weighing them down and yet are refusing the One who has power to lighten their burdens. God has promised to give rest to all who come to Him. However, it is sad that many still dwell on alcohol, drugs, pornography, and other sinful things for relief. Some are deeply involved in sorcery. Some worship creation instead of worshipping the Creator. Others believe in other people such as rich and powerful people, kings, presidents, or themselves. Some are filled with hatred, lies, greediness, idols, and other things. Some are full of rage. Some are involved in human trafficking or robbery. Others are into witchcraft. Some are involved in all kinds of sexual practices and all kinds of addictions. Though, many of these people want to get out, they don't know how. They are trapped. Why? This is because there is no human who can set him/herself free. We all need the One True God. He only has power, but we all must cry out to Him.

The kingdom of this world never makes people content or satisfied. We cannot fix our eyes on something to survive. For example, we will become disappointed if we fix our eyes on our government and its power. Only God the Heavenly Father has the ultimate power to set humans free. In the USA, the president has about 2 million staff members. Besides managing this staff, he also must manage his own life, family, and almost everything that goes on in the nation and around the world. Unfortunately, even some companies who find it hard to manage their 10 or fewer employees take delight in insulting presidents. In my opinion, it will be better to offer our prayer support if we have nothing to give to presidents, and encouragement rather than insults or discouragement. Their task is heavy, but if we pray for them, God will lead and guide them. They need helpers and not opponents. A president is a mere human being just like the rest of us. They can be filled with evil, make many mistakes, and take the law into their own hands just as we all do when we disobey God. That is why they make many promises but can fulfill only a few. For this reason, the world cannot depend on human leaders for survival. Our responsibility is to pray so that they too will get to know God and depend on His leadership.

We all make mistakes; no one is perfect. For this reason, we need to pray and ask God in every election. So that God will appoint the right person at a particular time and keep praying while they are in power. We need those that God chooses for the time, as it is written in **Romans 13:1–2**. That is not to say they will do everything right, but it means God will have put them there for a reason: maybe to bless if we rely on God, or to punish if we fail to rely on God and pray. Thus, in every way, we need God. We need His Kingdom of love, patience, and power to rule in our midst because we are powerless without Him. He is all-powerful. So, we must rely on Him, and have Him handle all our problems, if we don't want to become disappointed. Our survival is only guaranteed according to God's rules.

The Kingdom of God brings contentment. Humans are never satisfied because our wants are unlimited, but in Christ, we crave nothing of the world. So, let's become kingdom minded, because we can't focus our attention, interest, and passion on perishable things for contentment. We will become disappointed and heartbroken if we put our hope in man or things other than God. In Him, we become satisfied and content. Discontentment causes people to lose their peace of mind. They become depressed, worried, and troubled because of dissatisfaction. The truth is, craving anything more than God and His Kingdom will bring nothing but unhappiness. So, we must depend on God. Therefore, our prayers must be for God's Kingdom to be established on earth to drive out wickedness. Praying these will help save the world. We are here temporarily. Thus, we must have a Heaven mindset.

How can *God's Will* Be Done on Earth as It Is Done in Heaven. We can only live a holy life when we get to know and understand God and His Plans for the earth. In this case, people must give their will to God so they can live their lives on earth according to the plans God has for their lives. Without *God's Will*, none of us will live for Him. That means we will never live to fulfil our purpose here on earth (Jeremiah 29:11). So, allow me to ask you these questions: are you living for God? Are you in *His Will*? Do you know anyone who needs to know *God's Will*? God's Kingdom will bring *His Will* into place in you. This is important because it is in *His Will* that we can find our purpose in life. The questions we must ask ourselves and others are these:

- How can *God's Will* be known to all people?
- How can *God's Will* be done on earth as it is done in Heaven?
- Why is *God's Will* important?

Salvation is *God's Will* for Humanity. In God, salvation is at the top of the list. Jesus' mission on earth was about salvation. He came to reconcile us back to our Father in Heaven. He reveals the Father and makes it clear that we are not just ordinary, but God's Children who have been allowed to build a relationship with Him through salvation. We don't have to be confused about who we are if we understand the Prayer of the Lord. We are children of God because His Prayer shows us our identity; we don't have to question our salvation and our identity because it is already perfected in Christ Jesus. We don't have to be afraid anymore because the love of God in Christ cast out fear. We don't have to think God is far from us because He is closer than we can ever imagine. We are no more in spiritual bondage; our past sins are forgiven. We don't have to worry about tomorrow, nor do we have to be afraid of the future, for God, our Heavenly Father, holds the future in His hands. We must be happy and content because we already have the victory.

We are accepted and loved with an everlasting love. We are set free and are seated in Heavenly places with Jesus. Our righteousness is in Christ Jesus, and we are filled with the Holy Spirit and His power to do greater works. This means we are authorized to win souls, pray for the sick, and do greater things for the Kingdom of Heaven. We as heavenly children can help people get to know who they are and find their identity in Christ. We are to help the lost find their way through the power of salvation in Christ. We are not to keep it to ourselves but share the gospel of Christ to all for salvation to take place. We must not be afraid of any strategy of the enemy, because the One in us is Greater and Mightier. This is our responsibility in this life, and prayer gives us the power to do it. In that case, we must pray to do the Kingdom's Work because many people can't find their way.

The world and our needs. Humans have physical, emotional, and spiritual needs. Psalm 20:7 says, "Some trust in chariots and some in horses, but we trust in the Name of the LORD our God." If every good thing come from God, we can depend on God and not on chariots and horses. Therefore, where people seek their needs are very important. In Ecclesiastes 1:2, King Solomon wrote, "Vanity of vanities, all things are vanity." Thus, we must be careful and not to dwell too much on worldly things. We can ask God for all our needs, but salvation is at the top. Today, some lives are cut short because they focus on different things instead of salvation. In Matthew 6:33, the Lord said, "Seek ye first the Kingdom and its righteousness, and all other things shall be added unto you" What are those things?

The World and Forgiveness. Evil comes in many forms. It can be unforgiveness, which is why the Lord said we must forgive. Unforgiveness is what we are witnessing in our world today. For example, I will do no harm to anyone if I forgive and let go of what was done to me. However, if I fail to do so, I will take matters into my own hands. Most people are out for retaliation except those who choose to forgive. This is because when unforgiveness become a spirit, it lives in a person and rules over that person. That is why many people refuse to forgive; they are being controlled by unforgiving spirit. They struggle within themselves, but they can't escape because the spirit of unforgiveness is living inside them and controlling them. In families, workplaces, the government, and almost every area of life, we see many troubles due to unforgiveness.

According to Jesus in **Matthew 6**, "God the Father will forgive you, if you forgive others." This means you must forgive to be forgiven. The world would not have become a miserable place to live if we have learned to forgive and let go. We live with ill intentions, such as revenge and grudges, and as a result, the fear of retaliation has gripped people. We judge and condemn; people have been shot, harmed, and even killed because they couldn't forgive. This has blocked people from seeing God's plans for their life; many Christians suffer because they fail to forgive. I was once a victim, but thankfully, I have been delivered. However, I also pray and ask God to help me overcome unforgiveness each day. To do this, I have learned to sacrifice my freewill to God.

Many occurrences over the years prove that our world needs healing. Evil has caused so much trouble of which unforgiveness seems to be the major issue. People who can't let go of the harm done to them are always looking for ways to take revenge. Therefore, forgiveness is substantially important because, without forgiveness, we become disqualified to use the Holy Name of God. Today, what the church must do, is to pray for the world as we pray for ourselves to be free from all unforgiveness. Let's ask for forgiveness, be forgiving and make peace with ourselves, with all families, and with everyone so that God will heal our land. Everyone needs forgiveness. Let's then pray for God to teach us the right way to forgive without holding anything against anyone. This will bring healing to the whole world.

Prayer: Lord, please help us make forgiveness our everyday affair and practice. Amen!

Temptation and Evil in the World. Today's world is filled with evil due to temptation. Sin is polluting the world because evil is everywhere. Believers and unbelievers alike are tempted in many ways. In some ways, we overcome, but in many ways, we fail. Sin entangles and enslaved humanity; even those that hate sin, are doing it and have no idea how to free themselves. This can be in a form of anything contrary to God's Word. How can humanity avoid temptations and be delivered from evil? The answer is this: we can never win over evil without God and His deliverance Power. We, as humans, can't because we have no power to save and deliver ourselves out of sin. Only God can. So, let's submit under God and His mighty hands. Each day, we must pray and ask God to lead us not into any temptation that will cause us to do evil. If you see nothing wrong, then think of why people have become money lovers and why innocent children are being kidnapped, raped, molested, abused, and murdered. Aren't we supposed to protect these little ones? Why are we the ones killing them through abortion, hatred, war, and other means? Why should little children suffer from sicknesses, diseases, and starvation due to our own evil ways?

Not only children, but many people have been killed due to hatred. Knowing the one behind the troubles of humanity will prepare your heart to ask for the mercy of God to rule. Let's do our part as children of God ask our Father to bring His Kingdom down on earth. Satan is the source of all evil. Before you blame people for anything, know who to blame for everything first, so you will know what you must do to help people come to their senses and not be trapped by Satan in his wickedness. We all have freewill to do whatever we please, but that freewill prevents people from doing right sometimes. This means allowing *God's Will* is the best solution. Our only victory over sin is when we surrender to God. May God help us to overcome sin.

We will pray seriously if we do understand what temptation and evil means. We usually talk only about trials, but we forget about temptations. Why Jesus prayed in such a way? While on earth, He too was tempted. Therefore, He is aware of temptation and what it means to be tempted. With temptation, the devil attracts to entice or seduce; and you will fall into his trap if you are not alert. Jesus wants to protect us from that, and it is only when we pray. If trials and temptations are inevitable and will come, then depend on Christ victory. What I know is that trials cannot be prayed against, but temptations can be prayed against. This is because trials are to help us grow, whereas temptation is to cause us to fall. How? Trials build our stamina and make us stand strong as it is written in 1 Peter 5:10, but temptations cause us to become weak. In temptation, Christ overpowered the devil with the Word. With His trial, He had to ask the Father by saying, "If it be Your Will, let this cup pass by me." Jesus was aware, otherwise, He wouldn't have said, "and when you pray say, lead us not into temptation."

Jesus was tempted in many ways. He was tempted by Satan and humans, but He overcame them all. Hebrews 2:18 says, for as He suffered being tempted, so He can help us overcome temptation. He can protect us against the evil one if we surrender our free will to Him. If we learn from Him about dealing with temptation, then we shall overcome. We must apply the Word just as He did to overcome.

Jesus said that we must ask. This means that if we pray, we will be protected. The Lord will not allow us to be tempted. If we are tempted, it shall not be beyond what we could bear. If we fall into it, He will make a way for us. As it is written in 1 Corinthians 10:13 "No temptation (trial) has overtaken you except what is common to mankind. And God is faithful; He will not let you be tried beyond what you can bear. But when you are tempted, He will also provide a way out so that you can endure it." In James 1:13-16, we are told, "When tempted, no one should say, God is tempting me. For God cannot be tempted by evil, nor does He tempt anyone; but each person is tempted when they are dragged away by their own evil desire and enticed. Then, after desire has conceived, it gives birth to sin; and sin, when it is full-grown, gives birth to death." Don't be confused with this Scripture.

Jesus was led into the wilderness to be tempted by Satan. This is because Satan wants to tempt humans all the time. That is why another name we use to describe him is the 'tempter.' The good news is, whether it be temptation or trial, God knows them all, and He has the power to help us through or prevent it. Remember when you are being tempted, do not say, "God is tempting me." It is not *God's Will* to tempt us, but rather lead us away from temptation; it is His job to deliver us from evil (the trap of the evil one).

Temptation means Satan is trying every means to seduce, lure or entice you. This means you have not yet committed the crime. The crime you commit is when you fail the test. God knows that as long as Satan is in our midst, he will test us because that is what he plans. He tempts us so we can sin against God. That is how we become polluted by evil. Temptation is a desire that entices us individually. If we fall into it, it will pull us away from God's presence because He is a Holy God who cannot look upon us because of the sin we committed until we repent. So, what is the simple truth? Pray daily and say, "LORD, lead me not, lead my family, my friends, Your church, and people not into temptation; and deliver us from evil." To be delivered means that you are asking God to help you not to do evil or be rescued from being enticed.

Lord's Prayer helps us pray fervently. The world must be protected and be delivered from evil. If you are told to jump from the building top, you will think the person who told you to jump is not in your best interest. However, this is exactly what the enemy, who wants our downfall, does. Christ knowing this has taught us how to resist him. That is why He wants us to pray daily saying, lead us not into... God sees when Satan wants us to jump from the building top. So, let's pray and say, "Lord, lead us not...." With this, we are asking the Father to send us His angels to encamp around us so we can be protected. Christ has defeated the devil through His Blood; therefore, we have every power to live our lives as overcomers.

Sin is a very serious matter, but in our world today, it is what is ruling. Nevertheless, God does not condone it. The Bible says that no thief, no blasphemers, no liars, murderers, or adulterers will inherit the Kingdom of heaven; yet we get trapped sometimes. Jesus Christ broke the barrier between us and God with love by paying the price for our sins. Thankfully, some of us have come to see the light, but some are still in the dark by chosen their own way. We sometimes wonder why God sent Christ if He knew He was coming to suffer at the hands of humans. Yes, God chose this approach to show us the wickedness of humankind. With Christ, we get to see how painful life is. We see this from birth, how babies are born, and the path they choose. Then after all the suffering in this life, the baby grows into an adult, and then he passed from this life, but there is a purpose for this. The purpose for coming into this world is to know the Father and have a relationship with Him before we die. Because after this life, there is life eternal with God.

God brought salvation to the world. However, for centuries, some people have chosen to allow sin and Satan to rule over them and have remained to be wicked through actions and deeds. God is not a murderer to send His Son to be killed, rather He sent Him to be the payment for sin. He could have sent Jesus not to endure this pain, but He did it all for a reason so that mankind could truly know the difference between wickedness and kindness. Why am I saying all this? In many parts of the world, Christians are being persecuted because of their faith in the same way that Christ and His followers were persecuted. What crimes have they committed? None! Rather, they are hated and persecuted for their faith. This shows the wickedness of humans. Nevertheless, God still wants the truth to be told so people will have no excuse in the end.

Know what God deserves. Jesus tells us that the Kingdom, the power, and the glory belong to the Father." This means Heaven earth must adore Him. Giving thanksgiving to God, glorifying Him, and honoring His Name, is our daily offering to our King. However, are we doing just that? If solving our world's problems depend on how we respect and honor God, then we have responsibility to honor Him as the King of all. He alone has the power to perfect us. And so, may we hunger for God's Kingdom by worshiping Him in spirit and in truth! It is the only way to eradicate the evil kingdom of Satan from among us.

Chapter 21 – Conclusion

This book as a very special book. The reason is that it came about through my encounter with the Lord concerning His Prayer, as I have already explained. In fact, I take *the Lord's Prayer* as our emergency alert system because it is a Prayer that covers ever area of life. For example, each time we hear an alert on our phones, TVs, or radios, it is a city's police, or fire department alerting us of danger. It can be floods, a hurricane, tornado, a heavy rain, or an accident. In emergency situations, the fire dept sends alerts to help people prepare. They warn us to have plenty of water bottles, food, candles, or in some cases, even sandbags to secure our homes. In The Lord's Prayer, we have everything that prepares us to be safe; and if we pay attention to that, we shall be ready to face anything. For this reason, let's take The Lord's Prayer as our everyday emergency alert system to help us to be prepared. Whatever warning we receive from the Holy Spirit regarding what lies ahead, we should pray about. Each day that we wake up in the morning, we must listen to the voice of the Holy Spirit concerning life. ***He is the One who brings the warning sign and alerts us of any danger ahead.*** He sounds the warning bell to alert us of what needs to be prayed for and about.

This is how we prepare ourselves. Do you know God, and if yes, then ask yourself if you have a good relationship with Him. We must ask God the Father through Jesus the Savior for the Holy Spirit to show us what must be prayed for. Is there any problem anywhere in the world? Is any trouble ahead of us and our household, in our neighborhoods, in the city, in the country, in the government, or anywhere around the world? Do we need to change our ways of life, or repent? Who needs salvation? Does anyone need the Lord and His forgiveness? Are our ways honoring God? Do you know how to Hallow God's Name and exult Him? What about the church of God? Are churches practicing holiness? Do you know how important it is to pray for holiness? **What** about God's Kingdom? What about *His Will* for us? Are we living according to God's plans and purposes for our lives here on earth? What about your needs and that of the world? Are your needs being met? What about forgiveness? Do I need forgiveness, or I must give forgiveness? Everyone must know the importance of knowing God as our Heavenly Father; know His Holy Name and serve Him as He requires of us. But how many people in my circle and in the world do I think know God, give Him thanks, praise His Name, and worship Him? Are people truly living according to God's law?

The time has come for each believer to be engaged. It is a time to join prayer groups, immerse yourself in prayer, and be a part. Be engaged and get deeper in the things of Heaven through prayer. Be in the word of God, pray, and share, because if you do, the Lord will lead and guide you to touch many lives. There is no more time to waste. Today is our day. The disciples did their best. Today, the second coming of the Lord must be on everyone's heart even though we have no idea when He will come. But if we look at the signs around us, we can see that time is running out. So, we must engage in strategic prayer. Through prayer and the word of God, we shall be empowered and equipped to send the gospel to all.

In the public, you must pay attention to your environment. If there is something that needs intercession and the Holy Spirit brings it to your attention, you must pray right at that moment. Do not wait to get home first. Pray right away and pray again when you get home. When necessary, add fasting, and pray as the Holy Spirit directs. Let's say that the Lord wants you to pray for the sick. The Holy Spirit will bring to your attention the need to pray for someone who is sick. Because healing is under the subject of "Give us this day our daily bread", it means healing for the body is needed daily. So, you will pray for the person's needs for healing as well as all sick people you meet. Maybe, when a homeless person on the street asks for money and you do not have it, you can talk with them about salvation and pray for all other homeless people. Do it at once if the Holy Spirit prompts you. Whichever way the Holy Spirit prompts you to assist, do so all to the glory of God.

As you begin to pray, the Holy Spirit can even bring many things into your mind and help you pray for them all. It is all about intercessory. So, once you are praying "Give us this day our daily bread," it will not be only for your needs but everyone's as well. The Holy Spirit will bless you with much work if you are open to His leadership. You will be surprised to see how you can pray for many needs in a short amount of time. And you will be surprised to see the impact your prayers will have on the Kingdom's Assignments. There may be people who need protection. You can pray for protection for yourself, your family, and all people. Preparing your heart to pray when you hear the voice of the Holy Spirit will bring many blessings. You may be driving, and yet be praying. So, pray for drivers when the Holy Spirit prompts you to pray for a driver on the road, do so right away. All these can be short prayers, but they can be effective.

When you are at home cooking, or in your prayer closet praying, you will be reminded to pray about something or for someone. You can go on your knees, lay down flat, or just start meditating on the Word of God at that moment even if you are cooking. Always begin your prayer by asking the Holy Spirit to lead you. It is the ideal way of praying according to the Will of God. It is important to give thanks, praise God and adore Him before you ask for anything or make a request. This is the Will of God as it is written in Psalm 100. You can bring your request before the Lord after you are done giving Him what belongs to Him, and thanksgiving and praises are all His. So, keep in mind what belongs to God because it is important.

With thanksgiving, you give thanks to the Lord for all His goodness.

With praises, you admire the Father's Greatness, Goodness, and Power.

With request/supplication, you ask for your needs and the needs of others. That is for every need around the entire globe.

Whatever it may be, ask for yourself and others. Make sure the Holy Spirit is leading you and that He is the One in charge. Always invite Him to guide you, though He already lives in you. If the Holy Spirit is in control, you have nothing to worry about. Keep in mind that without Him, you can never pray effectively. We are commanded to pray to the Father in Heaven, in the Name of Jesus Christ, the Son, and with the help of the Holy Spirit; there is no way around it. We ask for forgiveness and repentance for all our wrongdoings.

Evil is very real, and it is deadly. But in our present world, evil has become so rampant that it is being assumed as something that is fake. This has made sin become addictive because sometimes we forget to realize how deadly it is. Some people even think Satan is fake, but Satan and his demons are not fictional, they are real. We may not see him standing in front of us. But if you take all the cruelness in this life into consideration, then you shall see that, indeed, Satan (evil) is real. People can choose to reject God today, make fun of Christianity, and live their lives as they please, but tomorrow may not be a fun time for them if they continue. Today is the day of grace. Sin is caused by evil, and evil is caused by temptation, and temptation causes us to sin against God. This makes sin a cycle if it is practiced. How can we turn to God and make Christ as the Lord and Savior? Lack of knowledge of the Savior is ignorant, and that ignorance will destroy you if it continues. But as we can see, people still ridicule and mock God and Christ because they know them not. What can we do as Christians to help? There are many false churches, teachers, and many fake church goers. If we have come to know the truth, then what can we do to help others come to know the same truth? Can we insult, humiliate, or judge them to win them for Christ? I am sure you can agree with me that the answer is 'no.' We can only help them by showing them the true love of God. So, let's become peacemakers and be called children of God **Matthew 5:9**.

We are called to pray; therefore, if we pray for the lost, and tell them about God's salvation through Christ, then God will work in their hearts. When Jesus came, He loved the unlovable, showed the way to the lost, saved sinners, and helped the poor, and we can follow His example. We cannot save them, but God will listen to our prayers and call them to Himself. We can talk and debate, but it will do us no good if it was not done with genuine love and compassion. We should pray, and speak with them, if possible, in a loving and compassionate manner, and show them the right way to God for their sins to be pardoned just as we pray for our sins to be removed. When we sin as Christians, we know what to do, but what about unbelievers? They have no idea what to do with their sins. Because of this, they continue to sin, but salvation will show them the way to the only Merciful God. Sin is deadly; therefore, we cannot relax, or gather information about people just so we can use it against them, point fingers, and think of them as sinners. But we must bear in mind that evil does not deserve to dwell among humans. This is not to say that we must pamper sin. No, that is not what I mean. Whatever we do, we can rebuke sinners, but it requires love and compassion, not a judgmental attitude because it divides. So, if we are divided, then we are helping Satan build his kingdom on earth instead of God's. If you have good intentions for what you do, and it is still causing confusion, then pray for God to show you a better way. God can give you compassion to speak to people about how they can change their ways rather than insulting them. You may be destroying the work of God. The devil tempts people many ways, but sometimes, the same people that can help them are the same people that condemn them.

Believers needs prayer support. The downfall of many believers is a lack of true love, love of money, and power struggles. It is time for us to care and pray for everyone, so that those spirits will play no part among believers. For example, preachers and their families are being attacked all the time. They can also become lovers of money. This is because the devil's goal is to make sure their messages are being polluted, but again, we are called to pray that God will use His servants who are called by His Name in a very effective way. We are called to stand in the gap for all people and our world, and not just praying for ourselves. So, let everyone start to have a prayerful attitude, and to know that we have no better choice than to read our Bible and pray daily, and pray for everyone including priests or preachers, missionaries, evangelists, and everyone.

People struggle because the voice of God is not heard, and the joy and peace of God's love is no longer felt within their soul. The word of God is explained. It cures, stills the soul, and calms the heart. It helps us turn our hearts and minds to the thinks of God where we can find an ending peace. Can we share this Good News? The time has come. What can we do? As believers, our part to play is to ask for forgiveness for ourselves and for the whole world. God's messengers must get up and sound the alarm so people will have no excuses. All the evils that have taken over this planet are outrageous, but the end to them all is near. The good news is that they are all coming to an end soon, but it won't be pretty without God's gift of salvation. **God has plans for the wor**ld. In this, His righteous Kingdom must come, and *His Will* must be done. If you know all these basic Christian Prayer concept, then you are on the right path, because our duty is to pray for God to bring more into His Kingdom of Salvation.

Sin is rooted in pride and rebellion, and Satan is the cause. John 8:44 says that he is the father of all lies. The devil is the deceiver. God created Satan perfect, but he chose to become evil. Psalm 139 tells us that we are wonderfully made, but we can also choose the same path as Satan and walked away from God's grace. May God forbid! For that matter, keep in mind of what the Kingdom of God stands for, to help you live right. The reason why humans are filled with evil is because Satan creates all kinds of evil through lies. To get followers, he must lie about God by involving deception and deceitfulness. Today, I am sent to remind every true child of God to become aware of what is going on. Many people are struggling, even church leaders. If you get to know how the devil works against humans with temptations and evil, especially people of God, you will not spend a day without praying for church leaders, pastors, all believers, and unbelievers! If we pray, confusions will be taken away; those who need to be helped will be helped, and the ones that need salvation will get to know the truth.

In living our lives in the Kingdom of God here on earth, we cannot do whatever pleases us, because His Kingdom is pure. So, in this Kingdom, we cannot continue to do whatever we want and say, God is merciful. Yes, He is, but remember, you have no idea of your days on earth; therefore, whenever you are tempted to do anything that is contrarily to the *Will of God*, pause, take a deep breath, and ask yourself if what is tempting you will be found in the Kingdom of God or will bring glory to His Name. Compare that to God's Word and keep in mind what the Word says about temptation and what it leads to. Keep doing this each time you are being tempted, and you will overcome evil. The Word of God helps us to determine the difference between what is right and wrong. As we know, it is not everyone who says, "Lord, Lord will enter into the Kingdom of Heaven...." **Matthew 7:21** says only those that do the Will of God. We then know that even some that claim to be Christians are wolves in sheep's clothing. God has given us a conscience that helps us to know the difference between good and evil so we will not give in to selfish cravings and desires. In order for this to take place, we must abide by the word of God because it is not automatic. In addition, the Holy Spirit will cause our conscience to have feelings of shame and guilt, which will lead God's people to repent because they are the right emotions that guide us to a sound mind that dwells on the things of God.

It is imperative to pursue holiness. This is very important because the Bible tells us that without holiness, we can't see God." There are consequences to sin; therefore, we must make every effort to live a holy life. Every Christian has besetting sins we constantly struggle with. It can be gossiping, lying, anger, boastfulness, pride, or lust etc. But believers do not have to struggle with these sins because our righteousness is in Christ Jesus; therefore, we must ask for His help in whatever we are struggling with. If there is anything we must strive for, it is holiness. We must pursue it with the help of Christ. As children of the Holy God, our responsibility each day is to make sure our thoughts, doings, and everything are aligned with Christ. We must think right, act right, and say the right things, so nothing will defile us.

If you know what is coming into the world, you will pray for the world. Many troubles are yet to come upon the earth. But let me remind you of a few of them. In **Revelation 16:17–20,** John wrote about His dream. In this, he explains of what is coming on the earth. He wrote that when the 7th angel poured out his bowl into the air, a loud voice came out of the temple from the throne. The voice said, "It is finished! "Then there were flashes of lightning, noises, thunder, and a big earthquake. This was the worst earthquake that has ever happened since people have been on earth. The great city split into three parts. The cities of the nations were destroyed. And God did not forget to punish Babylon the Great. He gave that city the cup filled with the wine of his terrible anger. Every island disappeared, and there were no more mountains. Giant hailstones fell on people from the sky. The hailstones weighed about 100 pounds each. People started to curse God because of the pain. Wow!

Here is a one question I have for you: On that dreadful day, would you find yourself praising God or cursing Him? Answer for yourself. Are you prepared for what is ahead? The seventh angel will pour his bowl into the air, and it will not be like watching a movie; this time, it will be real. A loud voice will come out of the temple saying it is done! There will be voices, thunders, lightening, and there will be a great earthquake like one we have never experienced before. The cities of the nations will be destroyed; everything will be destroyed. So, the question is, where will you be? Are you prepared for whatever is coming?

If everything in this life is going to be destroyed just as in the days of Noah or in the time of Sodom and Gomorrah, then how must we live our lives here today on earth? Let's see some of the modern-day countries and their attractiveness. I am sure it is everyone's dream to visit some of these beautiful places, even if not all. Sadly, they will all be destroyed one day. Sad, right? But yes, they will be destroyed one day. Think of the World Trade Center and its downfall.

New York City –We know of NY and its Prospect Park's darling little boathouse, borough, and museums. The island of Manhattan and its stratospheric buildings, the choice is yours. You can enjoy all day with beautiful sight seeing. But just as the 'The Twin Tower was destroyed in the twinkle with an eye, so shall all be.

Singapore – People who have been to Singapore can tell you what a feast for the senses it truly is. Its skyline, the Marina Bay, illuminated buildings on the waterfront; the Botanic Gardens and the garden bays are what will take your breath away.

Queenstown, New Zealand – Known as the "adventure capital of the world."

Istanbul, Turkey – The city and its hilly cobblestoned streets are just amazing!

Paris, France (The City of Light) – there's something to make the heart go aflutter around every corner, be it an iconic monument, a cozy sidewalk café, boulevard lined with creamy stone Haussmann-era mansions, or display of a patisserie boulangerie (French bakery) can take your breath away.

San Francisco, California – Set on a peninsula between the Pacific Ocean and San Francisco Bay, the steep city offers beautiful hilltop views of skyscrapers, bridges, mountains, and surrounding water. The Golden Gate Bridge, etc., are just few of its amazing sceneries. What about LA (CA), Palermo, Italy, and Cape Town (South Africa**).**

Dubai – Of all that I have mentioned, think about Dubai and its complex constructions. They will take your breath away. But sadly, they will all be destroyed one day. Isn't that sad!

So, keep in mind that just as humans pass from this life, so everything else that we see in this life will pass away. Regardless, God will judge every sin. We can cruise all over the world to these nice places, eat at nice restaurants, have fun, and enjoy ourselves, but earthly enjoyment is brief. Therefore, it is not what matters. It is okay to enjoy life because that is a part of life. However, our everlasting enjoyment after this life is more important; that comes only through obedience. For that matter, we as humans, cannot live our lives as we please. That is why Jesus wants us to know the Father in Heaven; have a relationship with Him; know about His Kingdom; sacrifice our 'freewill' to

Him; hate evil; love God; love others as we love ourselves, and worship God rather than worshiping money or idol. This is *God's Will* for us.

Today, despite all the warning signs, many are still living their lives as in the generation of Sodom and Gomorrah. Many people have taken matters into their own hands; they behave as if they retain the whole world, and there is no judgement. In **Galatians 6:7,** we are told, "Do not be deceived: God cannot be mocked. A man reaps what he sows." **Hebrews 9:27–28** says, "it is appointed for man to die once, and after that comes judgment. Christ has been offered once to bear our sins; but the second time, He is coming to judge as we read in **Isaiah 2 & 3**.

We must be alert because sin has run rampant in our world today, and it is getting out of control, every place on earth is covered with sin, even the church. Our only solution is God's Word and prayer, because as sin was not taken lightly in the past, so it will not be taken lightly in our time. **Matthew 24:37–39** says, "...For as in the days that were before the flood they were eating and drinking, marrying and giving in marriage, until the day the flood came, and took them all away." Please read **Luke 17and Revelation 16**. It is us living today that are going to face this dreadful day of the Lord on day.

We have no idea when this will take place, so why wait? No one want to be caught by surprise. So, today is the time of grace. **2 Corinthians 6:2** says, "...behold, now is the day of salvation." It our time for preparation**, just as we prepare to travel, so we must prepare for that dreadful day.** So, the next time you travel to any of those beautiful cities, also think of what will happen to those cities one day, maybe even while you are still there. The truth is it is not just the cities, because if all these cities are going to be destroyed, then where would you be? Answer for yourself. Give your life to the Lord if you haven't done so yet because no one knows tomorrow; only God knows. Jesus came to bring us hope, so, don't be confused of this. And don't try to seek peace and answers from wrong places. Because if you do, you will torment your mind, and you will struggle with misery and hopelessness. But you can seek the Lord while He may be found.

Nothing causes us to sin more than yielding to temptation. Temptation leads us to sin against God. I am not excluded. We all sin now and then because of temptation, and the devil is not tired of tempting. But we can be aware when we follow these things:

- Be alert.
- Submit to God. (Give Him your freewill)
- Resist the devil.
- Read the word of God.
- Pray in faith and wait upon God in prayer.
- Live in holiness and stay closer to God.

Meditation –I will now finalize everything that has been said through Biblical Meditation. It is what completes the Lord's Prayer. *The Lord's Prayer* makes meditation so easy. How? It is what each line is about. Aside from praying with it, you can also use it in meditation. In **Joshua 1:8** and Psalm 1, we are told about the importance of meditation. But what is meditation? Christian meditation connects our spirits to the Spirit of God and His Kingdom of righteousness daily. Let me show you how. With the Salutation, "Our Father," you give your respect to God. You can meditate by thinking of God and who He is (His attributes). With His Name, you can meditate.

What does God's Name represent? With His Holiness, His Kingdom, *His Will*, His Provisions (including Protection, Forgiveness), and His Power and Glory, you can meditate all day long. You can mention His Name "YAH-WEH," and as someone said, you will take it as the air you inhale into your lungs. How? The answer can be found in **Psalm 73:23**, "My flesh and my heart may fail, but God is the strength of my heart and my portion forever." That's awesome! So, you can use God's Name, *His Will*, His Kingdom, Holiness, Provision, Protection, Forgiveness, His Power, Glory, and Honor, Salvation, to do meditation.

Start your daily meditation by inviting the Holy Spirit to lead you. As we know from **Romans 8:26**, prayer is not the work of any man but of the

Holy Spirit. Therefore, it is not a show, but a work of the Kingdom. The truth about prayer is that you cannot pray as much in public as you should in your closet; in your closet, there are many things to be prayed and interceded for. This is because there are. When we are alone, that is when we can have the time to wait upon the Lord and hear from Him. In our world today, we need God through prayer support more than ever because there are too many problems facing humanity. The world has become too polluted by troubles due to evil. And through prayer meditation, we can come before God with all our concerns. In our homes, we can meditate fand pray or peace for families, communities, political arenas, schools, hospitals, et al., and in our own lives. The world needs people like you and me who are full of compassion, because without that, it will be impossible to pray. You must have an intercessory heart. This does not mean being intrusive or interfering, but it means that you care about the world you live in. In **Ezekiel 22:30**, the prophet says on behalf of God, "I looked for anyone to repair the wall and stand in the gap for me on behalf of the land, so I wouldn't have to destroy it. But I couldn't find anyone." Thankfully, today, God has prepared you and me, through the blood of Christ, to stand in the gap because He has given us a heart of compassion.

This concludes all that I have learned from the Holy Spirit about the Prayer of the Lord, and I am sure there are more to **learn. Psalm 86** says, "Hear, O LORD, and answer me, for I am poor and needy. Guard my life, for I am devoted to you." In **Psalm 50:15**, we are told to call upon God in the day of trouble, He will deliver us... **Colossians 4:2** – Devote yourselves to prayer, being watchful and thankful. May the Holy Spirit empower us for good works. Read Psalm **119:105.**

Now let's pray.

Prayer: We pray and meditate that God the Father will bring salvation to all and help us to refrain from any sinful behavior so that there will be no room for evil. We pray that He will surround us with holiness to prevent us from falling into temptation. May compassion and love fill our hearts for all people, including the lost. May we love genuinely and care with compassion.

May we seek the grace of God and live according to that grace. May the mercy of God be with us and all that we do. May we live our lives to the fullest, trusting and relying on God and His strength and power every step of the way. May we be in His constant presence to behold His beauty. •*May the Lord be your light to show you the way*. •May those living in sin, repent of their sins, be forgiven, and be made whole. • May we get to know the Father and keep His Name Holy in all that we do. •May we give thanks, praise the Lord, and glorify His Holy Name all our lives. •May His Righteous Kingdom and His Perfect Will become part of your daily life. •May the Lord be your provider and protector to the end. •May you never become entangled by sin. •May you receive His forgiveness each day of your life and forgive as well. •May you not be led into temptation but be delivered from evil. •May the Good Shepherd find those that are lost and bring them home. •May they be taken away from the powers of darkness into God's Marvelous Light. •May those that are heartbroken be comforted; may they find hope in the Savior. •May those struggling in life find stability, and their worries be no more. •May those that are confused, have no love, and have no peace, find them in the Lord. •May they have the peace that surpasses all understanding and become anxious no more. •May those that are broken be mended. •May those that have no families come to join God's family on earth here. •May those that are lonely know they belong to God's family and God is with them. •May those that are mourning start to dance with joy in their souls. Amen.

This completes everything in the "Lord's Prayer." The Lord has given you everything you need to pray. You will build a stronger bond with God if you pray. You can live according to *His Will*; your needs will be met if you pray; you can overcome temptation; and you will know how to live a satisfying life. Therefore, you must pray, because the more we do, the more the world will be transformed. People will get to know the truth and they will turn to God. Holiness will rule on earth, God's power will be displayed among us, and *God's Will* shall become a part of us. We will see an immense transformation in our lives here on earth. People will live for *God's Will*, and God's Purposes and Plans will take root. If we pray, we will have protection against all evil, temptation will be overcome, and the glory of God would be displayed.

Prayer: God of Mercy, please help us to stand strong. May we be empowered to pray always, Amen! Dear Heavenly Father, let Your Kingdom come so that Your Will, will be *done.* I ask this for myself, my family, and in this world. Lord, have Your way and rule everywhere on earth with Your salvation as You rule in Heaven. *I pray for* Your Will to sanctify and mold me into the image of Your Son Jesus Christ. Give me the strength to live a pure life. I cannot accomplish this so, I need You. Lord, help me to surrender as I yield my will to You, for Yours. I pray that *You will help each one of us to live for you.* Help us to love You with all our hearts, souls, minds. Father, we pray against evil. May Your grace abound and overflow so we can do Your Will, in Jesus' Name, Amen!

Chapter 22 – The Prayer Lists—Use the Lord's Prayer for Prayer and Meditation

Give all your worries and cares to God, for he cares about you.

Prayers help us to know that we are part of God's Kingdom.

This last section covers things for which we can pray for and about. It includes praying for yourself, others, and for the whole world. You can also add anything that comes to your mind. Remember, your daily prayer of adoration connects you to the Heavenly Father and His Kingdom in a very special way. So, take a moment to adore Him. This includes Thanksgiving, Praise, and Worship. This is very important part of prayer which must never be ignored. Read **Psalm 103 &100.** Always keep in mind that forgiveness is another key to effective prayer; and so is faith – **Hebrews 11:6**. You can never have effective prayer with unforgiveness – **Matthew 5:24.** Praying for yourself, for others, and for the world are also important. Read **Matthew 6:6; 7:7; Luke 11:24; Hebrews 4:16; 1Timothy 2; and 2 Chronicles 7:14**. In prayer, meditation is vital. Take the time to meditate upon the Word of God, and don't ignore 'the moment of Silence.' This allows God to speak to you. This is because prayer is not a one-way, but a two-way traffic.

Why pray? In **Matthew 26:41–42,** we are told to watch and pray. In **1 Thessalonians 5:16–18**, we are told to pray without ceasing. Jesus prayed, but why, if He was God? Here is why: when Jesus Christ was on earth, He was both 100% human and 100% God. As a man, Jesus had a need for prayer. Therefore, He had to rely on His Father for guidance, strength, wisdom, and power to do everything on earth. He did everything to show us that we also must not rely on our own understanding, but in all our ways, we must acknowledge Him to direct us; as it is written in **Proverbs 3:6**. So, we must acknowledge Him in all our ways, so our paths will be directed according to the Will of the Father. Jesus modeled prayer for us because He wanted His followers to learn from Him. Prayer prepares us to become devoted, strong believers, and close to God. We get to know more about God and build our personal relationship with Him. And it also helps us to stand against the devil's schemes. Here are the ways we prepare ourselves for spiritual battle. The reading in **Ephesians 6:10-12** tells us that:

The belt of truth will protect us from being deceived.

The breastplate of righteousness will prevent spiritual pollution.

The feet fitted with the gospel of peace is the peace of God.

The shield of faith will help us to extinguish all the flaming arrows of the evil one.

The helmet of salvation will protect our heads and the mind from evil thoughts.

The sword of the Spirit is the Word of God. The Word helps us to conquer.

These are not physical tools but spiritual ones. If you know the Word of God, you will know and speak the truth. Your mind will be protected against evil thoughts; your feet will be guided to the right path; your mouth, your ears, shall all be anointed by the Holy Spirit for good work. This is how we prepare ourselves for spiritual battle. These helps us to pray in the spirit, on all occasions, with all kinds of prayers, and requests for all people. Jesus is our good example. **Romans 8:34** says, He intercedes on our behalf. In this verse, we read, "Who is to condemn? Christ Jesus is the one who died and was raised.

He is at the right hand of the Father interceding for us." Jesus is interceding on our behalf every day. He does not condemn anyone; rather, He intercedes for all people, both good and bad. He also wants us to pray for ourselves and for others in His Name.

Why do we pray for ourselves? As I stated earlier, so that you will not fall into temptation. You will love the Lord, your God, yourself, and people if you pray. You will also become strong and a devoted Christian if you pray. And you will receive power to do the Kingdom's Work if you pray and wait upon the Lord. As it is written in **Luke 24:49,** we must wait for the power of the Holy Spirit. This means that we are praying. Keep in mind that you will fall if you fail to pray. This means, pray if you want to stand as a strong Christian. Pray for the flesh and the spirit if you want to serve God better. **Matthew 26:41** says, the spirit is willing, but the flesh is weak. So, you must pray for both. Pray for the *fruit of the spirit.* Ask the Holy Spirit to give you wisdom, good character, love, peace, joy, compassion, faithfulness, humility, self-control, etc. Pray if you must travel; and do the same before you make any move. if you need God's blessings, healing, peace of mind, a good wife or a husband; a good career, or a good friend, pray. Pray in all circumstances. Pray, pray, and pray for and about everything!

Why we pray for people and even our enemies? Matthew 5:44 says, "But I tell you, love your enemies and pray for those who persecute you, that you may be children of your Father in heaven. He causes His sun to rise on the evil and the good and sends rain on the righteous and the unrighteous."

We are commanded to pray for all nations and leaders. Paul told the churches to pray for him, that whenever he speak, words may be given him so that he will fearlessly make known the mystery of the gospel and declare it fearlessly. This applies to all ministers of the gospel, including missionaries, evangelists, and every believer who wants the gospel to go to the ends of the world. In **1 Timothy 2:1–2,** we are told to pray for our leaders and all people—for kings, presidents, and all those in authority, that we may live peaceful and quiet lives in all godliness and holiness." Why is this important? In **Jeremiah 29:7,** we are told to pray for the peace of the city.

We pray for our cities because there will be peace if God blesses our towns, cities, and nations. So, just as **Romans 8:34** tells us that Jesus intercedes on our behalf and does not condemn us, so must we also do. You must pray for all people including your leaders, and don't discriminate. For instance, if your party choice is 'Rain party and are praying for only for party 'Rain leader to win, but after Rain party leader failed, you stop praying for your leaders, then know who you serve – a party or God? The same goes to you if your party choice is Sunshine, or whatever party you belong to. Why praying for our leaders is important? **Romans 13:1** helps us to understand that God chooses leaders for specific assignments. Therefore, we must be careful not to pressure God for a leader because if we do, it can become a chaos. For instance, when the Israelites pressured God for a king, He chose king Saul, but the end result was not appealing.

God chooses according to the time. He can choose a leader to punish a nation if we fail to obey and pray. For that matter, it is very important us to humble ourselves, pray, and seek His face in every election, not just for our cities or countries, but for the whole world. Why this is important is because one small trouble in another city, country, or nation, can affect the whole world, as can be seen recently in Russia's invasion of Ukraine or Israel and Palestine. So, we cannot just sit back and relax because our city or nation has not been affected. You never know when you will also be in trouble. We do the same for people and their problems. In the same way we send aide to other parts of the world when there is a natural disaster, so we do also by our prayers.

Call to prayer:

We are called to pray; so, let's get busy. Get involve in God's work through prayer and pray for everyone and everything. It will be wonderful for churches all over the world to set a day aside for prayer, sorely for the church everywhere around the world. Not once a year, but once a week or at least once a month. This will make a huge difference in the body of Christ. If we want to see 'church growth' protection against church attackers, and unity and not division, then we must pray. And pray for righteousness to reign. We must join in prayer wherever we are, because prayer can bring about a great change. I pray that people will form more and more prayer groups, and individuals will also pray seriously each day in their closets using the Lord's Prayer as their guide to effective prayer. This will make a huge difference in the body of Christ, and in our world today.

We must learn from the Master who taught us to pray, and the Holy Spirit who helps us to pray daily. **This is what I understand in my spirit: when the Lord was about to begin His work on earth, He started with 40 days prayer and fasting, and He ended His work with prayer. This means that prayer is the key to starting and finishing the Kingdom's Work as required of us.**

There are **many** things to tackle, and there is no time to waste. A fervent prayer that includes fasting will enable us to accomplish a lot! If you can fast, then do so sometimes; if you can't fast, pray. Always keep in mind that it is not just about praying, but it is about praying to get the work done as the Master requires. Therefore, we need to focus. Prayer is the key. This means, if we focus on the purpose of *The Lord's Prayer which* remind us that we have an awesome Father, we can communicate with Him better. So, let the understanding of the Lord's Prayer help you to know this awesome Father we have; become connected to Him through prayer and His Word, and allow your worries to be His worries. Many things are about to happen, and if we are not connected to the Father through Jesus Christ as one family, we will miss the true purpose of our existence. If you are saved, then you need the Word of God, Prayer, and Faith to help keep you strong, build your relationship in Christ, and serve Him better. If you are not saved, then you need salvation first.

We all need to ask for the gift of discernment to detect the Truth, to keep us from being deceived, because the deceiver is working very hard against the Christendom. Each one of us must get involved in prayer. 'Pray-for-me' kind of Christianity is okay, but it is not what we need at this point in time. We must have a prayer partner (s) whom we can pray with. We must know the plans that the Lord has for each one of us. It is written in **Jeremiah 31:34**, "No longer will they teach their neighbor, or say to one another, 'Know the Lord,' because they will all know me, from the least of them to the greatest," declares the Lord. "For I will forgive their wickedness and will remember their sins no more."

Nothing can change God's plans and His perfect Will for humanity. Therefore, we must keep calling upon His Name until His plans are fulfilled. There are many reasons for why we must pray, but let's place emphasis on these for now. As you follow the prayer list, it will bring even more into your mind. May the Lord empower you to pray fervently according to *His Will*. And may He bless you and reward you greatly for all the time you spend in prayer toward God's work on earth! May God bless us all in Jesus Mighty Name. Amen!

Keep in mind that the rule effective prayer is reading Scriptures, study what you read, allow the Holy Spirit to help you understand what you read, meditate upon it, pray, and Wait for God to speak to you through that. Here are some of the things to guide you to pray daily. Again, and again, allow the Holy Spirit to lead, guide, and intercede as you pray. As it is written in **Romans 8:26,** it is the Holy Spirit that helps us to pray. May the Lord empower you to pray, and may He bless you as you pray! Amen!

Prayer beginnings.

Our Father:

*God is a Great Father who gives freely. He gives us rain in due time and causes the sun to rise on the good and the bad – **Matthew 5:45.** For that reason, we give thanks to Him for all His Goodness through salvation. We give Him thanks for His Great love, His Mercy, His Grace, and for His Faithfulness. We do this for ourselves, for our families, for the church of God in Christ, and for the whole world. The goodness of our Heavenly Father helps us to give thanks, but we also praise and worship Him for who He is. By so doing, we are sacrificing to Him our offering. In this case it is the *Kingdom*, the *Power*, the Praise, the *Glory, Thanksgiving,* and *Dominion.* They all belong to Him forever and ever. These are the kinds of offerings that God the Father deserves.

Hallowed be thy name:

*The Name of God must be Hallowed in all that we do. This is our reverence to Him. The Holy Name of God makes Him the Greatest of all! And for that matter, we exult His Holy Name through our services and worship.

Thy Kingdom Come:

*Pray for God's Kingdom to come. If you are tired of all the evil in this world, then you won't be silent. Instead, you will give your time and wealth for the Kingdom's Sake and pray for God's Kingdom to come so that righteousness will rule.

The *Will of God:*

*Pray for *God's Will* for your life, for the lives of your children, and their children's children. Pray for *God's Will* in the church. Pray that the church will operate through the power of the Holy Spirit. And continue to pray for God's plans for the world. Humanity must sacrifice *our free wills to God.* So, pray that we will come to the complete knowledge of God's plans for the world – **John 3:12–20.**

Give us this day our daily bread:

*Humans' needs are insatiable. Let's ask for our needs with grateful heart. Whether physical, emotional, or spiritual, they all come from God. As **James 1:17** declares, "Every Good gift comes from above." So, pray for your needs and add to your prayer lists of the needs of others. And pray that God will help us become content with what God gives and not greedy. Pray for the world and its troubles. Prayer for God's provisions and blessings for the world. *Pray for peace, love, and harmony for the world. *Pray for food, shelter, clothing, water, air, and good relationships.

Forgiveness:

*Pray for God's forgiveness for yourself, family, the church, and the world. Pray also that we can forgive one another, love our enemies, and pray for those that persecute us, as we are commanded to do.

Lead us not into temptation; and deliver us from evil:

*We pray against temptations that may cause our downfall: *Pray for protection for all people against evil. *We pray against any sinful nature and any form of evil practices which may cause us to do evil and sin against God. *Pray against any disobedience spirit. *Pray that the devil cannot use anything to distract us, and that our purposes on earth will be fulfilled.

To God be the Kingdom, the power, and glory forever: Worship God. Amen!

Pray for God's work and salvation for the world:

Pray for outreach ministries – salvation – **John 3:12–20 & Romans 3:23.** Pray that gospel of salvation will reach to all people over the world. *Pray against attacks on Christians. *Pray for people to turn away from their wicked ways. *Pray for genuine repentance and forgiveness. *Pray that we will give reverence to God.

Prayer for God's power, unity in the church, in the family, and prayer for the world:

Pray for God's anointing and His power to rule in the church. *Pray for the body of Christ to be united. *Pray that the children of God will love one another, have faith, and trust God. Say a prayer for every believer each day: Church leaders, priests, fathers, all preachers, pastors/ministers, evangelists, mission work, deaconesses, elders, deacons, new converts, and backsliders. *We pray for unity in the family; unity in our communities, in the church of God in Christ, at workplaces; and in political arenas. *Pray against division in every area of life. May God help us to work through our differences.

Pray for church groups to be effective:

Pray for the worship team; *men's & women's movements; *children ministry; *youth ministry; *tithes and offerings; *church benevolence programs; etc.

Pray for righteousness/holiness/purity:

Pray for kindness and humility; *love, unity, and patience; *courage and power; *truthfulness and obedience; and *pray for repentance.

Pray for the fruit and the gift of the Holy Spirit:

Pray for the Holy Spirit anointing; *We need the power of the Holy Spirit to do God's work. So, *pray for love, peace, joy, trust, faith, faithfulness gentleness, kindness compassion, self-control, genuineness, mercy, etc. Pray for the favor and the blessings of God: *Pray for satisfaction and contentment; *pray for wisdom, discernment, knowledge, and encouragement. *Pray for prophecies, dreams, and visions, miracles, and healings.

Pray against evils spirits that seek to operate in churches.

Pray against every sin: any evil intentions and wickedness: love of money, anger, hatred, jealousy, envy, gossip, adultery, pornography, idol and witchcrafts worships, etc., will have no control over any child of God.

Pray against all kinds of addiction:

Alcoholic addictions; drug addictions; smoking addictions; shopping addictions; food addictions; sex addictions (pornography, gambling, games, etc.).

Pray for good decision-making:

Pray for everyone to make a good decision and choose the right path (All people, both young and old).

Pray for genuine love and respect:

God, ourselves, others, our elders, our children, and even and our enemies.

Pray for families and God's blessings upon families:

Pray for togetherness; pray that God will keep all families in perfect peace, love, understanding, and true affection, and mutual support. *Pray for protection; *Pray for pregnant women, nursing mothers, and barrenness for all our family descendants (nuclear and extended family). *Pray for prosperity (against poverty) – aging successfully and become successful. *Pray for high self-esteem (boldness and confidence); *Pray that all our needs be met in God's way and not in wrongful ways.

Pray for married couples and singles:

Pray against troubles in marriages that will cause divorce.

Pray for all singles:

Pray that God will have mercy on those that are looking for their soulmates that God will bring them their soulmates, and not who the enemy sends on their path.

Pray against abuse:

Pray against violence: domestic violence, child abuse, spousal abuse, and animal cruelty.

Pray for people to choose a healthy lifestyle:

Healthy eating Habits, exercises; *positive mindset and thinking.

Pray for truthfulness and protection for gov't officials and their families all over the world:

Pray for presidents, vice presidents, and secretaries of states. *Pray for the police academy and those in the military. *Pray for judges, lawyers, juries, and ambassadors. *Pray for unity, the fear of God, and understanding for our leaders. *Pray the fear of God to rule over them. *Pray for God to lead and guide them to His truth.

Prayer for prisoners:

Pray that **incarcerators** will seek God and His forgiveness; *pray that they will repent wholeheartedly and find peace. *Pray for people who are in trouble. *Pray for those that have been wrongfully convicted.

Pray for the work of our hands:

Pray for businesses, workers, traders, store owners, and market people. *Pray for farmers, businesses, creative ideas, and inventions.

Pray for the unemployed:

Pray for those who have no jobs or have lost their jobs and seeking employment through job trainings. *Pray against poverty and homelessness.

Pray for the medical field:

Pray for doctors, pre-med students, and nurses (from the director of nurses to nurse aides.

Sicknesses and diseases:

Pray against all kinds of diseases affecting humans; and may those that are sick recover fast.

Pray for counselors and psychiatrists:

Pray for psychological issues – those with depression, worries, and those with anxieties.

Safety and travelling mercies:

May God grant us travelling mercy wherever we go**. Pray for** drivers, pilots, ship's crews, bike riders, motorcycle riders, horse riders, joggers, hikers, etc.

Pray for the world:

Pray for all people and all firms. *Pray for nations, cities, towns, villages, and everywhere around the world. *Pray for protection. *Pray for love, peace, and against hatred and greediness. *Pray for every race, every culture, every tribe, language, and people for cultural acceptance and against racism. *Pray for an understanding of why God created us differently. *Pray **against crime and against** every evil intention or are tempted to do evil – shoot or kill another person, murder the innocent, traffic humans, kidnap, deal with drugs, lie, bully, harass, intimidate anyone, steal from others, cause unhappiness, etc. *Pray against, sexual immorality, adultery, prostitution, and homosexuality, disbelief, false worship, and witchcraft practices, and atheism. *Pray that all who delight in doing evil will be set free from their traps through salvation.

Prayer for the world and against natural disasters:

Pray against natural disasters – floods, tornados, hurricanes, fires, earthquakes, etc.

Pray for safe environments:

Pray for homes, communities, streets, schools, churches, workplaces, airports, and everywhere to be safe for humans. Pray against thieves and bobbers who come to steal, kill, and destroy.

Pray for healthy environments:

Pray for environmental issues and all the world's problems – Nature, humanity, animals, trees, fish, ocean, rivers, lakes, rain, sunshine; and pray against pollution and global warming.

Prayer for blessings and favor for your daily life:

Pray for goodness and mercy to follow you each day. *Pray against generational curses and pain/sickness & diseases.

Pray for *God's Will:*

Pray that we will sacrifice our free wills to God.

Answering Prayer:

We know *God* listens when we *pray.* **Jeremiah 33:3** says, "Call to me and I will answer you, and will tell you great and hidden things that you have not *known.* "Read **Psalm 20 & 1John 5:15**.

In summary:

Pray that God will help us take care of all our issues in our cities and in our nations all over the world. Pray for protection for all nations. Pray for all nations and leaders to honors God. *Pray for peace and against war. *Pray for a spiritual awakening in every country. *Pray for the prosperity of nations its people. *Pray for justice to be upheld in every part of the world. *Pray that believers can worship God in spirit and truth. *Pray for freedom so the Good News will continue. *Pray for people to know the truth and be set free. *Pray for God's Holy Spirit to dwell in us and use us to do the God's Kingdom Work on earth.

We pray in the Name of our Lord Jesus Christ, with the help of His Holy Spirit, and with thankful heart, Amen!

Prayer: Dear Lord Jesus, we thank You for everything that You have thought us about prayer. Father, may You be blessed now and forevermore.

I'm sure there are more to these; What else can you added?

May God bless us all as we pray, Amen!

The end!

Personal Prayer Notes

Personal Prayer Notes

References

- Dr. Allender, B. Dan. 'The Healing Path – How the Hurt in your past can lead you to a more abundant life' (The literary agency of Alive Communications, Inc.,). Colorado Spring, 2020.

- https://en.wikipedia.org/wiki/Christian_population_growth#:~:text=However%2C%20this%20rate%20of%20growth

- https://hbr.org/2006/05/why-innovation-in-health-care-is-so-hard

- https://www.everydayhealth.com/emotional-health/big-ways-forgiveness-is-good-for-your-health

- https://www.mnpsych.org/index.php%3Foption%3Dcom_dailyplanetblog

- https://www.ndtv.com/india-news/fear-and-faith-inside-the-last-days-of-an-us-man-john-allen-chau-killed-by-remote-tribe-1952049

- https://www.niehs.nih.gov/health/topics/agents/air-pollution/index.cfm

- https://www.sermoncentral.com/sermons/the-beauty-of-heaven-glenn-pease-sermon-on-heaven-255709

Epilogue

Involve yourself in the Kingdom's Work.

Both John the Baptist and Jesus Christ began their ministries focusing on the Kingdom of Heaven. This shows the importance of the Kingdom's Work—**Matthew 3**; **4**; and **5**. So, involve yourself in the Kingdom's Work and make a difference today! If you want to get involved, you can contact us, check our website, or find a support group at your local church.

Prayer: Numbers 6:24–26—May the Lord bless and keep you. May His face shine upon you and be gracious to you. May the light of God shine on you. As you choose to use this book as your prayer guide, may you see a great change in your life, your family, your church, your community, and the world like never before. May you and your children, and your children's children, become God's instruments of glory. May the Mighty Hand of God be on you and everything you do from today forward. May God Almighty, the Great God we serve, use you for His glory. May you never be confused about what you are called to do for the Kingdom of God. May God's blessings and His Power, Anointing, and Favor be your portion today and forever, in Jesus Mighty Name. Amen!

www.ingramcontent.com/pod-product-compliance
Lightning Source LLC
Chambersburg PA
CBHW051303120626
46547CB00015B/2067

9798989673711